FRIEND OF THE FAMILY

11/30/15

Evin ⎯⎯⎯⎯⎯⎯⎯⎯⎯⎯⎯

I do hope you enjoy
this book as much as I
enjoyed being an FBI Agent

Regards and Keep up the
Good Work.

Ed Robb

FRIEND
OF
THE FAMILY

An Undercover Agent
in The Mafia

*Ed Roll
aka Tony Rossi
aka Kurt Wolf*

D. LEA JACOBS

The Compass Press
Washington, D.C.

Edited by Thea Clark
Cover and text designed by Stephen Thomas Previtera

Library of Congress Cataloging_in_Publication Data

Jacobs, D. Lea, 1954_
   Friend of the family : an undercover agent in the Mafia /
by D. Lea Jacobs.
      p. cm.
   ISBN 0_929590_19_8 (alk. paper)
   1. Robb, Ed. 2. United States. Federal Bureau of
Investigation__Officials and employees__Biography. 3. Organized
crime investigation__United States. 4. Undercover operations__
United States.
5. Mafia__United States. I. Title.
   HV7911.R612 J33 2002
   364.1'06'0973__dc21
                                    2002007709

*This book is dedicated to Howard Owen,
Dennis Danvers, and Tom De Haven,
writers whose novels I admire, and whose
company I treasure.*

AUTHOR'S NOTE

I'd like to thank Ed Robb for the months he spent telling me his story, and for the friendship I enjoy still.

John Lowe was instrumental with his advice, humor, and goodwill to both Ed and me during the writing of this book, as well as now.

Owen Laster of William Morris, Inc., has been a faithful agent and a leavening influence on me for a few years now, for which I expect one day to be appropriately grateful.

Dean Howells, publisher, has been a tireless advocate of this book, as well as a nettlesome editor, the best kind.

I'd like to express my admiration for the entire law enforcement community of every town, city, county, state, and federal organization in America. Your character and courage are all too often invisible. I hope this work helps shed light on your service and sacrifices.

Friend of the Family ranges over many of the covert operations, both minor and major, in the awesome undercover career of Ed Robb. Many personalities are included; you'll find an index of undercover operations, agents, and targets in the back. Also, many individuals with personal knowledge of the players and cases in this book weighed in with candor and support. They too are listed in the back, with my appreciation.

Ed Robb became the archetype for the contemporary FBI undercover agent. The agents he worked with were brave and ingenious men themselves; together they broke new ground in covert police work, inventing on-the run many techniques and strategies still in use by the Bureau. I hope you will enjoy reading about these real American heroes, and their very real enemies.

D. Lea Jacobs

TABLE OF CONTENTS

INTRODUCTION

Friend of the Family is the true and gripping story of one of the first and one of the best FBI undercover agents to work against the Mafia.

The war between the mob and law enforcement agents has been a popular American drama since the days of Al Capone and Eliot Ness, but the costs of organized crime in terms of ruined lives and political corruption have generally been less well appreciated. The FBI did not begin a serious campaign against the Mafia until the late 60's. Shortly thereafter, it had become clear that the mob was so well insulated by its own culture that only infiltration by undercover agents could provide the evidence necessary for effective prosecution.

Ed Robb was a pioneer in this dangerous work. He was the lead undercover agent in one of the Bureau's earliest major operations, code-named Coldwater, which took place on the west coast of Florida where I was then assigned as Supervisor of the Bureau's Organized Crime Squad. Initially designed merely to close down a Mafia-supported garbage collection racket and illegal gambling operation, Ed was instrumental in developing it into a major undercover effort which might have nabbed the kingpin of organized crime in Florida, Santo Trafficante, had not a mob war broken out which forced us to shut down the operation. During several years in his Coldwater undercover role, Ed worked his way up the mob ladder to become known among the criminal underworld as a powerful mob figure in the West Coast area of central Florida.

After I had been assigned to Bureau Headquarters as Deputy Assistant Director in the Criminal Division with various responsibilities including organized crime, Ed undertook another major operation named Pizza II. Again, he, along with other undercover agents, worked his way up the ladder until the operation resulted in what is still considered one of the largest drug busts in history.

Organized crime is still widespread and powerful, but it has lost much of its former immunity to prosecution and certainly its aura of invincibility. In recent years, the witness protection program, along with the effective use of the RICO Statute, has helped crack the armor of omerta. But it was the courage and skill of Ed Robb and a few others like him that turned the tide. His undercover work in penetrating the Mafia is truly remarkable considering the pressures and dangers he faced on a daily basis for several years.

Friend of the Family is the tale of an exciting and perilous life inside the mob. It is also the story of the early efforts by the FBI to take the fight into the Mafia's den. Ed Robb and a few other dedicated and professional undercover agents led the way in this assault on organized crime. Each one of them is a real American hero.

Anthony E. Daniels,
former Assistant Director, FBI

CHAPTER ONE
Sitdown

Jimmy East called for a sitdown. Dinner at Earl's Wine Cellar in Tampa. East was fifty-nine years old, a kindly gentleman with the power to order murders, a captain in the Lucchese crime family. He took a cut from every line of organized crime in his west coast Florida territory in return for his family's permission and protection.

Around the table in the private room were East, JoJo Fitapelli, Rick Mazzenga, Tony Rossi, and the three Agostino brothers—Bernie, owner of Cousin's, Jimmy East's favorite restaurant, and Nick and Ray, the restaurant's chefs.

The Agostino brothers were special. Bernie had a patch of hair on his nose that made him look like a rhino, Nick had a twitch, and Ray walked with a pronounced limp. The three brothers bragged of being seasoned shoplifters. They often "boosted" as many as five hundred record albums a day for sale to a guy in Miami for a buck apiece. The floorwalkers in the stores never kept a close eye on Ray, the cripple. Ray was the best thief in the bunch.

Lucchese associates Rick Mazzenga and JoJo Fitapelli were garden-variety thugs, pot-bellied ex-New Yorkers who preferred the sunshine and slower pace of Florida. Neither owed his membership in the crew to brains or strength; they were present, and they could be dangerous, because they were loyal.

Tony Rossi was different. He had keen eyes and a powerful, blocky build. He was a dark man with a brooding manner that told of the tough things he'd done, the hard places he'd been.

1

Though Tony had been a member of the crew for only five months, he was recognized by Jimmy East and the others— especially JoJo who had vouched for him with East — as a good earner, a stand-up guy, an up-and-comer. He knew the rules and respected power. He was one to be watched.

The others in the crew didn't realize just how different Tony Rossi was, or how intently he was watching them.

The conversation around the table went from women and horses to other associates and updates on several of their ongoing schemes. With Jimmy East's green light, Tony was opening a bottle club and gambling joint in Holiday. East asked him how it was going.

Tony waved his breadstick as he described the location he'd selected, an abandoned tennis club on Rte. 19. He announced the name for the nightspot. "We're gonna use the theme 'King Arthur's Court' and all that shit."

"Yes," East agreed, "that's nice."

Next, East asked JoJo Fitapelli for an update on a scheme he was working, a garbagemen's association in the Clearwater area. The association had recently held its second meeting. Some of the members were reluctant to pay their dues, JoJo said, until they were satisfied that the organization could deliver on its promises of price-fixing, guaranteed routes, and the "discouragement" of competing garbage collectors. They also wanted assurances that those running the association were in fact hooked up with New York crime families.

Jimmy East was sanguine. "Don't worry, JoJo, I'll make a few calls. It's done, alright?"

The antipasto and a dry Chianti were served. The men ate with gusto until Jimmy East leaned back in his chair to raise a more serious topic.

"Hey, we got a problem," he said, passing his hand over the group as if in benediction. "The FBI is watching us."

Tony Rossi held on to his poker face while his heart pumped adrenaline through his body.

East continued. "The Feds got their eye on every move we

make at Cousin's Restaurant. I know, because I've seen the pictures they took of us there."

Tony's mind raced. How could Jimmy East have gotten a look at confidential FBI surveillance photos?

Jimmy East looked straight at him. "Look, Tony, and you too, JoJo. We got to be careful. So no more business at Cousin's. Don't go there and don't try to reach me there. And another thing: be careful of strangers. I think the FBI is gonna try to slip an agent in on us. The rule is now no new guys, no one you haven't known forever, understand?"

Tony Rossi understood, better than the others. He was the new guy. He was also an FBI agent. Special Agent Ed Robb.

He stifled the fear. He looked at his hand, caught in mid-air with a roll of prosciutto stabbed on a fork. It wasn't shaking.

Good.

Then Ed figured what had gone wrong. Two weeks earlier, he'd gotten a call from an agent in the Tampa FBI's Organized Crime Squad. The agent said that he'd shown some surveillance photos—taken during a Lucchese sitdown at Cousin's presided over by Jimmy East—to a snitch he was working on a different case. The agent thought the informant might be helpful in identifying some of the faces. The snitch knew a few of the guys, but not all of them, and asked to keep the photos overnight so he could show them around.

Now Ed began to sweat. The informant had indeed shown the surveillance photos around: he'd shown them to Jimmy East. The snitch was spinning his agent, playing both sides of the street.

That's it, Ed thought. I'm dead. The snitch must've ratted me out. This was perfect, just like a Mafia movie. It's the ideal setup; they invite you to a nice dinner, laugh and smile, everyone having a good time. Then they lay the cards on the table and whack you right after the Sambuca and cigars.

Ed waited for the unveiling to start, for the first look askance and the first suspicious question. Bernie Agostino, one of his brothers, or Rick Mazzenga was surely about to grin at him and say something like, "Yeah, Tony. Now that Jimmy mentions it, where the fuck do you come from? Who the fuck are you anyway? JoJo, what do you know about this guy?"

Ed became keenly aware at that moment of how alone he was, how he was no more than a chameleon in this deadly jungle. If his cover had been blown, what could he do? He was faster and bigger than any of them but he was unarmed, and any of them could pull a trigger or thrust an ice pick. He was cornered and outnumbered. He was theirs for the taking.

He felt a strong urge to be elsewhere. He could jump from his seat and run but he was at the opposite end of the table from Jimmy East, the farthest spot from the door. Unarmed, he would never make it. Still, there had been no overt accusation, nothing more than a reference to the FBI that had set off his alarms. There had been a major screwup in the Tampa Field Office, no question about that. But how big? Better to play it out a few more minutes, he thought.

The pasta was served. Ed excused himself from the table and went into the nearby men's room. He left the bathroom door cracked and leaned his ear close to listen to the conversation. If anything threatening was whispered about him while he was away from the table, he would know he was busted. He checked the window over the toilet. He might squeeze out of it into the alley but it would be tight and he could easily get stuck halfway in and out. A great way to go, he thought, shot while hanging out of a bathroom window. No, if things broke badly, he would rely on his old football training to bull through them and sprint out the front door to the street.

After a few minutes of eavesdropping, the throbbing in Ed's chest subsided. Everything seemed normal around the table. No one had hinted at a problem with Tony Rossi. Ed washed his hands and returned to his seat opposite Jimmy East. No more was said about the FBI. The conversation moved on.

After dinner, on the drive back to New Port Richey with JoJo, Ed's confidence in his cover was buoyed. He talked about tapping into bank night depositories to let JoJo see he was thinking about bigger game. Ed was elated; he had passed a crucial test that night. It was clear the Lucchese mob knew the FBI was on to them, with plans to infiltrate the crew. Not only had he escaped detection, he had actually been elevated to the inner circle of confidants warned by Jimmy East.

Toni Rossi was not a dead man. Indeed, his career was just beginning.

CHAPTER TWO
Making the Man

The sitdown took place in July 1979 during the early stages of one of the FBI's first and most successful penetrations of the mob. For years, many FBI agents had been eager to take on the Mafia from the inside but J. Edgar Hoover, for reasons unknown, had prohibited any undercover work in organized crime circles.

Experts on the history of the Bureau have put forth their own theories, the most accepted being Hoover's fear that an agent, operating in the Mafia's world of greed, self-gratification, and violence, might succumb to temptation, cross the line, and embarrass him and his beloved Bureau. Perhaps he couldn't believe that one of his straight-arrow agents could pose effectively as a criminal or that, if he could, he shouldn't be on the force. Whatever the reason, during the forty-eight years of Hoover's directorship, the FBI made no effort to penetrate the Mafia. That didn't happen until well after Hoover's death in May 1972.

Today, the Bureau's training programs benefit from considerable undercover experience. Mob rules and protocol, the moves to make and not to make, what to expect and how to react, can be taught. The mind-set and pathology of mob soldiers and capos are generally understood and can be imitated in training, and the innate personal and psychological traits an agent will need can be sought in the selection of candidates for undercover work.

It is recognized that the successful criminal undercover

agent must embody a collection of opposites. He must be so honest that he can tell a lie with a straight face, so incorruptible that he can feign and even deal in corruption without being tempted. He must have such a steadfast personal identity that he can metamorphose into another character and return to himself unaltered; he must have an ego strong enough so that he can pose as a loyal lackey. He must be so independent and self-reliant that he is still on his own course when following a crowd. He must be a quiet and detached listener with a mind alert enough to retain nuggets of critical information whether from people of high intellect or of low, stultifying ignorance. He must be physically tough enough to threaten violence convincingly so as to avoid it, even prevent it. Above all, he must value law and order so dearly that, in its pursuit, he can talk, move, and posture like an authentic criminal.

But the initial criminal undercover agents, known as UCAs, had to draw on only what they brought with them into the FBI as recruits. Ed Robb, one of the first UCAs and, in the end, one of the best, proved to have highly developed natural talents for this line of work. His career provides a history of the formative years of criminal undercover work in the Bureau, and a study of Ed Robb himself becomes a look at the archetypal criminal undercover agent, because the model used and taught in the FBI's training today is based, in large part, on him.

* * *

Edgar Straessly Robb was born two days before Christmas, 1937, in Pittsburgh's Northside suburb. His mother named him after the crime-busting, straight-talking, then American icon, J. Edgar Hoover, with no inkling that her son also would become a historic figure in the Bureau.

Early in life, Ed began to identify with the heroes he saw in countless movies and comic books and especially among the real-life heroes of World War II. He determined that one day he too would become a strong man. He would fight for right, for justice, and for his country.

In Ed's neighborhood, the heroes were the tough Italian guys who belonged to gangs. They committed petty crimes as tests of manhood. Ed could not be found lacking. He hung out with the gangs to smoke and thumb his nose at law-abiding citizens; he adopted their swagger and lingo, but he was acting. When his gang broke windows or stole gas, he would go along, but couldn't bring himself to throw a rock or lend his weight to a crowbar to break a lock. When it was time to be home, he left quickly. Growing up in a tough neighborhood taught him how to read people, to recognize bluff from real threats, and how to react to either.

At Thiel College in Greenville, Pennsylvania, many of his classmates came from Pittsburgh, Youngstown, Erie, and Philadelphia, some with mob names like Genovese, Ciancutti, and Martino. These sons and daughters of the mob were proud of the fact that they weren't ordinary: they were connected.

Ed graduated in 1959 after a four-year football grant-in-aid, playing both ways as an offensive and defensive lineman. He loved football, the honesty of the contact, the jarring truth of the game. He also loved Gretchen Hoffman, a strong-willed blonde from Warren, Ohio, with a steady gaze and calm smile. They were married in their senior year.

After three years at various jobs, Ed joined his father-in-law's construction business. Harold "Toughy" Hoffman was a land developer, a short, heavy man with a direct, no-nonsense manner and a ready temper. He was a friend of Jackie Presser, head of the powerful, mob-connected Teamsters Union. Under Hoffman, Ed learned both sides of the development game, the business and the blisters. Earlier, Hoffman had been the biggest coin-operated machine vendor in Ohio and western Pennsylvania, supplying slot machines, Wurlitzer jukeboxes, table shuffleboard, and pinball games to bowling alleys, restaurants, and bars. He got out of the lucrative business because he grew weary of the mob's increasing shakedowns for protection money. Toughy sold out while the selling was still good and healthy.

By 1966, Ed was working hard and living well. He was young and strong with a future in his father-in-law's business. He enjoyed construction work in the same way he'd enjoyed football. It was honest and rugged, the best of the traits he attributed to himself. But he never forgot his childhood dream of being a hero, of standing up against evil and putting his finger in its chest.

That year, Ed applied and was accepted for a deputy's position with the Sheriff of Trumbull County. For the next three years Ed worked the graveyard shift, from 5 p.m. until 1 a.m. His duties included responding to the expected late-night disturbances, convenience store holdups, domestic tiffs, drunk and disorderlies. Every Christmas, Ed drove his deputy's car to collect bottles of booze from Sheriff Barnett's many friends and business connections.

As a deputy in Trumbull County, Ed again saw the La Cosa Nostra names he recognized. At night he broke up the Italian kids' fights, gave them speeding tickets, and drove them home when they were too drunk to walk. He played poker with the older men who joked of "owning a judge" then said no more. He was aware of, and grudgingly admired, the mobsters' extended families, their honor, their notorious loyalty and power.

In 1969, his third year as deputy, Ed applied to the FBI. In June, after several mental and physical tests and a meticulous background check, he received a letter of acceptance from the FBI. Ed Robb was to report to Washington on the first of December.

* * *

On that snowy day when he hefted his luggage and walked to the front door of his home, Gretchen was not pleased. She was now a mother of three, living in a big house in a neighborhood developed by her father. She wasn't angry with her husband, but she'd been asked to trail behind him while he followed his dream. The FBI was not her dream; it wasn't even a pleasant thought. Ed's dream threatened to pull her up by her roots. She loved him too well to try to take away his life's goal. She just didn't know, watching his footprints press into the snow over the sidewalk, whether she could share it.

* * *

Ed joined the eleventh New Agents Class of 1969 on December 1 in the Old Post Office in Washington, D.C. Among the fifty recruits, there were no women and no blacks. There were a few Italians, Hispanics, and Orientals but for the most part the class looked a lot like America's opinion of who ran things in 1969. Hoover's agents did not reflect American diversity because they were not intended to; an FBI agent was a paragon, an ideal.

First, a mountain of official and classified manuals was slammed on the desks before each candidate. Next came the badges. Ed's crest was number 4038. Then, an Assistant Director took the podium and advised the trainees of their single greatest duty: Do absolutely nothing to embarrass the Bureau or the Director. Nothing. Never. That included drinking, womanizing, improper handling of finances or Bureau property, excessive partying, anything concerning morals and conduct. The slightest scent of controversy could send you packing.

For eight hours a day, Ed examined the investigative mandates and authority of the FBI and studied how to write the many reports the Bureau used. He learned the nature of physical evidence, including fingerprints, tool marks, hairs and fibers, and the mysteries of forensics, ballistics, and serology, plus how to submit all of these and more to the lab with the proper paperwork to preserve the chain of evidence. He studied the FBI's most sophisticated equipment and how to testify in court. He attended lectures on foreign counterintelligence, federal and local police cooperation, and the conduct of background checks on federal employees. He took courses in constitutional law, criminal psychology, and federal criminal procedure. In the fifth week, the training was expanded to include physical instruction at the FBI Academy at the Marine Base in Quantico, Virginia, just outside Washington. Ed excelled in boxing and wrestling. He worked on martial-arts holds called "come-alongs" and fired .38-caliber Colt or Smith & Wesson revolvers.

The classmates did not compete against each other in any part of their training. They weren't even allowed to play softball, because that would generate a losing team. Every one of you is the best, the recruits were told; no FBI agent is average, and if you're average, you're out. Hoover crafted this "above average" myth to enhance pride and confidence in his agents but it also fostered the famous attitude of superiority that since the 1930s had made the Bureau widely despised by state and local law authorities across the country.

On April 20, 1970, every member of the class graduated. Each trainee had been hand picked and screened far too painstakingly to fail. For his first assignment, Ed had submitted his preference for Albany or Boston, somewhere in his familiar northeast. That choice ran afoul of another Hoover dictum: a new agent could never learn the ropes well enough in familiar territory. In fact, Hoover wouldn't allow an agent to return to his hometown until he'd been in the FBI for at least eighteen years.

Ed was assigned to Knoxville. He drove there alone, leaving Gretchen and the kids behind in their big house in Warren.

CHAPTER THREE
Warming Up

It got hot in Tennessee. Ed wore the Bureau uniform at all times on the job, dark suit, stiff white shirt, tie and snap-brimmed hat. His Bureau car was not air-conditioned. Hoover said air-conditioned cars made the agents lazy.

After six weeks in Knoxville, Ed was sent to Oak Ridge, home of the Atomic Energy Commission Research Facility. It was a strangely cosmopolitan community, blending government scientists with the quiet, rooted ways of a small Tennessee town. Ed's territory covered two counties, Scott and Morgan. These were the soul of Appalachia, with their rolling green hills and hushed valleys mostly closed to outsiders. Only one hard-surfaced road cut through both counties.

The local Sheriffs' main duties were to break up domestic disputes and collar moonshiners. To the local authorities, a federal agent was an object for both skepticism and awe. Ed asked the Sheriffs to call him whenever they made an arrest. Their conversations were always casual, and the local Sheriffs enjoyed doling out information sparingly.

"Ed," one of the lawmen might say when he phoned, "I got me five new felons here in my jail."

"What'd they do, Sheriff?"

"Oh, they was up to no good. One fella killed someone."

"Tell me about it."

"Well, I don't know. Ain't much to tell. From the sound of things the man mighta needed killin'."

Chats with the locals were also slow, rambling affairs.

Ed visited the general stores searching for information. He sat on the front porches with the men after the day's farming was done, whittling on a stick, all the while wondering what he was making as he shaved a small limb to a point. He'd eat some peanuts, talk some weather, farming, and catfishing. At last, one of the citizens would ask, "What is it y'want, Ed?"

Ed's year in Tennessee provided invaluable experience that would later keep him alive while he was in the heart of the mob. He began his study of stillness, the ability to lie in wait for a piece of information to surface, just as a hunter waits for his quarry to break cover. He perfected a poker face, a distance— even indifference—in his mien that spoke of strength and confidence. Even in his stiff suit and hat, he learned his first lessons on how to be trusted by the distrustful.

* * *

In February of 1971, Ed was transferred to the Field Office in Richmond, Virginia. Three months later he was told to report to the Charlottesville Office, seventy miles west at the foot of the Blue Ridge Mountains. He moved his family there. By this time, anti-Vietnam War activities had become a preoccupation for the FBI. Campus demonstrations, peace marches, and public uproar were aimed at every American icon, including the FBI. Resident Offices were broken into and ransacked, the most notable example of which was the burglarizing of the FBI Office in Media, Pennsylvania, masterminded by the Berrigan brothers. The FBI's longstanding targets—the Klan and the Communists —were shunted aside to make room in the Bureau's sights for the Weather Underground, the New Left, and the many splinter cells of domestic unrest.

This year of turbulence marked the beginnings of the FBI's undercover efforts. Whereas Hoover had refused to infiltrate organized crime, he showed no such hesitation when kids and priests were pillaging his offices. Ed began to see a new style of agent around the Charlottesville Office and at Quantico. Behind their backs, the other agents called them "Long Hairs." They were dirty, smelly, and unshaven, dressed in rags, and their cars were often hand-painted microbuses. They and their vehicles were like moving billboards, stippled with anti-war slogans, peace signs, and psychedelic rock-and-roll logos. The Long Hairs kept to themselves on the shooting range; they smoked a lot and hid behind sunglasses day and night. The Long Hairs were resented by the regular street or "brick" agents because they were off on their own, making independent decisions, seeming to lack discipline and structure. Their beat-up cars, bead necklaces, scraggly hair, and "Right on, man" lingo were flower-power pollen in the face of the legendary FBI paragon, the snap-brimmed, blue suited, square-jawed, steely-eyed G-man.

In early 1971, the FBI learned that a cell of the New Left was planning to bring thousands of hippies to Washington, D.C., to occupy and take over federal buildings during their May Day celebration. Hoover was incensed. He put out a call for one hundred Special Agents, all more than six feet tall, all in excellent physical condition, to volunteer for protection and surveillance assignments. Ed was one of "Hoover's One Hundred."

The demonstration lasted three days. Downtown Washington became a tangle of bodies. One of Ed's jobs was to pull apart the interlocked arms and legs of the "human carpets" lying in front of the Justice Department, so government employees could get to work. No buildings were shut down, but government officials made mass arrests, putting everyone they collared into RFK Stadium.

There were rumors at Quantico about the Long Hair under-cover agents who "never came back." No names, just tales of once clean-cut Special Agents who disappeared into the ranks of the grungy and remained, no longer guarding against it from the inside. Ed was fascinated with the thought that an alternate iden-tity might become so strong that it could take over. How did this happen? Weren't these agents just playacting? Wasn't the role just an extension of the self, a new suit of clothes on the same frame? Or had these few lost agents created a second persona that was so believable and authentic, so persuasive, that it could actually consume the Special Agent hiding inside the dirty jeans and headband and replace the original man? Perhaps Hoover's fears were justified.

Ed was drawn to the challenge of working undercover, of operating outside but still inside the FBI. He watched the Long Hairs carefully. Add a shower, he thought, some clean clothes and a better car, and that's for me. An FBI undercover agent. A year later, on May 2, 1972, Hoover died. Ed heard a broadcast from the Richmond Field Office over the two-way radio in his Bureau car.

"Attention all agents. We have sad news. The Director died this morning in his sleep." That was all. Ed paused but did not mourn.

*   *   *

Only a few months after Hoover's burial, the FBI's first significant criminal undercover operation took place in Washington. Ed was not a part of the action but he followed it with interest. It was code-named The Sting, after the movie of the same name. The FBI set up a storefront in downtown Washington as a cover for a fencing operation. Agents worked the streets undercover, steering thieves to bring their stolen goods to the store, which was rigged with hidden video cameras and microphones to record all transactions. After six months, the agents put the word out that there was to be a big party in the back of the store, where those who'd done business with the fencing operation could finally meet "Mr. Big," a reputed Mafia capo from New York who was at the other end of all the stolen goods.

The night of the party, the crooks came one by one to the front of the shop. A big bouncer stood at a door leading to the rear of the building to greet them.

"How you doin'? Glad you could make it. Go on in back. The party's happening."

The thieves sauntered into the large warehouse space in the

15

rear where fifty men and women ate, drank, and danced to loud music. Just then, each thief was greeted again.

"Hello. FBI. You're under arrest."

One at a time, the thieves were handcuffed, searched for weapons, and whisked to a side room where a magistrate waited with a gavel behind a desk. Just as quickly, the thieves were unobtrusively taken out a back door to a waiting police van and hauled to the District jail. More than one hundred burglars, robbers, and thugs were jailed that night. The Sting was such a success and brought the FBI such positive publicity that the decision was made to increase the Bureau's undercover efforts.

A few months later, in another part of Washington, the FBI conducted an identical sting, again with a big party at the end. The second was just as successful as the first, with another hundred arrests. This time, the sign over the storefront read "GYA Enterprises." It meant, "Got You Again."

Later that year, one of Ed's close friends from his class, Dick Genova, made a name for himself overnight for an undercover job he did in Buffalo. Genova, an Italian from New Haven, managed to become the chauffeur for Sam Pieri, the Mafia boss of Buffalo. Genova was acknowledged as the first FBI agent to penetrate a criminal organization. Ed's interest in undercover work soared.

He went to his supervisor in the Richmond Field Office and asked to be assigned some covert work around Richmond. He also let it be known in FBI Headquarters that he was actively pursuing criminal undercover assignments.

Until then, criminal undercover investigations had been undertaken mainly by city police. New York, Los Angeles, and other metropolises were far ahead of the FBI in both training and tactics. With Hoover's demise, the Bureau was finally free to mount its own covert operations against organized crime. With The Sting and Genova's coup, Ed saw a new game opening up in the FBI's playbook. A few bold men were stepping up, and they would be pioneers in the FBI, an elite cadre when the game began. Ed Robb wanted a place in that lineup.

CHAPTER FOUR
The Barbout Game

In late fall, 1972, Ed got a call from the Richmond Field Office. An agent there needed help developing information on a jewelry store holdup. The agent's sources said that a local bar owner might have gotten his hands on some of the gems. Ed's assignment was to hang out at the bar and see what he could turn up.

The bar was in a predominantly black part of town. It was a dark and shadowy afternoon when Ed walked in. He wore a powder blue polyester leisure suit with a cobalt silk shirt opened down his chest to display a weight of cheap gold-plated chains. In his pocket was forty dollars of FBI money. He was accountable for every cent of it. The outfit he purchased at his own expense.

Ed perched on a barstool and ordered a Dewar's and water. He finished the first round quietly and ordered another. The bartender chatted with him—the usual small talk of sports, the weather—while the barroom gained a few more customers. Ed sat back to let events come to him, just as he had done on the porches in Tennessee. His barstool might have been a rocker, the bartender a farmer; it didn't matter because the way to draw them out, to gain their confidence, was the same.

Ed was just a two-bit hoodlum in an inky saloon; the clothes, the drinks, the smoke, the small talk said it all. The other patrons shared a moody quiet, watching instinctively to see who was brethren and who was not. Ed acted disinterested; direct questions and attentive listening would stand out here like a police radio. His instincts told him clearly, on this first undercover foray into the criminal world, that the key was curiosity. The successful covert agent shows none; he makes others curious about him. The agent must suppress every temptation to find something out. Just wait. Bait the hook, let it dangle.

After an hour, the bartender, with no prodding from Ed, reached under the bar for a velvet bag and a loupe, a jeweler's magnifying glass. He laid them out in front of Ed. The bag contained a dozen small gems.

"What do you think?" the bartender asked.

"What do I know about stones?" Ed replied irritably. "They could be shit, I don't know. You tell me they're good, they're good."

The jewels were put away. Ed made no comment. He knew better than to feign knowledge of gems of which he was ignorant. Fake it and someone will catch you, then you're blown.

The bartender poured Ed another Dewar's and water, then leaned on his bar and looked up at the TV. Virginia State Senator (later Governor) Douglas Wilder was on the news.

"Did you see that big-ass pinky ring Wilder was wearing?" the bartender asked.

"No, I didn't."

"Well, next time, watch. It came from that Schwartzchild burglary."

Ed took a swallow of Dewar's. "The fuck do I care?"

When he returned, Ed told the Richmond agent what happened in the bar. The FBI later recruited the bartender as an informant, without revealing Ed's cover.

At home that night, Ed hung up the powder blue leisure suit and silk shirt in his closet, hoping he'd need them again. He told his supervisors he needed to learn about gems and jewelry. He didn't even know how to use a jeweler's loupe. How could someone be sent undercover in a jewelry heist investigation if he knew nothing about stones? On his own, Ed located a jeweler who taught him the fundamentals of gem appraisal and how to hold the loupe in one eye.

This episode exposed the FBI's ineptitude in covert operations. The Bureau was starting from zero. Ed Robb had to make it up as he went along.

* * *

By the summer of 1973, the FBI had begun keeping records of volunteers for criminal undercover work. No more than a dozen agents signed up. Ed sent a letter to Headquarters requesting that he be put on the nationwide roll. He set out his appearance, background, and qualifications. He was knowledgeable of the criminal elements in the construction and trucking trades. He had also attended the FBI's gambling school, a two-week course at Quantico where a casino was set up complete with magnets and other cheating techniques.

In November, Ed got a call from the Pittsburgh Field Office asking if he'd be interested in penetrating a gambling network that might be connected to organized crime in the city. He agreed to take a look.

At the Pittsburgh Office, Ed met with Special Agent Dean Naum, an experienced criminal investigator and now undercover operative. Later, he would realize what a foolish move this had been. Dozens of FBI agents and employees in the building saw him and Naum walk several times into the office of the Organized Crime Supervisor to discuss the case. Indeed, he had been lucky. Within a year, a secretary in the Pittsburgh Office was arrested and prosecuted for revealing Bureau secrets to her mob-connected fiancé. Thereafter, whenever working undercover, Ed kept every contact with the Bureau on a need-to-know basis only, and refused to enter any FBI Office.

Ed and Dean were to infiltrate an illicit, high-stakes dice game, called Barbout, popular among Pittsburgh's Greek community. The two agents would be introduced into the game, played in nearby Erie, by an informant. The plan was to sit in on the game, see the money change hands, pass some marked bills, and then decide whether to bust the game that night with an armed FBI squad waiting outside or to keep it going as a lead to information on other mobsters or corrupt public officials.

The Barbout game was targeted for several reasons. First was the suspicion of corruption that always attends illegal gambling. It's common knowledge that a sizable and ongoing game cannot survive without protection from the police, who in turn may be acting on orders from an appointed or elected official. That means payoffs. The first place to look for this kind of corruption is among local lawmen. A dirty sheriff, a ranking cop, even a judge can make it known in enforcement circles that a particular bar, club, or set of persons should be left alone. Even the honest cops will often look away, reluctant to turn in a fellow officer, refusing to cross the thin blue line that defines their brotherhood.

The Barbout game also was targeted as a possible gateway into the city's underworld. Illicit games draw underworld figures and become the center for other criminal activities such as conspiracies, fencing stolen goods, and prostitution. More importantly, illegal gambling pays organized crime's overhead. It fuels and finances other mob enterprises. Unsuspecting players who rack up huge losses soon find themselves exposed to a downward spiral of Mafia influence. Their debts climb at the usurious interest of 4 to 5 percent weekly, which is called "juice," "vigorish," or, more commonly, simply "the vig."

Payment of debt is enforced at first by gentle prodding, followed inevitably by more coercive and violent means. The losers may trade favors to ward off collection or hand over ever-increasing bits of their legitimate livelihoods in exchange for relief. Gambling is the principal path through which the mob inserts itself into legal businesses, quiet communities, and the chambers of public officials.

The FBI had already gathered a good deal of evidence of corruption in Erie and Pittsburgh from surveillance, confidential sources, and other overt means, but not yet enough to warrant arrests. The investigation was faltering; the next step was to insert undercover agents. Because of the inherent dangers to the agents, undercover operations must always be the last resort.

Ed and Dean drove to Erie in a rented Buick to meet another

agent and an informant. The car had been rented by a Pittsburgh agent through a friend who ran a dealership. When Ed learned where the car came from, he winced at the stupidity. What if someone suspicious of him and Dean checked out the tags? The Buick could be traced to the dealership, then to the owner, to the owner's friend, to the FBI. It was dumb and dangerous. Another lesson.

Ed dressed in a salmon double-knit leisure suit and brown silk shirt. Around his neck hung a shark's tooth necklace, gold bracelets jangled on his wrists. Ed believed that one of the ways the bad guys could spot a cop was by looking at his shoes, so he wore high-heeled, grey Florsheims polished to a gleam. Next to him in the Buick, Dean Naum was outfitted similarly but without the flash, his shoes a little scuffed.

Ed picked the name Edward Anthony Rossi for himself, answering to "Eddie." His undercover Social Security number was only two digits from his true number. His fake background was as close to Ed Robb as it could be. Eddie Rossi came from Pittsburgh and had worked in the construction trades. He'd knocked around, gotten in some trouble here and there, made a living doing whatever he had to do.

They headed into Erie where Ed considered another danger. He had grown up in nearby Pittsburgh, attended Thiel College, and lived in Warren, both only two hours away. What if he encountered an old acquaintance? What would he do if someone called out his real name in public? Ed planned simply to brush off the acquaintance immediately and walk away. He'd explain later if he had to that the encounter was just some guy he'd ripped off, or he'd screwed the guy's wife or owed him some money on a gambling debt—anything to justify a quick and uncomfortable departure, before the confused old pal could say anything more than "Hey, Ed?" These tactics would be included in later FBI training, but in those days Ed had to make them up on the run. Who knew if they would work?

Dean Naum, a Greek American, went by the undercover name Dino Stamos. He and Ed concocted the story that they were in Erie to do market research for a new fast food chain. This was a good cover because no one really knew or cared what "market research" was. They even had cheap business cards printed. Eddie and Dino had grown up in the same neighborhood, their fathers had been "in the war" together, and they'd hung out as kids. They'd "done a few things together" since.

If anyone were to inquire further, Ed's pocket response would be, "Hey, fuck you. You writin' a book? I don't ask you what you do, do I? What are you, a cop?" Ed wanted Eddie Rossi to be an authentic bad guy and he knew that real bad guys drop no names, tell no long stories. The criminals would expect a cop to act anxious, talk too much, be too eager to fit in. A cop would know more and ask more than he should. If Eddie Rossi could be wary and defensive, the real crooks might want to talk to him, the way men in prison murmur to the dark, quiet guy locked in the next cell.

When they reached Erie, Ed and Dean entered the Holiday Inn bar and ordered beers. Within minutes, Ed's stomach flipped: across the room sat Babe Palamaro, an old frat buddy and football teammate from Thiel. Ed felt an insane urge to shout, "Hey Babe! How the hell are you? Lookit! I'm working undercover for the FBI! Who'da figured?" Instead, before Babe could turn their way, Eddie and Dino left their beers and slipped out the door.

* * *

Ed and Dean made arrangements to meet the Pittsburgh agent and his informant at a Ramada Inn in nearby Edinboro. The informant, called Chucky, told them the Barbout game was run in downtown Erie in a building across the street from City Hall near the police station. Clearly, thought Ed, someone had purchased some protection.

According to Chucky, the game was operated by Anthony Sciotti, known as Sy, a made guy with the Pittsburgh crew of John LaRocca. Sciotti took a piece of the action from the Greeks for allowing the Barbout game on his turf. Chucky had also heard that bosses James Licavoli from Cleveland, and Russell Buffalino and Sam Pieri from Buffalo, were in for a cut. This broke a mob rule that no two families could be partners in any criminal enterprise. It also meant that the game, though run by the Greeks, was perhaps subject to a tug-of-war between several Mafia families. These possible tendrils in and out of the Barbout game made it a valuable target for the FBI.

Chucky said the best way in was to get next to Sciotti. Sciotti ran the Calabrese Club in Erie. Chucky could handle the introduction. Ed was leery of Chucky, as he would be of informants throughout his undercover career. He understood the pivotal role of snitches. They initiate an operation and give it credibility, but they are turncoats liked by no one on either side of the law. Often, an informant is motivated by greed, like Chucky. Good information on a topic of priority to the FBI can bring a professional informant a quarter of a million dollars a year. Some snitches work on contract or regular payroll with the Bureau. Sometimes, they're just cop-groupies, fringe criminals who like to hang out with the police and pretend they're cops, frequently asking for such absurdities as badges or credentials, even a gun and shoulder holster. Or, an informant may be working off a debt to the cops who have him nailed on other criminal activity. The most common motive is revenge: A criminal's spurned girlfriend can be an invaluable source. The mob eats its own so routinely, with so little reason or remorse, often with beatings and murders, that the ones who live to tell about it sometimes do.

A snitch's information is always suspect. He may inflate his facts to make the information more valuable. A $100,000 card game becomes a million dollar game. A cop who's being paid off actually only accepted a free beer off-duty. The law itself recognizes the unreliability of an informant. While his information can justify the initiation of a covert operation, there must first be independent corroboration of the information to establish probable cause before permission to initiate a wiretap or a warrant for search or arrest can be issued.

An informer becomes dangerous if he feels he is too valuable to the investigation. He may try to control events, call some shots, be in on the planning sessions. He may even threaten to reveal an agent if not satisfied. The smart undercover agent moves an informer through as fast as possible. Use him to get to his network, make his contacts your own, then get him out of the case immediately. The Italians have a word to describe someone who is unpredictable, a loose cannon, dumb because he's confused rather than stupid: stunad. Chucky, like most informants, was stunad.

During the initial conversation at the Ramada in Edinboro, Ed and Dean learned from the Pittsburgh agent that two other agents from the small number of undercover volunteers had tried several weeks earlier to break into the Barbout game. Ernie Haridopolis from the Little Rock Office and Nicky Gianturco out of New York—a Greek and an Italian—had met Sy Sciotti but never got close to the game. Chucky claimed it was because they smelled like cops. They tipped too big.

At the Calabrese Club in Erie, Ed and Dean were stopped at the door by a mountainous man with bulging muscles. Ed learned later that this bouncer was the Pennsylvania arm wrestling champ. The hulk told them the Calabrese Club was private. Members and invitations only.

"Right." Ed was confident. "We were invited here to meet with Mr. Sciotti."

The big man changed his tone. "You know Sy? OK. Be right back."

The bouncer waved his hand and another leviathan took his station at the door while he disappeared to tell Sy of the visitors.

Anthony Sciotti came to the door. His dusky sharkskin suit moved without a wave or wrinkle. His greying hair was slicked back, pushing his Roman nose and suspended cigarette out from his face even further. He was short, in his mid-forties, with the tough guy's look of disdain. Chucky made the introductions. When he shook hands with Eddie and Dino, the gold around all of their necks ting-a-linged against their bare chests.

Ed and Dean told Sy they'd heard about him from some friends of theirs who'd traveled through Erie in the past few months. They said Sy Sciotti knew where all the action was in town. The friends had introduced Eddie and Dino to Chucky here, and Chucky said he knew Sy. Sy hangs out at the Calabrese, Chucky says, Let's go tell him hello.

Sy welcomed them to the Calabrese Club and bought the first round. Ed and Dean made no mention of Barbout or any other illegal activities. For the next three days, the two agents hung out in their growing collection of leisure suits to meet up with Sy and Chucky at the Calabrese, eat dinner, pound down Dewar's and water and talk trash with Sciotti and his pack of slick friends.

When the two agents left Erie to continue their "market research," Sy gave them hugs and told them both to be sure they called him as soon as they came back through town. Ed knew they had to leave for a few weeks; staying any longer might look as if they'd been sent there. Besides, if Eddie and Dino were actually the shady characters they claimed to be, why weren't they out earning? The market research story was purposely flimsy, designed to appear as nothing but a smoke screen for some other felonious activity it was time the two got back to doing.

Ed and Dean said their goodbyes and left. They had just spent a weekend in the company of a known underworld figure without backup, recorders, or weapons. Their only protection from Anthony Sciotti was the relationship they were forging with him.

* * *

Two weeks after leaving Erie, Ed phoned Sciotti. He and Dino were coming back through. Could Sy recommend a good motel?

"Yeah, Eddie. You and Dino stay at my motel."

"Sy, you got a motel?"

"I live there, alright? And maybe I got a piece of it."

"Sy, you live in a motel?"

Ed's information had been that Sciotti had a wife and kids in Erie. The mobster drove a white Lincoln Mark IV, money floated around him like cigarette smoke. But he lived in a motel?

The place was a step down from a Holiday Inn, a rung up from a flophouse. Ed and Dean made the decision to take rooms there in order to build Sy's trust and friendship. Later, Ed learned that the motel was indeed Sciotti's sanctuary; he was protected there by the staff who guarded his privacy and his whereabouts. He had a master key to all the rooms.

Ed and Dean met Chucky in the afternoon. At Ed's request, Chucky arranged for them to play in a crap game held in the back room of a tobacco and candy shop downtown. The game moved fast and the two agents dropped $500. The men running the game probably were cheating with weighted or shaved dice of the sort Ed had used in gambling school at Quantico. He and Dino played like marks, losing the Bureau's money on risky, high-stakes bets. The logic was that, if the two new guys played and lost big, then they probably weren't sharpies, and if the game didn't get busted they were probably not cops.

Not all of the twenty people in the back room of the store were players. A few were big guys with guns under their coats to protect the game from being robbed. Holdups are a constant problem for the mob: illegal gambling activities are prime to be knocked off by rival crews, street toughs, or disgruntled losers. Being caught in the middle of a robbery also is a risk for the players. You could be rolling high one minute, and the next find yourself in a crossfire.

After the game, Chucky was dismissed. Ed and Dean went to the Calabrese Club for drinks with Sciotti. Sy met them wearing a black leather jacket, sharkskin pants, pastel silk shirt open, lots of jewelry, and shining patent leather shoes. Ed knew he and Dino were getting close to Sy when he invited them into the back room of the Calabrese to hang out and play some cards. After an hour, a bunch of guys came in, all wearing the same black leather coats as Sy.

"Hey, Eddie," one called, tugging proudly on his lapels, "you want one of these fuckin' coats?"

"Yeah. Lemme see one. You got a 46 long?"

The guy pulled aside a curtain to reveal a rack of coats, the rod bending under the weight of all the leather.

"Hey, hey!" Ed clapped his hands and walked over to look at the stolen goods, called "swag." He opened one up and looked inside. The label had been ripped out.

"How the fuck am I supposed to tell what size it is with the label torn out?"

The guy let go of the curtain, sizing Ed up. "Why you want to know about the label? The fuck you care about a label?"

Ed saw the test.

The guy continued: "How do I know you're not a cop?"

"Yeah," Ed replied, shrugging his shoulders once as if readying himself for some action. "Yeah, maybe I am a cop. And if I am, you're in a world of shit, pal. Tell you what. Take the fucking coat and shove it up your ass, tell me how it fits."

Ed took his seat at the card table. A hush descended on the room for several seconds. Then, like a cork popping back to the surface, the mood regained its form. Banter covered the strain. These guys were used to this sort of tough talk. In fact, Ed's challenging, bellicose response was the proper one required of a regular, "stand-up" guy. No one should get off lightly after accusing another bad guy of being a cop.

Ed had no intention of making a case out of the stolen coats. They were nothing compared with the opportunity of getting next to Sciotti, a made Mafioso. Perhaps the scene over the jackets had in fact been a test orchestrated by Sy. A cop would probably have laughed the accusation off and bought the coat, collecting evidence. Ed thought it unlikely the altercation was planned but it heightened his awareness of the scrutiny he and Dean were under. Crooks all have one thing in common: paranoia.

The next night, Sy hosted a dinner at the Calabrese. Eddie and Dino were invited. Sciotti sat at one end of the table, Ed was at the other. Next to Ed sat a long, thin man in a sharkskin suit

27

with skin pale as milk and blue eyes like lasers. His laugh was a jerking pant through his nose. His name was Ray Farita; Ed recognized him. Farita, a Cleveland wise guy, was a suspect in a federal bombing case. Later, Sciotti confided to Ed that Farita was a mob hit man, specializing in taking out family members who had fallen into disfavor. His trademark was a .22 round to the back of the head.

The conversation at the table never ranged far from schemes, scams, vengeance, and broads. The talk took a nasty turn when the name of Jimmy "The Weasel" Fratianno came up. Fratianno, formerly a "button"—a made member—in the Licavoli crew in Cleveland, had become notorious in mob circles as an informant for the FBI. The Weasel used to make regular trips to Erie. Everyone at the table knew him and all agreed what a "yellow-fucking-rat-prick" he was. He had better not come around Erie now, they said, or he'll get clipped. Cut up and fed to the fucking fish.

After an hour of pasta, meatballs, Chianti, and bread, Sciotti issued a warning to the group that there was going to be an FBI raid on several Erie bookmaking operations. There had been an earlier raid, he said, to gather evidence and now they were coming back to make the grand jury arrests. The word was that the FBI was holding sealed indictments for Sciotti and twenty other mobsters.

After dinner, Sy whispered to Ed, as if Eddie Rossi were the only man in the room who could be trusted, that he had somebody in the U.S. Marshal's Office in his pocket. Sometimes, he said, the Pittsburgh FBI Office shared information as a courtesy with the U.S. Marshal. That's how Sy got his tip.

When the dinner broke up, Ed and Dean went to the Holiday Inn bar to hang out. Dressed like gangsters, they sat in a dark booth, watching a dozen obvious FBI agents in blue suits, snap-brimmed hats, and cheap shoes, drinking in the bar. Ed called the Erie contact agent from a pay phone.

"Call off the raid," he said.

"Naw. No way they know," he was told.

"Look, dipshit! I know, don't I?"

The next day, while Ed and Dean hung out at the Calabrese, the raid went down. Reports of the arrests filtered into the back room, to the card table, to the laughing Sciotti and his crew. When the FBI struck around town, they turned up only a few marginal characters, no one important. Sy chuckled: The guys the Feds arrested were just schmucks that he wanted popped, guys he specifically did not alert to the coming arrests. The FBI had done him a favor by getting these guys off the street.

After the raids, Ed, Dean, and Sy ate at the Calabrese Club. The two agents began to press Sciotti to get them into the Barbout game. Sy was reluctant. The Greeks were a tight and suspicious group, he said. They didn't welcome new people easily; the game had plenty of players and they weren't looking for more.

Ed knew how large a favor he was asking. Vouching for someone within the underworld ties you to that person. Your name is on him always. If he turns bad, gets out of control or, worse, if he winds up a cop or a snitch, then you get punished by the family for his sins as if they were your own. Putting your name on the wrong guy could get you killed.

While Ed talked with Sy about the Barbout game, two black men got out of a taxi and attempted to enter the Calabrese. They were told at the door that the club was private, with no black members. The men made a mistake. They walked past the huge bouncer who had spoken to them politely but firmly. Ed watched from his booth as the two blacks were dragged to the parking lot by the bouncer and a few others and beaten, calmly, professionally. Ed's every muscle tensed; he strained to keep his seat. Trying not to wince, Ed steered Sy's attention to another topic.

During the investigation in Erie, Ed had become involved in another FBI gambling sting in Virginia Beach where he was also posing as the shady high roller Eddie Rossi. By now, Rossi had been fully born, with a driver's license, business cards, an address, even a phone number in Pittsburgh where he could be reached on weekends. The FBI had installed a red phone in Ed and Gretchen's bedroom in Charlottesville that rang to a Pittsburgh number; Gretchen and the kids were told never to pick up that phone. Ed wanted to bring Sciotti into the Virginia Beach web, to impress him, and perhaps involve him and his Pittsburgh famiglia. Ed explained to Sy a scheme he was hatching: He wanted to run a casino on a hired boat that would operate in international waters, outside U.S. jurisdiction. Sy was intrigued. He agreed to talk more about the idea after he gave it some thought.

The next day, Ed and Dino arranged a meeting with the Pittsburgh Organized Crime Supervisor, Jim Fanning. In a breakfast restaurant, they reported that they were inching closer to Sciotti. The mobster was opening up to them, evidenced by the rack of leather coats, the early warning on the FBI raids, and the whisper of corruption in the U.S. Marshal's Office. Sciotti was a direct link to the ruling Pittsburgh organized crime family, perhaps even to the boss John LaRocca. Ed wanted Fanning to ease off on the bid to break into the Barbout game. It was getting to be a sore spot with Sciotti. Let us work him, Ed asked, let us see where he can take us. It's already gotten bigger than the game. No, Fanning told them. The mission is to break into the game and shut it down. That's all. Now go do it.

Ed and Dino left the meeting irked by what they perceived as a bureaucratic lack of vision. How could Fanning trade the enormous potential of a relationship with gangland figure Anthony Sciotti for one illegal gambling operation? Another game would just spring up in its place. But Sciotti could take them to the top.

When Ed returned from his meeting with Fanning, he noted instantly that his motel room had been tossed. Each time, before he left the room, he set up several tiny traps, telltale signs to reveal if the room had been entered. A tiny bit of scotch tape across the doorjamb would be broken. A hair, licked and stuck across the keyhole, would be split. His blue socks would not be laid out in the top drawer three in a row between two pairs of brown, as he'd left them. Ed expected this. It was an indication that he and Dean were moving in the right direction, toward the center of things. The search of his room was another milestone, a security gate on the way in.

At dinner with Sy, Ed made no mention of the violation of his room. Though they could not be sure, he assumed Dean's room had been searched too. We've passed another test, Ed thought, so maybe it's time to step it up a little with Sy and follow Fanning's orders. See how far we can push. Ed pressed again for an introduction to the Greeks and the game. Sy refused, a little more testily this time.

Ed knew his window was closing. Fanning had made it clear he was close to pulling the plug. Ed devised a plan, a now-or-never scheme to get into the Barbout game. He told Dino, who agreed. What was there to lose?

After dinner, Ed took Sy aside.

"Look, Sy, me and Dino, we don't really want to play in the Barbout game."

"Eddie, then why you been breakin' my balls to get in?"

"We figured maybe you get us in, we play a little, then we rob the thing."

Sciotti went ballistic, scalded by the proposal. Ed tried to explain how Sy would get half, there would be a couple hundred grand there easy, plus watches, jewelry, we'll clean 'em out and we'll split it. Sy could only shout back, "You're crazy. You'll get us all killed! This is my hometown! Get the fuck away from me with this!" The mobster was furious. He stomped off, calling over his shoulder for Eddie to stay away from him.

When Ed got back to his room, it had been ransacked. There was no attempt to hide it this time. Dean's room had been searched as well. Dean came to Ed's room and said he was going down to the bar to talk calmly to Sy. Maybe Ed should stay put. Hours later, Dean returned to tell Ed he and Sy had made the peace. Dino had explained that his partner sometimes shot his mouth off without thinking, that Sy shouldn't put too much on what Eddie said about robbing the game. Eddie gets stunad sometimes, that's all. What can you do? Despite this assurance,

Ed slept with one eye open, afraid of retaliation from Sy or the Greeks. If trouble came down on Ed in this motel room tonight, he was dead. He had no backup, no surveillance, no secure phone, no weapon. He had not cleared the robbery scheme with the Office. It had been one of those shoot-from-the-hip, on-the-spot calls an undercover agent makes alone, for better or for worse.

It really wasn't such a bad plan, he thought. Appeal to Sy's greed, the soul of a gangster. Get into the game, play a little, lose some marked bills, look around, memorize some faces, and leave. Explain later to Sy that there was too much heat in the room to rob it that night; we were just scouting. Next time.

Or maybe it was a crazy idea. There was a lot of interest in the Barbout game from a lot of angles, probably more than Sy could control. There had to be a payoff going to someone high up in the Erie police or city government. That's delicate, not something you mess with. Somebody bigger than Sy would be mad. Whatever, Ed thought; I had to try something. I hate losing.

The next morning Eddie, Dino, and Sy said their goodbyes. Ed told Sy he'd stay in touch. Yeah, he admitted, it was a stupid idea to think about robbing the game. Sorry about that.

Back in Pittsburgh, Ed and Dean were debriefed. Fanning told them they had failed and to go back home. As far as Ed knew, the Pittsburgh Office made no use of any of the information he and Dean developed.

Ed continued to call Sciotti to maintain his link with the mobster. Over the next few months, they chatted several times. Ed continued to mine Sy for leads and mob gossip. Once, Sy mentioned "that thing in Virginia Beach. Is that still on?"

"Yeah. I'm working on it. You want in, Sy?"

Sy told Ed of a twist he'd come up with for the offshore casino. He'd give Ed a list of big shots, dirty politicians, rival underworld characters, and high-stakes gamblers from Erie. Ed would take them all out on the casino boat. Once outside U.S. waters, Ed's gang would fleece everybody, then sink the boat. No witnesses. Ed agreed to consider it. Such a list from Sciotti would be invaluable. But did this monstrous scheme come from the same guy who wouldn't rob the Barbout game?

Not long afterward, after several conversations, the phone calls and planning between Eddie Rossi and Sy Sciotti stopped. Sy went to prison on a gambling conviction, without ever knowing that the dangerous, crazy Eddie Rossi was an FBI undercover agent.

CHAPTER FIVE
Talon 2 and the Marriott Abduction

Criminal undercover operations quickly won prestige inside the FBI. The Field Offices that ran successful covert operations—resulting in multiple arrests of big-name criminals or corrupt public officials—got favorable attention from the news media as well as accolades within the Bureau itself.

Herb Clough, in charge of the Norfolk Field Office, initiated a storefront sting in 1974, code-named Seawall, in the sprawling oceanfront city of Virginia Beach. Clough gave Seawall two years, then closed the operation after netting more than three dozen street-level burglars and thugs, the typical catch of a storefront bust.

After the success of Seawall, Clough wanted to engage in another, more ambitious undercover investigation to penetrate a higher strata of the local underworld. The next target for the Norfolk Office would be organized crime. A new covert operation was mounted, code-named Talon. Though the Mafia was not yet ensconced in the city, Clough's street agents had told him the mob was making inroads. Clough wanted to take the pulse of organized crime in his territory.

The undercover agents of Talon penetrated the Virginia Beach entertainment scene. They made several criminal connections and a few cases including gambling, official corruption, and a non-mob-related murder. Most importantly, the agents developed confidential sources and information that led Clough and the Norfolk Office to believe the city had been selected by a New York crime family for investment and expansion. Carlo

34

Gambino, Jr., had become a regular visitor to Virginia Beach. He was the frequent guest of Tony Gargulio, a gangland figure relocated from New Jersey. Other names turned up by Talon investigators carried a lot of local weight: John Arragona, the coke freak son of a powerful land developer; Eddie Garcia and Roger Nonni, also big developers; and Peter Babalas, a Virginia Beach state senator whose unethical conduct made him, in 1987, the only state senator ever censured by the Virginia Legislature. The FBI observed all of these prominent men consorting with known Mafiosi.

When Talon was shut down, it left behind living roots in the criminal community. Informants had been recruited, leads gathered, suspicions aroused, names and faces collected and researched. Many of the criminals swept up in Talon traded lists of their associates in return for better sentencing recommendations from the FBI.

Clough and his staff devised a follow-up named Talon 2. The plan called for a fresh round of undercover agents to stir up Virginia Beach. The first agent sent in on Talon 2 was Charles McGinty, a slight, pale redhead. He was a type that had only begun to emerge in the mid-1970s: a computer whiz. He was installed in a penthouse overlooking the Chesapeake Bay. The apartment bristled with hidden cameras and microphones. McGinty's cover was to be a computer nerd named Chuck, an expert in electronic embezzling. Though he was knowledgeable in his criminal craft, McGinty was a rookie in undercover techniques. For months, he had been a fixture in Virginia Beach nightspots and restaurants, rubbing elbows in his blue suit, dark tie, and cheap shoes. He asked too many questions and left noticeably big tips. Chuck met no one and got nowhere.

Talon 2 needed someone to inject McGinty into the right crowd, but the Norfolk Office could find no one well-connected in the Virginia Beach underworld they could pay to squire Chuck. The Office decided to bring in another agent who looked and acted enough like a criminal to give Chuck some authenticity. Tom Kelly, the Assistant Agent in Charge in Richmond, got a call from Norfolk. Yeah, Kelly replied, we've got a guy who's been around. Up in Charlottesville. I'll send him down to take a look.

* * *

Eddie Rossi parked his red T-Bird in front of Sir Richard's Restaurant. He ambled in wearing a papaya leisure suit and the usual gold chains. He sat at the bar and ordered a Dewar's up. He drank, smoked, watched, and scowled. After a few rounds he asked the bartender if he knew Chuck. The man did.

"Tell him Eddie Rossi's lookin' for him." Eddie paid and left.

Ed repeated this act around town for several nights at all the known watering holes, to spread the scent around. If Ed could get accepted, Chuck must also be "OK." He must be, if this evil-looking bastard Eddie Rossi was in town to do a job with him and his friends.

One evening in Sir Richard's, Ed sat on a barstool chatting with a bartender, an Oriental who had been caught up in Talon 1. The man hadn't been charged but he had talked about a lot of things he shouldn't have told the undercover agents.

"Yeah, the Feds ran a scam down here," the bartender said. "I got to be friends with those guys. They treated me alright. I hung out with them, showed them around, and then they fucked me."

The bartender couldn't believe he'd been taken in. "The shit they were wearing and the way they acted. I should've known they were cops. But I'll tell you one thing . . ." he leaned across the bar to speak conspiratorially to Ed, ". . . they'll never get me again."

"No," Eddie Rossi agreed. "No fuckin' way."

In fact, the bartender was surrounded. Ed spotted a table of what he was certain were undercover local cops, all wearing the same outlandish gangster outfits he had on. Probably State Police, he thought, or Virginia Beach cops, running a small-time drug buy-bust. Later, he learned that the Virginia State Police were running an undercover operation out of Sir Richard's.

Ed had arranged to get phone calls at Sir Richard's that were placed by an agent at the Norfolk Office. On several occasions, he'd responded to the caller in suspicious, dark tones to imply that the call was about some criminal activity, enhancing his reputation as a collection guy. Tonight, he took a call at the bar. He screamed into the phone. "What? What? You tell him, you fucking tell him, that's the way it is and if he don't follow up like we agreed I'll come down there and straighten him up myself!"

The agent on the other end laughed. "Christ, Ed, you're in rare form tonight."

"Got it? Good! Fuck you!" Ed slammed the phone down.

Patrons around the bar backed away. He stood in a spotlight of anger. He glared over at the table of state cops and smiled: let them write that up.

* * *

Ed spent several weeks "looking for Chuck," leaving his imprint in the right eyes and ears. Finally, he began to appear in public with McGinty. At Sir Richard's or the Isle of Capri, they talked openly about scores they were planning. Ed got Chuck to dress in a more flashy, mobbed-up manner, with gold chains dangling down his thin white chest beneath an open silk shirt.

At this same time, Ed was in the final stages of the undercover operation in Erie trying to break into the Barbout game. He disappeared from Virginia Beach for a few weeks to wrap things up with Sy Sciotti. On his return, he moved out of his motel and into a bedroom at Chuck's spacious apartment. This gave the impression to all those watching that Eddie and Chuck had made a big score while he'd been out of town.

Bit by bit, it became clear that Ed was taking the lead in Talon 2. None of the targets wanted to talk to Chuck; they all vied for Ed's attention, passing on to him underworld gossip to curry favor with him. One such whispered nugget was that a longtime ACC basketball referee had accepted a bribe to fix a tournament game. Ed passed this info along, and the game ended with just the score Ed's source said it would be. Nothing came of the tip, but clearly Ed was on the right track.

But the really big boys—Gargulio, Gambino, Arragona, Garcia, Babalas—continued to avoid Eddie Rossi. Before he could run with their crowd and take Chuck with him, he needed to be recognized as a higher roller, a player of their own caliber. Ed spread the story that, before coming to Virginia Beach, he had been in Washington, D.C., extorting "queer politicians." He told colorful tales about his exploits. One of his most enthusiastic listeners was a professional gambler named John who owned a pizza joint. Ed made up a yarn about a gay U.S. senator who had been slow in his protection payments. Ed told John that, one night while the senator walked his French poodle, he drove by and blew the dog to mattress stuffing with a shotgun. The senator was left standing there with an empty leash in his hand. Ed swore John to secrecy, knowing the gambler would spread the story like wildfire.

Weeks later, Ed set up an act for John's benefit. He took the gambler with him to the Norfolk airport to make a connection. John came along to guard his back. Ed pulled up behind another car in the lot and parked. He got out and climbed in the passenger side of the car and began an animated talk with the driver. After a minute of angry gesticulating, Ed began slapping the driver around. When he was done, he returned to his T-Bird, tucking in his shirttail and rearranging his coat. The driver, a young agent from Norfolk, jumped out and followed, apologizing and pleading for "more time." Ed patted the kid lightly on the cheek, mumbled "Yeah, yeah," and drove away. He made John swear on his mother's grave not to tell what he'd seen.

By the time John finished relaying the scene to his pals, Eddie Rossi had broken both of the poor guy's arms.

* * *

By now, a year had passed in Talon 2, and Ed considered

himself a failure. He'd developed some good info and gotten in tight with some genuine scoundrels. But to date, in his four-year undercover career, he hadn't gotten one criminal arrested. That was how undercover agents kept score: whom and how many did you bust?

Chuck McGinty finally left Talon 2. Though Clough and the other supervisors were reluctant to admit it, they had tossed the young computer whiz in over his head. Rather than isolate the specific problems of corruption and gambling and insert the right agent for the job, they had sent in a specialist in white-collar crime and told him to look for criminals. Ed likened it to baiting a hook and hoping the fish would bite, instead of studying first what they were biting and then choosing the bait. The Norfolk Office had made a mistake, but they were learning.

Ed was alone now in the big apartment overlooking the Bay. He pondered what he could do to get next to the Gambinos and their connections. He needed an inspiration, a boost. He got it in the form of a new case.

* * *

The Manassas Resident Agency was abuzz. Street Agent Larry Lien had uncovered a plot to kidnap one of the world's richest men, J. Willard Marriott.

A Washington U.S. Park policeman, Paul Shepherd, had contacted a local burglar to help him find someone to assist with the kidnapping. The burglar was well known to the D.C. police, who were sitting on a strong case against him. Hoping to trade information for federal intervention, the burglar brought Shepherd's kidnapping plot to the FBI.

Local police don't like this sort of thing. They work hard to hang a conviction on a criminal to get him off the streets, then he tries to slide out of it by climbing in bed with the FBI. In return for his cooperation, the Bureau had to promise the local police that, when they were done with him, he would work for them to their satisfaction. Afterward, the burglar would get no guarantee of assistance from the FBI, just a kind word to his judge and the prosecutors. Take it or leave it.

Ed got a call from the Alexandria Field Office. He had been suggested for the job by Don "Big Daddy" Moore, the Assistant Director of the Criminal Division at FBI Headquarters. The lofty height from which this recommendation came was not lost on Ed. His reputation as an undercover agent was growing.

He arranged to meet the burglar on the Manassas National Battlefield, beside a cannon. The place was wide open, safe, and quiet, where the chances were small that anyone would recognize Ed or the informant. Ed told the burglar to have Shepherd phone him at a downtown motel. Then he told him to get lost; he was out of the loop, effective immediately. Eddie Rossi would take it from here.

Shepherd called Ed at the motel. The call was recorded. A meeting was set at Washington National Airport. The airport was under federal jurisdiction but was also in Virginia. Ed chose this site to keep the locus of the crime's origin within the federal domain. Kidnapping is both a state and federal crime, so if the FBI lost control over the prosecution, the case would land in the stricter Virginia courts rather than before the more liberal judges of the District of Columbia.

Ed arrived at the airport's North Terminal. Shepherd was seated on a bench near the Pan Am ticket counter, wearing a brown leather jacket. He was heavyset, balding. Ed's signal to Shepherd was the copy of War and Peace under his arm.

Eddie Rossi was dressed like a mob hit man in his chains, polyester suit, and sparkling shoes. He also wore something extra and unseen: a Nagra recorder strapped under his left armpit.

He sat beside the large man in the leather coat.

"I don't like cops," Ed said immediately. "I don't trust 'em. If you was trustworthy, you wouldn't be a fucking cop."

Paul Shepherd was apologetic. He didn't enjoy being a cop, he said. He was sick and tired of protecting all those rich folks who didn't give a shit. He's the one who put his ass on the line every day and they go home safe to their big houses and he ain't got shit to show for it. He's sick and tired.

Shepherd had played Santa Claus for Nixon at several White House Christmas parties. There, Shepherd saw more opulence than he could stand, more tuxedos, gowns, caviar, chamber quartets, crisp linen, and high ceilings than he thought was fair. He felt mocked, a man like him who worked in jackboots and leather gloves riding a Harley Davidson. He deserved more because, in his eyes, he had damn well earned more. And he meant to get it.

J. Willard Marriott, in his late seventies, was a longtime supporter of Richard Nixon. Officer Shepherd had met Marriott while on duty at several White House soirees, many catered by Marriott's company. Shepherd also had encountered Marriott at the White House while playing Santa. He had gotten even closer to Marriott during Nixon's second inaugural ball. Marriott had enlisted the U.S. Park policeman to run weekend errands. Sometimes Shepherd picked Marriott up at home and drove him to meetings with Nixon.

Shepherd told Ed his abduction plan. Ed would stake out Marriott's house in a van provided by Shepherd. After the domestic staff went home, Ed was to enter a side door that Shepherd would make sure remained unlocked. Ed would bind Mr. and Mrs. Marriott, then roll the old man up in a carpet and carry him to the van. He'd drive out the George Washington Parkway to an address in Virginia where Shepherd, his girlfriend, and brother would be waiting.

Shepherd told Ed to drive him from the airport to check out Marriott's home in D.C. From there, they continued to Virginia to Shepherd's girlfriend's house, then back to National Airport. They made arrangements to meet the next week.

Eight days later, Ed drove an FBI camper, equipped with hidden video cameras and tape recorders, to a Ramada Inn in Fairfax just across the Virginia line. He called Shepherd. When the officer arrived, Ed went into his act.

"Paul, are you sure you want to do this?" he asked. "Cause

you seem kind of unsure. We don't have to go through with this." Ed tried to talk him out of the kidnapping, all of it recorded. Shepherd was adamant; he was sick of being broke and Marriott was going to pay him half a million for his years of loyal service on the force, so on and so on.

Ed had him cold. Later, with this recording playing in front of a jury, Shepherd couldn't claim entrapment by the slick FBI undercover agent Ed Robb. Paul Shepherd had his chance to back out, right there on videotape, and he rejected it. The cop was now a criminal. This videotape was later used as a training tool at the FBI Academy. Shepherd went over the plan one more time. Ed did everything except advise him of his Miranda rights. Ed said, "OK, we'll talk soon," and set the date. He left in the camper.

The next day, Ed presented the case and the evidence to the U.S. Attorney's Office for the Eastern District of Virginia. The Assistant U.S. Attorney determined that there was probable cause and sufficient evidence to prosecute. He had arrest warrants issued for Paul Shepherd, his girlfriend, and brother. The Marriotts were advised to take a trip out of town for a week or so, until the arrests could be made. Shepherd and his crew were taken down the next day. They were eventually convicted in federal court of conspiracy to kidnap. Shepherd got twenty years.

Marriott was grateful to Ed when he learned which agent had saved him. He invited Ed and his family to his Virginia farm and mansion, and even struck up a correspondence with him. This attention from the hotel baron made Ed uncomfortable; he'd done nothing more than his job. What did make an impact on him was that he finally had an arrest for his record. The breaking of the Marriott kidnapping case received national publicity. Of course, Eddie Rossi's name and face were kept out of the limelight but those whom he wanted most to know what he had accomplished—the FBI and Gretchen—knew. Ed's spirit was buoyed. He packed his bags and headed back to Virginia Beach and Talon 2, where nothing had been going well.

Eddie Rossi would no longer wait passively for Talon 2 to

crack open. He moved to the attack with a plan certain to rock-et him up to where the monied mobsters and dirty politicians in Virginia Beach would acknowledge, even embrace, him. His scheme was ambitious, maybe too big to handle. But now, in many ways, so was Ed Robb, flush from having saved old man Marriott.

Ed's plan took its cue from the current events of 1976. The world was thirsting for Middle Eastern oil. Newscasts and the front pages were awash in rich Arabs; their castles, flowing robes, playboy relatives, and bulletproof Mercedes had become worldwide icons of unfathomable wealth.

An Arab. That's what I need, Ed thought. I need a sheik.

The plan called for the FBI to set up another undercover agent, Richard Farhart, as an Arab prince and surround him with an exotic retinue in the fashionable Cavalier Hotel. The purpose of the prince's visit to Virginia Beach would be to investigate for his royal family the possibilities of owning a horse track. Pari-mutuel betting was being considered for the first time in the Virginia Legislature. Politician and connected-guy Peter Babalas was keenly interested in the issue, as were several other Talon 2 targets, all real estate developers who would do anything for the chance to get close to such a wealthy financier. The sheik, in flowing kaftan and blinding jewelry, would step out of a stretch limo at Sir Richard's, flash around a roll of bills large enough to choke a camel, and share a pleasant meal with Eddie Rossi. Later, installed in his suite of rooms at the Cavalier, the prince would entertain guests and petitioners in the lavish style of a sultan. At his right hand, as local advisor and chamberlain, would sit Eddie Rossi.

Ed submitted the plan on paper. He broke down every element, even to the roles of the agents who'd be kissing the sheik's rings. He traveled to Pimlico in Maryland to study how a track was operated. His construction background would allow him to appear knowledgeable in front of the developers and politicians who would be invited to meet the sheik. He estimated a budget, a time frame, and projected a strategy. Eddie Rossi would

43

encourage the sheik to accept proposals from Talon 2 targets. As a result, Rossi's status would rise high enough to penetrate the Gambino circles in Virginia Beach.

The plan felt strong. Ed submitted it to FBI Headquarters. They turned him down. There are too many fishing expeditions going on right now all over the country, he was told, we don't need one more. You've had a year in Virginia Beach and you've turned up nothing. Time to shut down, Ed.

It was the Barbout game all over again, Ed thought. Another operation ready to break wide open with just a nudge, and the bureaucracy kills it. He could not know that three years later, the FBI would use a very similar scheme in what would become one of the most famous of all FBI undercover operations, code-named ABSCAM.

Talon 2 was a victim of a flaw that the FBI shared with other bureaucracies. Each investigation is a project; it becomes the preserve of the people who devised it and instigated it. When an operation takes a long time, as Talon 2 did, supervisors and agents often get promoted or reassigned before the investigation can mature. Professional administrators can't put their careers on hold for the sake of one case. Inevitably, with the change in management comes a change in styles, priorities, and strategies. Though the undercover agent is always at the center of an operation, it's still essentially a team project. When the team is broken up—as it was when Herb Clough, the agent who brought Ed in on Talon 2, and several other supervisors had been transferred near the end of the investigation—support for the op can fall apart, especially in those cases where results have not been immediate.

When the order came down to close Talon 2, Ed left town quietly. He stayed quiet. Ed Robb was a foot soldier.

CHAPTER SIX
Coldwater

Foiling the plot to kidnap Marriott enhanced Ed's reputation in the FBI. With his other operations, he was now one of only a dozen experienced undercover agents in the Bureau. The tactics and techniques he developed and used became the subjects of study at Quantico. Supervisors in other Field Offices sought his advice on operations they planned. He traveled around the country giving seminars to budding undercover agents. He described his successes as well as the hard lessons of Talon 2 and the Barbout game. Ed was widely recognized as one of the formative powers in the FBI's still nascent initiative in criminal covert operations.

In the Charlottesville and Richmond Offices, his direct supervisors began to realize that Ed Robb now belonged to the FBI at large. He was no longer referred to as "Special Agent Robb" but as "undercover agent Robb." He had joined an elite corps within the Bureau, and he was champing at the bit.

None of the undercover assignments he'd worked so far had been as big as what he now wanted to sink his teeth into. He felt ready to use all he had been learning and teaching about the underworld and the criminal mind. He was ready to break into the mob.

His first chance came in February 1979, in a call from an agent Ed worked with during his weekend as one of Hoover's Hundred. Special Agent Ed Stewart was looking for a covert operative to penetrate the Pittsburgh Mafia. The city's gangsters were becoming heavily involved in the vending machine business. Ed wasn't surprised, recalling his father-in-law's experience with the mob in nearby Warren. The agent would be introduced into the crime family by Mel Weinberg, the informant who later became the key informant in the FBI's ABSCAM operation. Ed told Stewart he would come and look at the case.

An hour later, his phone rang again. This call came from Tony Daniels, the Organized Crime Squad Supervisor in the Tampa Field Office. Daniels was searching for an undercover agent to be inserted into an organized crime ring planning to run an illegal gambling operation in New Port Richey. There was also a strong scent of official corruption. Daniels had never met Ed Robb but he heard that Ed was an undercover agent who got the job done. Daniels needed the best, and people he trusted told him Ed Robb was it. Would Ed take a look at the job?

Ed couldn't have known it, but this call would engage him in an undercover operation lasting almost three years. The case would carry him to within one step of the highest ranks of America's organized crime families and place his life and the lives of several other agents in constant jeopardy. The operation would uncover murders, extortions, drug deals, robberies, illicit gambling, conspiracies, and public corruption, resulting in dozens of convictions. Its aftermath would leave many dead. This case would catapult the careers of many of the agents involved and solidify Ed Robb's reputation inside the FBI as a leading undercover agent.

*　*　*

Three days after the call from Daniels, Ed was in Waynesboro, Virginia, to testify in a car theft case. Now Daniels called to say he had cleared everything with Ed's superiors and a plane ticket to Tampa waited for him. Ed phoned Stewart in Pittsburgh and told him to hold off, he was flying down to Tampa to look at another operation. Privately, Ed was relieved: Too many people could recognize him in western Pennsylvania.

At the Tampa airport, Ed met Jim Kinne, the investigation's

contact agent. Kinne was a lithe, former Marine with handsome, sharp features under a clump of white blonde hair. He had a stubborn cowlick which, in a previous racketeering investigation leading to the conviction of Henry Trafficante, a brother of Florida crime lord Santo, earned him the nickname in Mafia circles of "Dennis the Menace."

Kinne checked Ed into the Sheraton across from the Tampa Field Office where he would meet Supervisor Tony Daniels and Case Agent Jack Case in the lobby. It made Ed uncomfortable to start his undercover work in Florida by meeting in public with three known FBI agents. But this was still their operation and they could run it their way—until he got involved.

Preparing to go down to the meeting, Ed saw his first Florida roach, a burgundy creature three inches long. It scuttled across the sink in his room. He jumped back and shouted at Kinne: "What the hell was that?" Ed had not been in Florida before. Kinne explained it was called a palmetto bug. Next, in his closet, he encountered a spider that seemed the size of a baseball. Ed turned to Kinne. "I'm taking the Pittsburgh job. I'd rather freeze my ass off than deal with these fuckin' bugs." Kinne pushed him out of the room into the hall. He chuckled in his New York accent, "You'll get used to it."

Ed Robb was the fourth agent interviewed for the job. None of the first three had been satisfactory. One agent smoked a pipe and spoke fondly of his hobby of bee keeping. "I can tend bar for the crooks and talk to them about bees," he said hopefully. Another agent assured Daniels that he would "never drink and drive" on duty and would "never accept sex from a woman" on the job. These, of course, were the right answers, but Kinne could tell the responses were sincere and this was a good, virtuous man, not one who could hold his own with gangsters on their own turf. The agent he was looking for would certainly show good judgment, keep his nose clean, and do nothing to embarrass the Bureau, but he'd also do what he had to do in each situation. A third agent they interviewed fit the bill but he could be in Tampa only six months before he was committed elsewhere.

Though Kinne didn't expect the investigation to go longer than six months, he could not guarantee it would be shut down within that time. This operation was one of the first FBI undercover stings to be designed by goals rather than duration, and Kinne, Daniels, and Case had their sights set high.

In the lobby, Ed Robb settled at a table with the three agents. They ordered beers and pretzels. Daniels said the Tampa investigation would be a Group 1 undercover operation. A Group 1 operation had to withstand intense scrutiny at the highest levels of the FBI before it could go forward. The FBI had to determine that all conventional investigative efforts, including wiretaps, surveillance, background information, confidential informant info, and physical evidence were exhausted in order to allow the insertion of an undercover agent. Group 1's were time consuming and very expensive. They could also lead to extensive government liability because the undercover agent skirts the edge of entrapment by actually entering the criminal process.

In contrast, a Group 2 operation—the more common undercover investigation—was of shorter duration and far less costly. Group 2's could be approved at the Field Office level, without major critical review. They were frequently done by local street agents rather than an outside agent brought in for the occasion. Group 2's were typically a buy-bust of a local drug dealer, purchasing stolen goods and busting the fence, or entering and then taking down a small-time gambling operation.

While Ed listened to Daniels, a one-inch palmetto bug ran across his plate. Again, Kinne assured him, "You'll get used to it."

The initial target of the investigation was Vincenzo "Jimmy" Acquafredda, an associate of the Gambino crime family out of New York. He had been sent to Florida to organize a union of west coast Florida independent garbage collectors. The union would be run, of course, for the benefit of the Gambinos. Garbage collection had long been a focus for mob influence in all the Eastern states; it could be an extremely lucrative business whenever competition could be squelched. In addition, the collectors, once organized, had to pay association dues, adding to the take.

Along with Acquafredda, the Gambinos sent down an introduction to a few family connections in Tampa. These men formed a loose-knit crew around Jimmy: Anthony "Fat Sonny" Santangelo, Joseph "Joe Pete" Pullicino, and Eddie Trascher and his son, Ricky.

Acquafredda lived with his wife in Port Richey thirty-five miles north of Tampa, where he owned and operated a garbage collection business, Gulf Coast Disposal. In 1977, he unwittingly told an FBI informant about his Gambino mission in southwest Florida and that he also intended to start a high-stakes, Las Vegas-style casino in a penthouse apartment in Port Richey. The FBI subpoenaed Acquafredda's phone records, traced his background to New York, and confirmed his underworld connections. He would be the central target of a federal inquiry into mob gambling and racketeering in the Tampa area. The investigation was given the name "Operation Coldwater," a translation of Acquafredda's Italian name.

Over the previous two years, the Tampa Field Office had exhausted every overt means to make cases against Acquafredda and his crew. The men were under constant surveillance and the informant was good, but no Title III permission for phone taps would be issued by the federal court without corroborating evidence. An undercover agent was needed to "tickle" Coldwater.

Ed told Daniels, Kinne, and Case that he knew nothing about the sanitation business, though he was well versed in gambling and official corruption. He could do the job, alright. But he would only consider the assignment on one condition: The three agents at the table would have to be open and honest with Ed, an outsider to their clique. "You got a beef with me or the decisions I make," he told them, "or if you don't understand my reasons for doing something, you come right to me. But I call the shots. No second guessing, no Monday morning quarterbacking." The Tampa team agreed.

After the meeting, Ed chatted with Daniels, who also came from Pittsburgh. He, like Ed, had played football in Pennsylvania and had been a Little All-America quarterback at Slippery Rock. Ed felt more comfortable.

The next day, he met with Daniel's boss, Phil McNiff. Ed repeated his condition that there be open communications between himself as lead undercover agent and all other agents on the case. He assured McNiff he could do the job but said that he didn't want to be told how to do it by agents who weren't there standing in his shiny undercover shoes. He had to be trusted—and his ten-year FBI dossier displayed that he could be trusted—or he'd be gone. McNiff said his only concern was that Agent Robb not drink and drive. Ed couldn't figure how an undercover agent running with a pack of Mafiosi day and night could avoid drinking and driving. But he promised McNiff he'd not get drunk and drive. That was enough. McNiff canceled all other agent interviews. Coldwater belonged to Ed.

He returned to Charlottesville to tell Gretchen he was on a new undercover case. It was in Florida and expected to last no more than six months. Ed knew, but did not tell Gretchen, that six months was no more than a guideline for Coldwater, a checkpoint, when the supervisors would evaluate the case and the staying power of the agent inside it. The cases being made, the supervisors' common sense, and the agent's mental stability were the only considerations for the duration of an undercover operation.

Ed also knew that a deep undercover penetration could change forever the mental makeup of the participant. Like the death of a loved one, a wrenching divorce, or any other extremely stressful emotional trauma, they are never forgotten and the effects are permanent. No agent ever leaves an extended undercover job as the same person he was when he went in. The strain and tension are unrelenting. The agent is drinking, staying out all night with killers, thieves, and psychopaths, coping with the dangers of living in the lion's den, dangers that rarely rest. Regardless of the agent's expertise, character, or mettle, the undercover experience always leaves its mark. Ed knew there were incalculable risks to an agent's psyche as well as to his life, because some undercover agents had never returned. He did not tell Gretchen any of this.

* * *

It was not Edgar Straessly Robb who said goodbye to his wife in their Charlottesville home the morning of February 27, 1979; it was his alter ego, Edward Anthony Rossi. Ed had completely shed his real name and identity: no monogrammed jewelry, no receipts in his wallet, no labels on his clothing that could be linked to Edgar S. Robb. He carried Rossi's credit card, secretly paid for by the FBI, and Rossi's Social Security number, traceable back to his birthplace, Pittsburgh, as well as an FBI fingerprint crime history. He wore Rossi's powder blue sports jacket, dark blue polyester pants, and white silk shirt open down the chest even in the winter wind of the Virginia mountains. There were the gold chains and rings and expensive Florsheim shoes. He'd spiffed up his fingernails with Gretchen's clear polish, the way Anthony Sciotti did his. Gretchen waved good-bye to the hoodlum in her driveway and closed the door against the chill.

Ed flew to Tampa, connecting through Atlanta. Waiting in the Atlanta lounge through a flight delay, he realized that people were stealing glances at him. He was in character now. For the Coldwater investigation, he chose to be known as "Tony" Rossi rather than his usual "Eddie." He could feel himself descending into the role like a diver, sinking slowly onto a dark, teeming reef. Tony Rossi was a professional blackmailer of homosexuals. He was a thug, con artist, gambler, boozer, immoral, money-grubbing bastard. For the foreseeable future, Tony Rossi would be home for the spirit of Special Agent Ed Robb. May as well settle in, Ed thought.

Ed never knew who might be watching and taking note of the figure he cut as Tony Rossi. He knew he had to be Tony at all times while on the case, in public and in private, starting now. He picked up The Wall Street Journal. Ed had learned that mobsters got lots of good ideas out of The Journal.

At the airport bar, a few pedestrians sidled up to him one at a time. They said hello, made small talk; he brushed them all off, some rudely. They were intrigued by his gruff demeanor and garish dress, drinking alone, glowering into the air. He looked like bottled trouble. This was the aura that Ed strove to perfect; his bearing was a magnet for criminal curiosity. He was certain that many of the looks, and even one or two of the conversations, were sent his way by other law enforcement undercover agents trolling the airport lounge for bad guys. Airports, like bus and train stations, are notorious congregation halls for hustlers, druggies, and pickpockets.

Arriving in Tampa, Ed called from a pay phone to Tony Daniels on his "hello line," a line that rang only in Daniels' office. Daniels answered it by saying, "Hello," a more secure greeting than "Hello. Tampa FBI. May I help you?"

A meeting was set for that evening at Howard Johnson's with Daniels, Jim Kinne, and the informant who would introduce Ed to Coldwater target Jimmy Acquafredda.

At the meeting, Ed stayed in character. Kinne and Daniels called him "Tony" to help feed his mobster role and to protect his real name. Ed spoke in rough and direct terms to the informant. He made it clear that only he, the lead undercover agent, would call the shots. The informant would do what he was told. When Ed was finished with him, he was history. If the informant did anything to jeopardize Ed's life, and Ed lived through it, he'd better believe he would pay for it. Fear, Ed knew from experience, was the key to these people.

What was the informant's reason, Ed asked? Why work with the Feds? Money, he was told. Just for the bucks. Professional informants were nothing more than turncoats for cash, without even the shred of an understandable motive such as revenge. Informants received no respect from either side of the law; the FBI called them by the same names as the Mafia—rats, snitches, stoolies, and louses.

Ed also made it clear to the informant that he and the FBI

could be trusted. If the snitch was stand-up, then Ed would treat him fairly and protect him. The snitch agreed to work with Ed on the case. Ed asked him what he knew about Acquafredda.

Acquafredda was a typical lower-echelon mobster, a working stiff who would do what he was told by his Gambino superiors. He was without scruples but had enough street savvy to be dangerous. Acquafredda would get involved in anything if the price was right: murder, dope, kidnapping, extortion, loan-sharking. He bore no respect for human life or dignity, including his own. He was, in mob parlance, a "mutt," one of the thousands of drones upon whose backs and trigger fingers organized crime makes its livelihood. These are the mobster wannabe's, the guys who do most of the real labor in hopes that, one day when their family's books are opened, they'll be recognized and given their "button," become "made," a "goodfella," be "straightened out."

In New York, Jimmy Acquafredda had been a union organizer in the garbage collection industry. He was a strong-arm enforcer, an intimidator, sticking ice picks into truck tires, throwing torches into dumpsters, keeping union members in line, and nonmembers quaking in their rubber boots. He also ran a "renegade truck," a sanitation truck secretly hired by the mob to impinge on union members' routes. The mob would then "protect" its members from the renegade truck by simply moving Acquafredda to another route, to prey on the next member's customers. He was eventually caught by the union and got into hot water with the membership. The Gambinos stepped in and sent him down to the Tampa area to work the same scam with their blessings and assistance.

To help set up a West Coast Florida Cartmen's Association, Acquafredda took a $60,000 loan from one of his family connections. The money did not go as far as he had hoped; Jimmy was a lousy businessman. The Florida garbage association was slow getting off the ground. Jimmy had to pay the 5 percent weekly interest on the sixty grand. Also, he had become embroiled with an unhappy wife and a demanding girlfriend.

To ease his rising financial burden, Acquafredda planned to start up a gambling operation in Port Richey. The informant told agents Robb, Kinne, and Daniels that Jimmy was staying out of the way of the New York Gambinos until he had his association and the casino running. If the Gambinos suspected he wasn't going to be able to pay back the $60,000, the family would send down a squad of goons to watch over their investment. Jimmy wanted to assemble his own crew; he wanted to be the boss in Tampa. This was the opening Ed was looking for. He would approach Jimmy Acquafredda with an introduction by the informant as an "unattached" guy, a good earner from Pittsburgh, a reliable, stand-up guy who knew the street and the rules, who didn't ask questions, who'd do "whatever" to make a few bucks, give Jimmy a piece of his action, and hang out. If Jimmy was putting together a Tampa crew, Tony Rossi was going to join it.

Ed had learned that bad guys carry a deeply rooted need to believe that another self-avowed bad guy is actually what he says he is. The true felon knows he has become isolated from society. He takes comfort and feels less of an outcast if he thinks he is among others of his own kind. He typically views himself as rough, rebellious, and intrepid. And the best undercover agents are bright, tough men themselves. They are the kind of individuals an outlaw hopes to see in his own mirror. Ed would play on the fact that Acquafredda would want to enlist Tony Rossi and that he would want to overlook any evidence that this Tony Rossi was not what he seemed.

In his hotel room after the meeting, Ed got a call from Jim Kinne. The informant had learned there would be a payoff later between Acquafredda and an unidentified Pasco County cop. It would go down at 7 p.m. in the Holiday Inn lounge in New Port Richey. To pull off the gambling operation, Ed knew Acquafredda had to own at least one highly placed law enforcement official. In return for money, the dirty cop would give Acquafredda early warning of warrants, busts, local undercover agents trying to infiltrate his crew or play at the casino, even the license plate numbers of police undercover vehicles. FBI surveillance was set up at the Holiday Inn for the payoff. Ed sat outside in Tony Daniels' car to monitor the transaction.

At 7 p.m., Pasco County Sheriff's Captain Joseph Donahue pulled up to the Holiday Inn in his squad car. Donahue was a supervisor assigned to Pasco County's Narcotics and Organized Crime Sheriff. Inside the cocktail lounge, he sat at a table with Jimmy Acquafredda and one of his crew, a young autobody mechanic named Lindsey "The Kid" Cherry. Acquafredda was seen passing an envelope under the table to Donahue, who put it inside his coat pocket.

Though the FBI witnessed the pass, it alone was not enough to make a case against Donahue and Jimmy. No conversations were overheard; intents could be inferred but not determined beyond a reasonable doubt. Perhaps Donahue's boss, Sheriff John Short, was on the take as well and the Captain was just the bagman. There were other reasons this evidence could not be used: Donahue could later assert from the witness chair that he had been conducting his own undercover operation into gambling and corruption in his territory. He might claim that the payoff was simply an example of how tight he had gotten with the perpetrators, just part of the role he was playing to sucker them in. This was one of the many pivotal reasons an undercover agent was needed in the case. An agent could witness, record, even participate firsthand in these criminal episodes. It was the only way Coldwater could build an airtight prosecution.

That night, Daniels and Ed devised their opening strategies. The first step would be to move Ed into a classy condo south of Tarpon Springs. The condo, in Pelican Point at Mariners Village, would be rented under the name of Anthony Rossi, who came with excellent references from banks, realtors, and former employers.

* * *

At a breakfast meeting the next morning, the informant

introduced Ed to Jimmy Acquafredda. The tale unfolded that the snitch and Tony knew each other a few years back in Pittsburgh, they'd done some things together on the street. Tony had been a stand-up guy and a close friend of Jerry Listner, a button in the Pittsburgh family. Tony had picked up some heat in the city extorting homosexuals. Listner told him to head down to Tampa and cool off, and he, Listner, would keep a watch over him. But just last month, Jerry was found floating face down in a swimming pool in Las Vegas. There was status in this. In the mob, being found floating in a watery rosette of your own blood in a Vegas pool meant you were somebody, you had big enemies. And it made Rossi's connection with Listner harder to check out. Jimmy had never met Jerry Listner but was impressed with the quality of Jerry's demise. The snitch patted Tony on the back.

"I can vouch for him, Jimmy. He's stand-up."

"So, Tony," Jimmy asked, "what are you doing in Tampa now?"

"Just keeping cool," Ed said. "Not looking for nothing serious. I got enough to hold me."

"Tony, I need people around me who know the rules. You know the rules? You know what I'm talkin' about?"

"Yeah, Jimmy. I know the rules." Acquafredda referred to the mob rules, the street protocols of respect, violations, and punishments of the Mafia.

"What do you think?" Jimmy asked the snitch. "You think we could use Tony here in the casino?"

The snitch agreed. Jimmy explained the gambling setup to Ed, told him he intended to operate the games out of his penthouse apartment. Was Tony interested?

"Yeah." Ed shrugged. "Sure. I'm around. The fuck."

Never say too much. Never claim to be an expert. Never look eager, pushy, or curious. Just dangle the bait. Let them come to you.

After breakfast, Acquafredda invited Ed to come up to the Port Richey condo where the casino would be set up. The apartment, on Bay Boulevard, was vacant except for a sofa and a few blankets and pillows on the floor. Acquafredda had moved out on his wife and shared the penthouse with Joseph "JoJo" Fitapelli. JoJo had been Jimmy's partner in New York on the renegade truck scam. JoJo was with the Lucchese crime family, protected through his powerful cousin Anthony DeMeglia (whom JoJo referred to as "Ant-ny"), a made guy in New Jersey. JoJo had received permission from the Luccheses to work with Acquafredda, a Gambino.

"This is my buddy JoJo from New York," Jimmy said entering the apartment. JoJo minced up his pudgy gut in his slick suit and high-heeled shoes and shook Ed's hand.

Jimmy explained that they were awaiting the arrival of the "furniture"—the gambling equipment—from Vegas. The casino-quality gaming tables would soon arrive via airfreight at the Tampa airport. It was a federal offense to bring gambling equipment into Florida, which did not permit casino gambling.

The "furniture" had been purchased and sent by Eddie Trascher's son, Ricky, a Las Vegas dealer. Along with the tables, Ricky was to forward a supply of Vegas chips. Each issue of Vegas-style chips is unique and can't be counterfeited or bought at a local game shop. The Vegas chips would prevent players from slipping their own markers into the game.

Jimmy walked about the apartment to explain where the tables would be and how the casino would operate. Ed peered out the penthouse windows. In the parking lot below were four Sheriff's deputies' cars.

"Jimmy, whoa. The fuck is this? There's cop cars all over the parking lot here."

"Tony, it's OK. They live in the building."

"Wait a minute. How the fuck you run a casino here with cops everywhere?"

"They're no problem. They've been taken care of. Alright?"

Ed backed away from the windows, acting afraid, as if he might be under surveillance.

"Yeah? What does that mean, they're taken care of? I don't like cops, Jimmy. I don't like this."

Acquafredda assured Ed that he had "the number two guy in the Pasco cops" in his pocket. We got him, Jimmy explained; he was into some other shit and we got him good.

Ed was hard to console. "I don't know, Jimmy. You can't trust cops. I don't think I want to get involved. I'm not getting myself jammed up over some fucking gambling."

Acquafredda repeated that everything was cool.

"Christ, relax Tony, we're all safe from the cops."

Jimmy explained that Ed's jobs would be doorman and bouncer. The stairway to the penthouse was locked to make the elevator the only access to the casino. Players had to call on the intercom and identify themselves before they came up. Tony Rossi would glare out the peephole and open up or not. Once inside, the prospective players would have to answer Tony's questions. Since attendance was by invitation only, guests would be required to tell him their connection. Players would also have to flash at least $2,000 cash before entering the casino. The idea was to have only vouched-for players with money in their pockets.

The game was apparently safe from police raids, under Donahue's paid protection. Ed had to be alert to newspaper reporters at the door, typically sent by an angry girlfriend or wife of a player who had lost a lot of her money at the tables. He also formed the first line of defense against armed robbers who might target the casino.

That night and the following week, Ed hung out with Jimmy and JoJo. They started their evenings at a local juke joint, Harv's Back Door, for drinks, food, friends, and dancing to Nicky Palmer's band. When Harv's closed down, they weaved their way over to The Club, an after-hours bar in Holiday operated by Jimmy Falzone, from Chicago. The pool tables and dance floor of The Club were empty before 2 a.m. It was a "bottle club," a private late-night spot where members brought their own liquor. The bottles were placed behind the bar with the patron's name on it. Members purchased only mixers.

At The Club, Acquafredda introduced Ed around. He met

one of Jimmy's pals, Anthony "Fat Sonny" Santangelo. Sonny ran Sonny's Nurseries, a garden shop in New Port Richey. He moved around The Club flaunting a roll of dollar bills as thick as his wrists. The FBI suspected Sonny of importing marijuana on shrimp boats from South America. Sonny invited Ed to drink out of his private bottle. By the end of the week, Sonny and Jimmy proposed Ed for membership in The Club.

Ed developed a routine in Florida. In the mornings and afternoons he met with Jim Kinne at the safe house to discuss the day's plans and pass on information. In the early evenings, he hung out at Pelican Point. There, he could drink and connect with a higher class of people than Jimmy, JoJo, Trascher, Fat Sonny, and the bar girls who drank away their money. He mixed with doctors, businessmen, and accountants on the deck at the clubhouse, then headed for Harv's Back Door and The Club to hang with the crew. Finally, with dawn mingling with the neon, the gang would file out for breakfast at Denny's.

To help penetrate Jimmy's crew, Ed needed to establish contacts outside the target group so the mobsters wouldn't feel targeted. An undercover agent must realize that not everything a criminal does is a criminal act. Bad guys play golf, have friends outside the gang, talk politics, and read The Wall Street Journal. Occasionally, an acquaintance from Pelican Point would stroll past on the street or in a bar and call out "Hey, Tony! What's happening?" The mobster next to Ed might ask, "Tony, who was that?" Tony Rossi would shrug. "Him? A guy, a dentist. I'm working on something. Forget about it."

Jim Kinne set up the Coldwater safe house near Pelican Point. The small house on a quiet street was the unofficial nerve center of the investigation. All the recording equipment used to monitor Ed's apartment was kept here. Before his daily visits to the safe house, Ed cleaned himself by driving evasively or randomly to check for a tail.

Ed's maroon 1979 Dodge had been wired with stereo microphones. The recorder was hidden in the trunk under the mat, secreted in the auto's body where he had to reach far up, feeling for it, to change the two-hour tapes. In addition to the recorder, the car also carried a tiny radio transmitter that allowed a chase car to monitor Ed's conversations. Both the tape and transmitter were operated by toggle switches beside the driver's front door, under the seat.

* * *

Ed centered his life around the night. He was drawn out by the sunset like some sort of ghoul, into the dark world of the mobsters. Waiting for him at Harv's, The Club, and nameless other bars and back doors were the denizens of this world, the scary little Italians with slicked hair and glinting gold, all garbed in slippery fabrics. The women cruised around hungrily in clouds of smoke and cheap cologne, their lips red and open. Ed was packed in with these people, jailed with them at small dark tables with glasses of Dewar's and water, Black Jack on the rocks, rum and coke sweating on the Formica tops. Cocktail waitresses in fishnets and spikes sailed through the smoke between the chrome chairs and the 10x10 dance floor. Disco tunes pounded in his ears. Though he knew there was always surveillance on him, he ignored it. He was Tony Rossi.

Ed concocted pat answers to ward off curiosity. The questions rarely varied; his replies were always short and brusque. Sometimes he acted offended at the clumsy attempts to dig into his background.

"Where you from?"

"Around."

"What do you do?"

"Whatever I gotta do."

"You got family?"

"Yeah. I got family. What's the name of your fuckin' book?"

Regardless of how innocuous his conversations may have been, no matter how focused or relaxed the company became, with jokes and stories pouring out with the alcohol, Ed could never let go, could never flow. Behind the laughter or silence of

Tony Rossi brooded the stone-hard visage of the FBI undercover agent standing a constant vigil, wearing a Nagra recorder strapped to the inside of his right leg beneath the groin. The recorder, the size of two cigarette packs side by side, was taped over a pair of panty hose he wore to avoid shaving his leg. Two tiny microphones were taped to his nipples. He cut a hole in his pants pocket and ran the on/off switch up into the pocket where he could reach it. This was the purpose of his presence among these people: not to drink and party with them but to record conversations of their intentions or involvement in criminal enterprises. The weight of the Nagra, the discomfort of the microphones attached to his chest—or, in the machines' absence, simply the job at hand and his training—never let him fully relax. Frequently, Ed found himself recording endless hours of idle chatter just to nail down one or two significant statements. Often, when the conversations did turn to crime, he played the devil's advocate, just to illustrate later to a jury that these men were dedicated to committing crimes even over his objections.

With Jimmy and the crew, Ed made it a point to drink only Jack Daniel's and water. Folk wisdom held that a man wouldn't get sick if he nursed good liquor. He had no choice but to drink; everyone else in the crew drank and he had to be a stand-up guy. The only reason for a gangster not to drink when in a bar would be if he were looking to pick up a woman. Ed wasn't looking for sex for two good reasons: He was married to a woman he loved and he was wearing panty hose.

* * *

On one of his first nights out with Jimmy and JoJo, Ed perched on a stool at The Club in New Port Richey. An attractive waitress sidled up next to him and introduced herself as Brandy. Ed responded pleasantly. Brandy put her hand on his thigh, one inch from the Nagra recorder taped to his leg. Ed moved slowly, fighting down the panic in his gut. He slid his leg from under her fingers.

"What's the matter, baby?" she asked.

"Nothing, baby, nothing." Ed nodded in the direction of Jimmy and JoJo. "This is business here, alright?" he said, shrugging his shoulders, rearranging himself. "Later."

He played the moment like it was no big deal, keeping cool. When Brandy walked away, his brow was misted with sweat.

Fear is the closest associate of an undercover agent. Like a cold slap of water it can keep him alert, eyes open and senses stretched. Or, working from the inside, fear—unrelenting and corrosive—can turn on him and destroy him. The undercover agent's fears are real. He dreads being discovered and the consequences that would surely follow, especially when inside the Mafia. His cover can be blown in ways large or small, by mistakes he can see coming a mile off or shocking screwups that spring out of nowhere: a little bad luck, a misstep by his support staff, a slipup by an informant, a touch too high on his leg.

Inevitably, even among the best undercover agents, fear sows the seeds of paranoia. Not long after the agent goes under, he hears the first worrisome whispers in his head: "They know who you really are. They're just stringing you along to set you up. You'd better not go to that meeting tonight or into this room alone with them." Left unchecked, such paranoia can become debilitating and dangerous. Each agent reacts differently to fear. Some turn to booze to build a soft, swirling levee to contain the dread. Others mask their anxieties behind bravado and swagger, going nose-to-nose with fear. Ed Robb recognized the power of fear. He knew from experience that the right amount of fear could work like the right amount of coffee or a stiff Black Jack on the rocks. Taken in small doses at the proper time, it can get you through a tough moment.

* * *

Acquafredda told Ed the "furniture" would arrive the next day, March 16, at the Tampa airport. Ed alerted Kinne, who set up surveillance at the airfreight terminal. Acquafredda was photographed the next day picking up the Las Vegas boxes in his truck, then transporting them to the New Port Richey penthouse. Ed was at the apartment to help lug the equipment upstairs. After helping uncrate the contents of the boxes, Ed could later testify that the "furniture" was, in fact, gambling equipment, transported illegally into Florida.

The first federal case against Vincenzo "Jimmy" Acquafredda was made.

* * *

The casino opened the night of April 20. Tony Rossi was a stalwart at the door, scrutinizing every player's credentials, connections, and bale of cash. Later in the evening, he cruised the games, assigned by pit boss Acquafredda to be on the lookout for cheaters and to "keep the peace."

At the casino were several Coldwater targets: Jimmy Acquafredda, who ran the games; JoJo Fitapelli, who dealt and handed out poker chips; Fat Sonny Santangelo, who'd put up money to finance the games; Eddie and Ricky Trascher, who had arranged the transport of the gambling equipment and now worked as dealers; and Pasco Sheriff's Captain Joseph Donahue, who let it all happen. Lindsey "The Kid" Cherry missed the first night of gambling. Ed had learned from Acquafredda that the Cherry family were longtime friends of Donahue's. Lindsey was the one who had introduced Jimmy to the Captain.

This first night of the game brought another target into the Coldwater net—Joseph "Joe Pete" Pullicino, owner of Mr. Pete's Riverboat Restaurant and Lounge in New Port Richey. Joe Pete, along with Fat Sonny, claimed to have given Jimmy Acquafredda $10,000 to open the casino. Joe Pete was not a made mob guy; he could never be. He was a native of Malta; he had no family lines to Sicily or Italy, a must for Mafia membership. Pullicino was an opportunist; he had his fingers in anything around him that stood a shot at making a buck. Ed got to know him as a self-inflated big shot, know-it-all, and bullshitter.

Joe Pete was also good natured, fun to hang out with, and well connected to Acquafredda, Fitapelli, and the crew. The week after the first Casino Night, Ed was with Joe Pete in St. Petersburg. A guy came up and asked the two of them what time it was. Joe Pete twisted his wrist around to get a look at his big gold watch. The man made a grab for the watch. Ed leapt at the would-be thief, bent his arm back, and sent him running. Joe, the loudmouth, told the boys what a stand-up guy Tony was, adding to his growing stature. A lot of successful undercover work, Ed knew, was just like this: Whenever Lady Luck landed in your arms, you needed to give her a squeeze.

By the time the casino shut down at 5 a.m., the house had lost more than $8,000. The big winner was a local builder, Vince Conrad. No one liked Conrad. He was considered a mouthy Italian with a fake last name. Joe Pete and Jimmy hated to watch him walk out the penthouse door with their money in his pockets. They told Ed, if Conrad won again at the next Casino Night, he should follow him out to his car and rob him in the parking lot. Conrad wasn't going to call the cops to report a robbery of funds won at an illegal gambling establishment and he wasn't going to sue.

The casino opened again for four nights in the next two weeks. Tony Rossi was there at the door or wandering the floor, quietly making himself known and appreciated. In attendance were all the principal targets of Coldwater as well as some new faces, some of interest to the FBI. Joe Pete played the role of a "shill." He gambled at the blackjack table and won or lost big, making the results known to all within earshot. He bragged or complained to other players that he was up or down as much as fifteen g's, just to keep the game's blood flowing. At the end of the night, Acquafredda collected Joe Pete's winnings or reimbursed him for anything he lost.

The afternoon before every casino night, Acquafredda gave Donahue $200. Sometimes Lindsey Cherry delivered the cash. Ed witnessed a few of the payments. But this still wouldn't be enough to nail down corruption and bribery convictions.

At dinner one evening with Joe Pete, Ed brought up the idea that he should handle the payoffs to the cop in Acquafredda's stead.

"Look, Joe," he said, "nothin' for nothin' but Jimmy's got his hands full. He's got enough problems, he don't need more. Why don't you mention to him to let me start handling the cop. I got nothin goin', no family. If Donahue turns on us, he can only jackpot me and not wreck the casino. I mean, Christ, Jimmy's a Gambino. They don't want that in the newspapers down here." Ed added, "Tell Jimmy about it like it was your idea, Joe. You're a partner in the game. Jimmy listens to you. All I want is an extra hundred bucks a night."

Pullicino said he'd look into it with Jimmy. Ed also lobbied with Lindsey Cherry, the go-between for Donahue and Acquafredda, to be allowed to take over the payoffs. Cherry was slowly attaching himself to Ed. The youngster believed Tony Rossi to be a rising star in the crew. He discussed with Ed the possibility of setting up a chop shop. Ed would bring in stolen cars and Lindsey would cut them up and sell the parts.

Jimmy was reluctant to hand his cop over to Ed, though he appreciated the overture. Jimmy warned him that he thought Ed took too many chances.

"Tony, stay low," he said, "and watch your conversations. The Feds got bugs everywhere. You gotta talk, go out in your car and do it." Yeah, Ed thought. Good idea. Right into my own recording machine.

That night, Ed was harassed by a New Port Richey cop who pulled him over and spread-eagled him across the hood of the maroon Dodge. The cop searched him, claiming that a 7-11 had been held up that night by a man fitting the description of Mr. Anthony Rossi, recently arrived in Florida with a long arrest sheet but no convictions. Later, Ed asked Kinne to check it out: There had been no 7-11 robbery that night. Ed was gratified; he had obviously made an impression as a local criminal. He was digging deeper, like a coal miner, one shovel-full at a time, into the rich vein of the Florida underworld.

* * *

Jimmy and JoJo split their energies between operating the casino out of their penthouse and setting up the West Coast Cartmen's Association. Jimmy complained all the time that the Association moved too slowly. "Some of the guys aren't getting in line," he'd say. "We're gonna have to beat them into line."

In early May, Jimmy mentioned to Ed that Sylvester Hutchins, a man with whom he had gone into partnership on a sanitation route down in Indian Rocks Beach, owed him $20,000. He told Ed to go collect.

Ed had to do something; he couldn't just refuse the order. Tony Rossi was supposed to be a tough guy, a collections and extortion expert.

"Yeah, sure, Jimmy. I'll do it. But it'll cost you half."

"Half? You want fuckin' half? It's my fuckin' money!"

"Sorry Jim, but that's the going rate."

Ed knew that if Acquafredda said yes, he'd have to stall, pretending not to find Hutchins, to avoid actually committing a crime or violent act. He was sure, though, that his offer was too rich for Jimmy's tastes. He was right. Acquafredda declined, cursing Tony. "I'll do it myself," he said.

Jimmy took an accomplice, a thug named Vinnie, to Indian Rocks Beach in Pinellas County. He confronted Hutchins, pistol-whipped him, and fired several shots into the air to make his point. Hutchins was terrified and went to the cops.

The Pinellas County Sheriff's Department opened a case against Acquafredda. They came to Pasco and surveilled him, marking him as an associate member of the New York Gambino family. Jimmy was arrested and faced extortion and assault charges in Pinellas. He went to his Pasco cop, Donahue, and asked him to take care of it. Donahue told him he'd do what he could but Jimmy had gone outside his territory. The Pinellas cops didn't take orders from Pasco County.

* * *

To add to Acquafredda's plight, the casino lost money each of the next five nights of play. Jimmy, Joe Pete, and Fat Sonny, the three financiers of the game, held a meeting. They were not going to lose any more.

At dinner on May 9, Jimmy told Ed that he was going to pick up two "cheaters" at the Tampa airport that evening. Around nine o'clock, Acquafredda entered the penthouse accompanied by two men Ed had not seen before. They were introduced around as Billy Jones and George Petry, just in from New York. Jones was a blackjack dealer, Petry his bodyguard.

Jones, a handsome man in his early twenties, dealt blackjack that night from a shoe. Ed had been taught at the FBI gambling school that you cannot cheat at blackjack from a multi-deck shoe. To his amazement, he saw it done by Billy Jones. The house won more than $10,000. A chunk of it came from Vince Conrad. During the long night, Billy explained to Tony Rossi that he was a member of a Gambino-run network of professional cheaters. He and his counterparts traveled all over the country upon request, cheating at any game or sport you could name including backgammon, tennis, golf, cards, croquet, Monopoly, even bingo. They took 50 percent of the winnings.

In the early morning, after the casino had emptied and Joe Pete returned his winnings to Acquafredda, Billy Jones showed the crew how he'd done it. He asked Tony Rossi what hand he wanted.

"Gimme an 18."

Jones dealt it from the shoe accordingly. He revealed a tiny pop-up mirror in the shoe allowing him to see the next card. He could play it or withhold it and play another card behind it. Ed did not know such a device existed.

That morning, Ed drove Jones to catch a flight back to New York. Jones said he was continuing on to Fairmont, West Virginia, where he was to deal at another game. Petry stayed behind in Port Richey to guard another cheater coming in for the next casino, announced for the following night, May 11.

Jimmy met the new dealer, Barry "Winter" Bienstock, at the

airport. Barry was a fat, pasty Jewish kid who never took off his sunglasses. With him at the blackjack table putting the magic shoe through its secret paces, the casino again took in more than ten g's.

On those nights when the cheaters were in the casino, Ed kept a close eye at the door for players whom he suspected were either made mob guys or well connected. He advised them, "Do yourself a favor. Don't play blackjack in here tonight. You want good action, go to Vegas, alright?" He knew Billy or Barry wouldn't stop cheating and there could be trouble if a goodfella or one of his crew got ripped off. Acquafredda only wanted money from "citizens," the locals, the innocent lambs for whom all mobsters reserve their ultimate disdain.

The night of May 11, the owner of a local trucking business, Tony Affetto, played and lost big money. Affetto was basically a decent man who, a few years earlier in Chicago, had gotten himself in the uneasy position of having to pay protection to the mob. When he fell down on the payments, they made it difficult for him to stay in business. He left the Windy City and relocated to Florida to start with a clean slate. However, Affetto brought with him what had got him in trouble in the first place: his love of gambling. At the door to the casino, someone vouched for Affetto. He waved his two g's and Ed ushered him in. Hours later, Ed saw him in a corner away from the tables, making a quick deal with Joe Pete Pullicino and his 5 percent juice. Ed watched in quiet sadness as Tony Affetto, another innocent, took the loan shark's money and then lost it back to the cheating blackjack dealer.

The next morning, Ed gave Jimmy and JoJo the excuse that he had a deal cooking out of town and had to be away for two days. He'd be back before the next Casino Night, the 14th. Ed flew to Charlottesville via a circuitous route. He called JoJo regularly from a pay phone for updates. Over the first months of Coldwater, Ed had developed a closer relationship with JoJo than with Jimmy. JoJo was single and could hang out. He was from New York and didn't have a driver's license so he often caught a ride with Ed from the motel where he lived. JoJo was affable, while Jimmy, always aloof, stayed buried under a mound of cares caused by too many women and too much bad business.

JoJo told Ed of a guy at The Club who was strutting around selling gold jewelry. He was "dropping names," mentioning "that guy from Tampa and Miami, The Old Man." JoJo was referring to Santo Trafficante, one of the most powerful under-world figures in America. Trafficante was the ultimate crime boss in Florida. Florida was an open state. Any of the major crime families could come there to do business but only after obtaining Santo's go-ahead and paying him his cut. The Old Man, as he was called throughout gangland, was a native of Tampa. He made his mark in Cuba in the 1940s and 1950s operating casinos in Havana under Batista with help from the legendary mob financier Meyer Lansky. When Castro threw Batista out, Trafficante got in bed with the new populist Communist government and survived as long as he could until Castro closed down all the casinos and threw him in jail. Mob lawyer Frank Ragano came down and bribed Santo's way out of jail before Castro could have him executed.

Trafficante then set up his operation in booming southern Florida. In the 1960s, he was allegedly recruited by the CIA to whack Castro. Another theory holds that the CIA contacted a different mob family to do the job, but that Trafficante got wind of the plot and, when the triggermen passed through Miami, he put them in a barrel and sent them to Castro as a goodwill gift. He even took blame in some circles, along with former Havana partner and New Orleans crime boss Carlo Marcello, for the assassination of John Kennedy and the disappearance of former Teamsters leader Jimmy Hoffa. Trafficante was ruthless, respected, and as strong and rich as any mob boss anywhere. Between him and Marcello, they controlled organized crime in the South.

Trafficante's name was a heavy one to drop. This act consti-tuted a major breach of mob etiquette: No one was allowed to "throw around a name" without permission. Even with an OK, the name could only be used to get something done, as a stamp of authority; never was a name to be bandied about just to impress people and carry on like a big shot.

"He's an arrogant cocksucker, Tony," JoJo said. "Says his name is John, says he's connected out of Chicago. Says he wants to meet with you. I gave him your number."

"Thanks, JoJo. I'll take care of it when I get back."

Before Ed returned from Charlottesville, the Tampa Field Office decided to upgrade his appearance a notch, as if he had made a score while out of town. When Ed returned to Tampa, the Dodge Coronet was dumped in favor of a cream-colored Bill Blass Lincoln Mark V. The Pennsylvania tags were registered to Anthony Edward Rossi, from Pittsburgh. The car was insured under the same name. Like the Dodge, it was wired for sound.

Back at the Pelican Point condo, Ed got the expected call from John. They agreed to meet in the parking lot of the Holiday Inn that evening. In the warm dusk, a short, dark-haired man in his early thirties sauntered across the tarmac.

"I'm John, from Chicago," he said. "I want to tell you about this guy Affetto."

Ed glared down at him. "Yeah? Tell me."

"He's my brother-in-law. I care about the guy. I'm putting you on notice, I don't want him gambling in your casino no more. He's got himself in dutch with some people in Chicago and he's gambling with their money."

"And who are you?"

"I'm with the right people in Chicago so forget about it."

Ed memorized the license plate number on the man's Cadillac Seville.

"John," Ed said, his tone cooperative now that the man before him had identified himself as a connected guy, "nothin' for nothin', but hey, why don't you talk to the guys that run the game? You know, I'm just the doorman. Look, I'll see what I can do, alright?"

Later, Ed gave John's description and license number to

Kinne for a background check. Next, he went to Jimmy Acquafredda and asked him to check on this little mutt out of Chicago.

The next day, Acquafredda caught up with Ed.

"Tony, I did what you asked and made a few calls. That guy John, he's Johnny Cascio. He's hooked up out of Chicago, with Mike Spilotro. He's been in the chop shop business, does some painting contracting. He stands up. But they said he's a bullshitter and don't take him too serious."

It would take the FBI three more weeks to respond to the Tampa Field Office's inquiry on Johnny Cascio from Chicago. This episode was another illustration of the value of criminal undercover operations. The successful undercover agent stands at the crossroads of all sorts of criminal activity. Though he remains charged with collecting evidence leading to convictions in an assigned investigation, he also has opportunities, like the one with Johnny Cascio, to develop random but precious bits of information that pop up like wild flowers.

The Casino Night of May 14th was another big success for the house. Barry Winter turned a $10,000 profit at the blackjack table. Barry and bodyguard George Petry were taken to the airport after breakfast with their 50 percent cut in hand.

The next afternoon, Jimmy declared to the crew that the casino would be suspended for a while. Captain Donahue had advised him that things down in Pinellas had heated up from the Hutchins beating, making matters hard for him to handle. Later that day Ed took Lindsey Cherry aside and put the idea in his head that the two of them ought to start their own game. Acquafredda, he said, had fucked up big time by pistol-whipping Hutchins. Just when we're making money. All Lindsey had to do was deliver the cop, Donahue. Tony would take care of the rest.

If Lindsey went next to Acquafredda and ratted Ed out about planning to take over both the casino and Donahue behind his back, Ed was prepared to eat a little crow and make the peace. But Tony's display of cunning and boldness would gain him even more status with JoJo, Joe Pete, Fat Sonny, and the rest of the crew as a mover and shaker, a "good earner."

Besides, Tony's machinations wouldn't come as a big surprise to Jimmy; he couldn't get but so mad. In the world of the mob, everybody screwed everybody. It was the way things got done.

CHAPTER SEVEN
Little Jimmy

Ricky Trascher stumbled into Harv's Back Door with his shirt torn and a bloody nose.

One of the crew asked, "What happened to you?"

Trascher pointed toward the door. "Two rednecks jumped me in the parking lot."

All the mobsters at the table leaped up at once, shouting for vengeance. They rushed outside; finding no one there, they grumbled back to their table in Harv's.

After a shot of whiskey and a minute of "You OK, kid?" from the gang, Ricky sat up and again pointed to the door. This time at the end of his finger were two tough-looking youths who strolled into the bar.

"Get 'em, boys," growled Acquafredda.

Six men lunged forward. The Nicky Palmer Band's volume skyrocketed. Ed moved first and grabbed one of the two strangers in a bear hug. He threw the large boy, struggling like a marlin, across the cigarette machine to make it look like he was hurting him. The other five attacked the second youth and dragged him to the bathroom where they pounded on him for a few minutes.

When they were done, Ed wrestled his kid over to the door and tossed him out alongside the other, bloodied boy. The mobsters shouted and laughed after them, wiping their hands as if from honest labor. The band eased off.

Two minutes later—Ed couldn't believe his eyes—the two toughs were back. The drummer launched into a loud solo and the fight scene replayed. Ed wrapped his same opponent in another bear hug and pulled him to the cigarette machine while the kid screamed "Guinea bastard!" The remaining crew members went to work on their target. When they brought him out of the bathroom this time, he was bashed and unconscious. They bowled him out of Harv's as Ed kicked his boy in the rear out the door.

The gang figured they had made enough trouble at Harv's for the night so they moved to The Club for some drinking and backslapping. At 4 a.m., Acquafredda pulled Ed and JoJo across the street to Denny's for breakfast. In a booth at Denny's, Jimmy told Ed he admired the way he'd handled himself at Harv's that night. Ed had taken on one of the rednecks alone. That showed balls.

"Now that the casino is shut down," Acquafredda said, "we got to start working on the garbagemen's association. Tony, I want to start using you as muscle."

JoJo objected. "Jimmy, no way. You can't bring in nobody new without permission. You know the rules. Tony's outside muscle and Little Jimmy's got to approve it."

Ed's ears pricked up. Little Jimmy? This was a new name, obviously a player with some clout, someone who had to be asked for permission.

"Fuck Little Jimmy." Acquafredda made a fist. "I'm the boss here. Little Jimmy ain't shit. I can do what I want."

JoJo was adamant. "Jimmy, no you can't. We went down to Tampa and made an agreement and you gotta stick to it."

As Ed listened to Jimmy and JoJo he realized their argument was opening an entirely new tributary of criminal activity. Ed knew the mob rules as well as either of these two mopes and he knew that Little Jimmy in Tampa, whoever he was, must be a Lucchese. JoJo, himself a Lucchese, was sticking up for Little Jimmy's rights. Acquafredda was a Gambino; it was only natural for him to chafe under the thumb of a rival family.

Here, with the name of Little Jimmy in Tampa, was the linchpin who held the two crime families together. If Little

Jimmy was the man who could bestow permission for the Luccheses and Gambinos to cooperate in the garbagemen's association, then he also must have obtained that power for himself. And the one man sitting on top of it all, the only godfather who could have granted Little Jimmy that ultimate approval in Florida, was The Old Man, Santo Trafficante.

Ed spoke up. "Whoa, whoa, wait a fuckin' minute here. I ain't gettin' involved in nothin' until this is straightened out. Jimmy, lookit, you gotta keep me out of the trick bag. I could get whacked, getting caught between two families like this."

Ed's objective was to draw out more information about Little Jimmy and his connections. Who was he? Why was Acquafredda hooked into him? If Ed showed reluctance, maybe Acquafredda would explain the situation better to convince him to come on board.

And he did. Acquafredda told Ed that he had been under a lot of pressure about the sixty g's in Gambino money he had brought down to Florida to set up the garbagemen's association. At JoJo's suggestion, Acquafredda had gone to Little Jimmy, a Lucchese capo from New Jersey, asking him to intercede on his behalf with the Gambinos in New York. Little Jimmy agreed and, of course, his price was to be cut in on the association. This was the agreement in Tampa to which JoJo referred. Acquafredda wasn't the sole boss in this situation; he had to ask for permission from the Luccheses to bring Tony Rossi in from the outside. This was a big development. Little Jimmy was a likely conduit to Trafficante, and both men might become targets for the FBI and Coldwater.

Ed and the Tampa Field Office had been talking about shutting down Coldwater soon. Their cases were already made against the casino operators and financiers; they figured Acquafredda, JoJo, or Lindsey Cherry would give up the cop Donahue in return for a lighter sentence. That would have completed the Coldwater brief—until Little Jimmy popped up. Ed felt a tingle as another wall barring his way into the almost impenetrable labyrinth of the Mafia cracked open for him. He felt sure that once he told his case agents about Little Jimmy, in Tampa by way of Jersey, Coldwater would continue with new energy.

JoJo held up his hand, as peacemaker.

"OK, look, we got no choice. Jimmy, we gotta go down to Tampa for a sitdown. We gotta do this thing. Tony, don't worry. We ain't going to get you in no trouble."

That afternoon JoJo told Ed a meeting was arranged for the next day, May 24th. He and Acquafredda were to confab with Little Jimmy at Cousin's Restaurant in Tampa and sort everything out. "So," he said, "forget about it."

Ed relayed this intelligence to Tampa agents Kinne and Case. A surveillance team was alerted and photographs were taken of the sitdown at Cousin's. At the table were Acquafredda, JoJo Fitapelli, Little Jimmy, Bernie Agostino—the owner of Cousin's—plus two men later identified as New York Lucchese family members Salvatore Sciremammano and Anthony Demeglia, JoJo's cousin.

That night, JoJo called to ask Ed to spin by his motel and pick him up. In the car, on tape, JoJo went over the details of the Tampa meeting. Acquafredda had been given the go-ahead by the Lucchese capo Little Jimmy to take over the garbage collection business in Pasco and Pinellas Counties.

"And you can come in with us, Tony. The man says it's OK."

"JoJo, you sure? I don't want to get jammed up. Between my people, your people, Jimmy's people, I can step on some toes real easy here and get in a world of hurt."

JoJo assured Ed that everything was in order. Ed made his first grab at the brass ring.

"I want to hear it from the man himself. I want a meeting with Little Jimmy."

JoJo laughed the suggestion off. Imagine, a mope like Tony Rossi insisting on a meeting with Little Jimmy.

"The fuck," JoJo snickered. "Right."

Right, thought Ed.

* * *

Tony Rossi was not a mope. In fact, Tony was making connections fast. He was not only gaining status inside Acquafredda's gang but outside it with the many groupies, sharpies, dealers, and buyers who orbit around mob crews.

From the start of his affiliation with Acquafredda, Tony Rossi began accepting and courting independent contacts. Johnny Cascio had come to Tony to keep his brother-in-law Affetto out of the casino. Lindsey Cherry was being tempted to start his own gambling operation with Tony and bring along Captain Donahue. JoJo told Tony all the secrets he could gather, currying favor with the newcomer. Acquafredda himself had given in to the meeting with Little Jimmy to gain Tony's participation in the garbage collection operation.

Quietly, Ed was moving up. Almost daily he was hit on by someone with a criminal suggestion or for a session of crooked pipe dreams. "Tony, got a minute? What do you think about this? I know this guy . . ."

Frankie Foggia was one of the first to come to Ed with a scheme. Ed had met Frankie at Acquafredda's casino where he was a regular player. Foggia was a Bonanno associate out of New York working in Florida as a masonry contractor. He was a typical mob fop, with slick hair and silk suits. He liked to shine: His gold chains, pinky rings, polished fingernails, Rolex Presidente, and two-tone Caddy gave him the glow of a Mafiosi sun-child. He appreciated Tony Rossi's style, the tough, sure way Tony handled himself at the casino door and among the gaming tables. Frankie was gay and kept it well hidden, or so he thought. He bragged constantly about his female conquests but the women Ed talked to complained that "Frankie never did anything" to them. Even so, the girls liked to hang out with Frankie because he was good-looking and had a wad of loose cash. He claimed to have been chased out of New York for sleeping with his boss's wife. Foggia approached Ed one night at Harv's Back Door.

"Hey, Tone. I get the idea you been around. Maybe you could help me."

"Shoot, Frankie."

"There's this guy, lives in Chicago. He used to be a big shot with the Boy Scouts. He's a closet faggot. I want to shake him down for 150 g's. What do you think? Can you give me some advice?"

Ed replied that, yeah, he'd done some of that work. You really had to know what you were doing. Extortion was tricky.

"Maybe you want to come in on it, Tony?"

No, Ed said, he'd left that shit behind. But he'd be glad to take a look at it when Foggia got close to doing the scam.

"We'll talk about it later, OK, Frankie? You got it."

He had had to put Foggia off. At the same time, it was important that he maintain Frankie's trust and interest enough to keep him sharing his plans. Ed couldn't participate in the scheme, nor could he pursue the relationship with Foggia fully to see where Foggia could lead. Ed had other fish to fry for the FBI.

On another night at Harv's, a member of the Nicky Palmer Band came to Ed with a load of stolen Army .45 pistols. The next evening Tommy, the keyboard player, tried to sell him some stolen gems. Ed replied in both cases that he didn't know anything about these items, guns or gems, but he knew someone who did and he'd put them in touch. Ed always left the door open: "Yeah, let's look into that." And he gave bullshit advice to sound like a big shot crook: "Be careful. Watch yourself. And watch the phones." He never acted too excited, or too bored. "Yeah," he'd say when the presentation was done and his last sip of Jack Daniel's downed, "I'll get back to you."

This swirl of criminal activity around Ed led him to approach Jim Kinne about bringing in another agent to make some of these additional cases. Ed requested Steve Salmieri, an agent from the Orlando Field Office who had also worked on Talon in Virginia Beach. Salmieri was trained in gem appraisal. Under the name Chico Navarro, he began to work on and off with Ed, building his own cases from the ones that spun out of Coldwater's center. Salmieri would be the first of several additional agents to be brought in before Coldwater was concluded.

Not all of Ed's growing list of connections were allies. Some were foes, but even bad blood added to Tony Rossi's status. Every bad guy needs a few enemies to flesh out the role. Tony Rossi was tough, a thug with street smarts. He lived in a world populated by other hard men, some of whom wanted to try their hand against him as he gained notoriety. For the most part, Ed let these muted, behind-the-back challenges slide. In fact, they pleased him as evidence that he was making waves.

On a few occasions, the provocations became face to face and unavoidable. Joe Cash was one such antagonist. Cash was an ex-cop whose dislike for Tony Rossi was so fervent that he made several calls to the Tampa Field Office claiming he could set Tony up so the Feds could bust him. Cash told the FBI that Rossi was involved in gangland slayings, drug running, and kidnappings. Ed had a good laugh when Kinne told him.

One evening, Joe Cash followed Ed into the parking lot outside Harv's Back Door. He moved in on Ed, telling a gathering crowd he was going to kick Tony's ass. Ed couldn't fight Cash; an undercover agent cannot engage in any activity that might later compromise him on the witness stand. A late-night brawl in a parking lot would not look good on the record.

But he couldn't back down from Cash's threats. There were witnesses; word would spread if Tony Rossi turned yellow.

Ed stared Cash down as the man's face reddened beneath his threats and bluster.

Finally Ed spoke, in an even, resigned voice.

"Joe, you wanna die?"

Cash laughed.

"Look," Ed continued, as if pronouncing a sentence, "you got a good chance of dying, real soon. I got enough problems on my hands without killing you. I don't need the hassle with your people, or my people. You wanna kick my ass? Go ahead."

Joe Cash's laugh stilled.

Ed walked up to Cash and spoke not only to his face but also to the ears of those around them in the parking lot.

"But let me tell you. You don't want to fuck with me. Because even if you kick my ass, there's gonna be a knock on your door later. You understand? Killing you right now isn't how it's done, Joe. That knock, that's how it's done."

Ed stood in front of Joe Cash, letting his words lay on top of the man's smoldering anger like a blanket over a flame. Then, satisfied he had held his ground long and hard enough, he got in his car and drove away.

The news got around about Tony Rossi, how he'd kicked Joe Cash's rear in that parking lot and how many rears he'd kicked in bars and parking lots all over Holiday and Port Richey. Gradually, the grumbling of jealous rivals subsided; it became established fact that Tony Rossi was not a man to be trifled with. Though his enemies did not go away, they quieted down to fade into the backdrop of his underworld life, part of the pedigree required of any authentic organized crime figure.

* * *

Ed wanted to meet Little Jimmy. JoJo was the key but JoJo wasn't sure Tony Rossi was a big enough player to meet a Lucchese captain. The answer was simple. Tony had to get bigger. Kinne, Case, and Ed devised a plan.

In mid-June, Ed approached JoJo about a big coke deal he was setting up with a guy down in Tampa. Would JoJo be interested in coming along and watching Ed's back? There would be something in it for him. JoJo agreed.

The next afternoon he picked up JoJo for the drive from Holiday to Fort Myers. Ed showed him a Hartman leather briefcase before he closed it in the trunk. The case was actually filled with newspapers, to weigh it down as if it had $100,000 inside. In Fort Myers, the two checked into a Holiday Inn under fictitious names, had dinner, sat at the bar, then called it a night.

At breakfast, Ed sent JoJo into the Holiday Inn restaurant first. JoJo stood near the door and checked the place out. He gave Ed the OK sign then sat at a table and had coffee. Ed entered and sat at his own table. After ten minutes Ed rose and walked to where Jim Kinne sat eating. The two chatted and Ed handed Kinne his car keys.

Kinne left the restaurant. Ed took JoJo back to his room and waited. After an hour, the phone rang: The deal was done. The two checked out of the motel, got a cab, and went downtown.

Ed's car sat on a deserted corner. He avoided it, sending JoJo around the block on a security patrol. When JoJo returned, they got into the car with Ed's spare set of keys and drove a few miles to the parking lot of a gift shop. Ed pulled in and opened the trunk. Inside was an identical Hartman briefcase to the one with the "cash" in it. Ed opened it to show JoJo the five footballs of cocaine inside. Each kilo of coke—in reality, flour and Epsom salts—was wrapped in Colombian newspapers from Bogota.

JoJo wanted to test the drugs. Ed deflected the request by telling JoJo he'd "dealt with this guy before and I know this is good shit. He knows better than to fuck with me."

They drove from Fort Myers to a Sheraton Hotel in Tampa. Again, Ed sent JoJo in first, into the men's room to check it out. JoJo watched as Ed handed the briefcase to the waiting drug dealer, actually FBI agent Bob Buresh. Ed received another identical Hartman case in return, and walked out.

Back in the car, Ed gave JoJo $2,000 for serving as lookout in the deal.

After the exchange, they drove to The Mardi Gras Lounge in Tampa, an afternoon gathering spot with cheap drinks and top-less entertainment.

"JoJo," Ed said across the table, his face flashing with the colored lights from the small stage, "I want to meet Little Jimmy. We're gonna have problems unless I get the go-ahead from your people direct. I ain't doing anything more with you until I meet the guy. That's it."

JoJo Fitapelli had a problem. Vouching for Tony Rossi with the Luccheses was a big responsibility. But the fresh $2,000 warmed his pocket.

He replied, "I'll set it up, Tony."

* * *

The next afternoon, JoJo led Ed to a table in a corner of Cousin's Restaurant in Tampa. A short, slender man rose to hug JoJo. His hair was as sleek and grey as his sharkskin suit. He wore sunglasses.

"Tony," JoJo said, motioning Ed forward, "this is Jimmy Fischetti. Jimmy, this is Tony Rossi I told you about."

Little Jimmy shook Ed's hand, then turned to introduce Bernie Agostino, owner of Cousin's.

Little Jimmy took his seat at the table and started the discussion with flattery.

"Tony, JoJo here tells me a lot of good things about you. He says you stand up."

"Thank you, Mr. Fischetti."

"So what can I do for you, Tony?"

Ed recapped Acquafredda's invitation to take part in the garbagemen's association.

"Hey," Ed said, holding up his palms and shaking them as he shook his head to make his reluctance clear, "nothin' for nothin' but I told him there was no way I was going to get involved without your blessings. Once JoJo told me who you were, I told him I wanted to hear it from you and no one else. That's the way it's supposed to be done."

"That's right, Tony."

Ed detailed for Little Jimmy his experience working for Acquafredda as a bouncer at the Port Richey casino and the disappointment everyone felt when the game had to be closed down just as they began to make money.

"Look," Ed said, lifting one hand, dicing the air with it, "I don't want to put the mouth on nobody, but Jimmy Acquafredda ain't doing the right things up there. He brought a lot of heat down on us by pistol-whipping that guy Hutchins. No disrespect, but he's out of control."

Little Jimmy agreed. "He's got problems. At home, in his business, problems." The old man told Ed of his own history with Acquafredda, how he had interceded with the Gambinos after they sent two thugs from New York to whack Acquafredda over the $60,000 he wasn't repaying fast enough. Little Jimmy, a made Lucchese, asked the Gambinos to leave Acquafredda alone, to give him a chance to straighten things out. This put Acquafredda in Little Jimmy's debt. But Acquafredda had not been showing the proper gratitude. Plus the Hutchins beating had drawn attention from the cops, a major blunder. He was indeed out of control.

The way Little Jimmy talked, Ed could tell he was gaining the man's confidence. In return, Ed was quiet, respectful; he had shown that he knew the rules and followed them. JoJo must also have told Little Jimmy about the big coke deal and how Ed handled Joe Cash.

Right then, Ed decided to pull out a plan he, Case, Kinne, and Supervisor Tony Daniels had concocted a week before. It was a scheme too bold for them to believe it could actually happen. But suddenly, with Little Jimmy's ear, with Acquafredda's fall from grace, with JoJo having primed the pump, Ed saw this was the perfect moment to unveil it. Tony Rossi had hung out with the crew long enough. He had to move up. Now, he was going to make his move to push Jimmy Acquafredda aside and create his own crew. Tony Rossi wanted to become the boss of Pasco and Pinellas Counties.

"Mr. Fischetti, I got some money to invest. I was thinking that Holiday would be a great place to open a club. You know, a real nice place you'd be proud of. We could move the casino in there; we could put the offices of the garbagemen's association in there and hold meetings. I want to ask you for your permission."

Little Jimmy looked at Bernie Agostino, nodded, and listened for more.

"I'll need the cop Donahue too, Mr. Fischetti."

Ed told Little Jimmy that he wanted control of all criminal activities in Pasco and Pinellas Counties including gambling, the garbage business, and prostitution but didn't want to "step on anyone's toes."

At the end of Ed's presentation, Little Jimmy asked him, "Tony, you hooked up with anyone?"

"No. I was around some people, but right now I'm not with anyone."

Little Jimmy considered the man in front of him, making a pitch for his own territory, turf that had already been granted to the Gambino Jimmy Acquafredda. Little Jimmy had the power to make the decision, granted to him by The Old Man, Santo Trafficante. Here was a chance to re-take Pasco and Pinellas for the Luccheses.

"OK, Tony. I'm awarding you your own territory. You got my green light for the club, the gambling, whatever. But remember, no junk and no 'whoores.' Too many headaches, alright? Forget about it. And you take over payments to the cop. If Acquafredda has a question, tell him to call me."

Little Jimmy said he would send as many people as needed "to do the job." There was no discussion of the Lucchese's cut but Ed knew it would be 50 percent of the profits after the club started making a score. With his ruling of "no junk and no whoores," Ed also knew, Little Jimmy was one of the old school who could make a distinction between proper mob activities and the dirty stuff, those which went against family values.

With hugs all around, Ed and JoJo left Cousin's. On the drive north, Ed was elated. Tony Rossi's star had ascended this night, and it shone down now over a new horizon. He had been claimed by a made Lucchese and given his own territory with the green light for a club, the cop, the garbage association, gambling, whatever he wanted to do. And the meeting had been photographed by surveillance agents and recorded onto the Nagra taped to his leg.

Ed clapped JoJo on the back. He held no fears that JoJo would be jealous of his success. JoJo knew he himself was not cut out to be a boss; he realized he was a mutt. But Tony Rossi had shown he had the right stuff to get to the top: balls, brains, discipline, and respect for authority. Tony was going to run things. JoJo would stay close.

"You know who that was back there, really?" JoJo asked, ever more eager to be of use to Tony.

"Who? You mean Little Jimmy? I know one thing. He ain't Jimmy Fischetti."

"He's Jimmy East."

The next morning, Ed turned the name over to Kinne. Jack Case entered "Jimmy East" on the FBI computer and came up bingo. Little Jimmy, Tampa Jimmy, Jimmy Fischetti, Jimmy East was Vincenzo Ciraulo, an organized crime fugitive wanted in New York on loan-sharking charges.

The Tampa Field Office decided to leave Ciraulo on the streets. He would solidify Ed's status as a Lucchese asset and provide the Mafia seal of approval for the opening of the club.

The club, as envisioned by Ed, Kinne, Case, and Daniels, would be the center for organized crime activities in Pasco and Pinellas Counties. Bad guys would sit, drink, and plot under its roof. In the middle of it all, sitting at the head table, his fingers in every pie, was to be the newly anointed Lucchese boss of Pasco and Pinellas, Tony Rossi.

CHAPTER EIGHT
The King's Court

Ed spent most of July setting up the club. He told JoJo not to tell Acquafredda of the meeting with Jimmy East, figuring there was nothing to be gained by a confrontation. He let it be known only that he had "the green light from the right people" to open the club. He'd make his move on Acquafredda when the time came. For now, Acquafredda kept himself busy and out of the way by getting the West Coast Cartmen's Association moving.

Ed found an ideal site for the club on Rte. 19 in the sleepy retirement community of Holiday, thirty miles north of Tampa. It was an octagonal building in the heart of a long run of fast food restaurants, strip malls, and vegetable stands. In its previous incarnation, it had been The Holiday Tennis Club. The building needed only minor remodeling to turn it from a health club into a nightclub. Joe Pete recommended a list of contractors. Ed had to get a business license, set up banking accounts, obtain liability insurance, negotiate a lease, deal with vendors, and do all of the chores any legitimate citizen would have to do. He did everything; the only help from the FBI was money. He estimated the cost of remodeling and licensing at about $20,000. Tony Daniels swallowed hard at the number and asked what he would be getting for his investment. Ed brought in a plan for a six-month extension of Coldwater so that the investigation could expand to include the Luccheses and Santo Trafficante.

The Holiday Tennis Club was owned by Richard Milbauer, a local attorney. Ed knew Milbauer from hanging out at The Club and Harv's. A childhood disease had left the lawyer with a deformed arm and a dragging leg. He was pale, shriveled, skinny, and bore a scummy reputation for degenerate sex and drugs. Milbauer disgusted most and was tolerated by the mob only because he had inherited a great deal of money and was easily separated from it. During their second meeting on the lease, Milbauer asked Ed about going into business together. The lawyer wanted Tony Rossi to help him find women to whore out. Ed refused. Jimmy East had made it clear. No junk and no "whoores." Late one night at The Club, the crew sat around scheming and playing cards when the idea came up to kidnap Milbauer and hold him for ransom. The notion gathered steam until Ed threw in a monkey wrench to disarm the plot.

"Fellas, wait a minute," he warned them, "everybody hates that motherfucker. Who we gonna hit up for the ransom?" None of the crew could propose a single name who cared enough about Richard Milbauer to part with a cent to save him. Ed negotiated a lease with Milbauer for six months renewable, at $1,200 per month. The Bureau's Legal Office said grace over the contract and the deal was done. Now it was time to give the club a name, a personality.

Ed wanted JoJo to participate to keep the mob involved. This would give them a sense of belonging and keep them from asking questions.

"JoJo, we need a name for the club and a theme. We got to get a logo, business cards, letterhead, all that shit." Ed knew of a club in Clearwater Beach, King Arthur's Court, which was going out of business. They drove down to look at the furnishings and bargained for all the decorations and dining room equipment. They bought suits of armor, spears, shields, a chandelier fashioned from a huge wooden wheel, pictures of medieval castles, heavy oaken tables and chairs, and primitive glasses that resembled mead flagons. The front door they bought looked like a drawbridge.

It was then that JoJo came up with a name for Ed's club.

"The King's Court."

"Yeah, JoJo." Ed liked it. "And I'll be the king."

The renovations began on the Holiday Tennis Club. After a few weeks, one of the carpenters disappeared. Five days later, the carpenter's family put in a Missing Persons Report, and the Sheriff's Office came around to question Ed. Tony Rossi was a suspect in the disappearance; the police figured that, instead of paying the guy, Rossi had him whacked. Soon after the carpenter disappeared, Richard Milbauer shot himself in the head with a deer rifle. Again, the police came to Ed. It seemed that Tony was associated with every questionable event with which he had even the most tenuous of connections. Ed was pleased at the attention. The constant harassment by the local police was a pain, but it did wonders for his reputation.

* * *

While Ed oversaw the arrangements for The King's Court, Acquafredda got the garbage association moving. Though Jimmy East had given Ed the authority to take over the association from Acquafredda, he could not do that. An undercover agent cannot assume a leading role in any criminal enterprise. He may sometimes participate—although never in a violent act—but can never initiate.

Ed attended his first West Coast Cartmen's Association meeting, held at the Holiday Inn conference room in Clearwater the evening of July 2, 1979. Jimmy Acquafredda, JoJo Fitapelli, Bernie Agostino, Rick Mazzenga, and representatives from eight private garbage-collection firms in Pasco and Pinellas Counties were there. FBI surveillance teams photographed each one entering the hotel lobby.

Ed walked in swinging a new Hartman leather briefcase. Everyone in the room started in on him: "Hey, Tone, you look like a legit businessman with that briefcase," and "Tony, you can write?"

Ed sat at the head table and opened the case with ceremony, pulling out pencils and pads to show everyone in the room the attaché was empty. The Nagra recorder lay hidden in the lining.

JoJo started the meeting. He announced that there had been an election for officers of the association, which, of course, there had not been. He gave the results.

"I'm going to be executive director. Jimmy Acquafredda is president. And Tony Rossi is secretary, because he's got his fuckin' briefcase."

JoJo reviewed the association's charter. The document was legal enough; it had been drawn up at Bernie Agostino's request by Henry Gonzalez, the personal attorney to Santo Trafficante. Ed had picked it up from Gonzalez.

The real mission of the garbage association was not stated in the charter. The goal was the total control of all sanitation pick-ups in Pasco and Pinellas Counties. The member operators were to pay initiation fees of $2,000 plus $50 per truck per month. In return, they would enjoy fixed prices, guaranteed contract awards, and the power to intimidate competition out of business. In addition, each member would receive "peace and harmony," which meant protection from violence to his trucks and family by his own association.

The ambassadors from the eight garbage-collection companies accounted for only half of the private sanitation businesses in Pasco and Pinellas. These men were not mobsters but they wanted mobsters to run the organization and keep everyone in line. They knew that gangland characters would do things they could not.

Acquafredda had tried for a year to get the association going but several of the independent operators had turned him down. He walked to the podium after JoJo and told the meeting the association had failed in the past only because "people didn't do what they were supposed to do. But this time," he pointed at Ed, Bernie, and Mazzenga, "we got the right people backin' us up."

Acquafredda said the group should get tough, double their prices, protect members' garbage stops, and eliminate competition. He made it clear that, if any member took another member's stop, he'd be forced to give it up. Rossi, the Lucchese Mazzenga, or Agostino would have a chat with anyone who stole another member's stop. If this visit didn't bring about the desired results, then the member should expect a visit by a baseball bat. If this didn't work, then as many people as it took would be "brought in to do the job." Acquafredda reiterated that the Mafia families behind the association would be the final enforcers of all group decisions.

JoJo spoke again to emphasize that the association was going to succeed "whether some people liked it or not." The group would handle all members' problems, including lending money, protection, and competition. He reminded the members that, if anyone resisted their efforts, they would be brought into line by beatings, burning trucks, and, if necessary, "more drastic action."

Bernie Agostino was the next speaker. He addressed the topic of customers. If a customer became dissatisfied with the service provided by an association member, no other collector in the group would pick up that customer's garbage, allowing the trash to build until the customer became more agreeable.

"Let 'em eat their garbage," he said to applause.

* * *

The renovations at The King's Court were under way. Ed was there every day, making his presence known, showing the place off to associates and potential members. The club was scheduled to open by Thanksgiving.

In mid-August, Ed disappeared from Florida for two weeks on a canoeing vacation in Minnesota with Gretchen. He left JoJo behind with a cover story about an out-of-town deal and instructed him to keep an eye on the job site and the mob crew, especially Acquafredda. Ed paddled on the calm waters and nestled by the campfire, but he could not discuss Coldwater with Gretchen. In the many quiet hours, he reflected privately on the progress of the investigation. Over the past six months, the FBI had made a number of cases: gambling against the crew, corruption on the cop Donahue, the fugitive Vincenzo "Jimmy

East" Ciraulo had been located, the garbage association members had entered into an extortionate conspiracy, even a link to Trafficante and his lawyer Henry Gonzalez had been established. The King's Court sting would become a reality in a few more months. Tony Rossi had been very effective. Was it time to call him away from Florida on some other shady business and insert a new undercover agent to take his place? He could introduce some new guy to the crew as his "longtime goombah." He would vouch for the agent and make it stick. He had convinced Tampa supervisor Daniels to extend Coldwater for an additional six months but the Bureau wouldn't make him stay if he could find a suitable replacement.

The FBI had an operation similar to The King's Court going in Arizona; Ed could tell the Florida crew that he was involved out there in another club. In case of an emergency, if Tony Rossi had to make an appearance, the Bureau could fly him in to Holiday. It would work. Gretchen wanted her husband back. Their son Matt was all-state in lacrosse and Ed wanted to see him play. His oldest boy, Mark, was a junior at Virginia Tech and daughter Amy was entering junior high. The lapping waters, the rhythm of the oars, the million stars, and his wife's arms told him for the two weeks in Minnesota, "You've done a good job, Tony Rossi. But Ed Robb's got plenty of life to lead at home. Let him go."

* * *

At that point, Ed Robb was ready to leave Coldwater. He decided he needed a contingency plan. Case, Kinne, and Daniels listened to Ed's request to be replaced as lead undercover agent in Coldwater. His reasons were good: his family beckoned, he had put in the agreed six-month stint, and all the original target cases were well in hand. A replacement agent could take the lead, allowing Ed to slide out on the basis of the Arizona cover story. Tony Rossi would still fly into Florida once or twice a month to check on things until the new boss was firmly entrenched. Then, finally, Tony would disappear. No one would notice: As long as the bad guys believed they were making money, their greed would swallow anything.

Agent Steve Salmieri was not going to be able to take over for Ed. As Chico Navarro, he had already been around the crew for a few months as a jewel thief, and was working his own cases, especially Johnny Cascio's Mafia connections in Chicago. Though everyone knew that Navarro and Rossi were connected, Navarro's role in Coldwater was already set as one of the guys who hung out. He wouldn't be seen as the next boss.

Daniels, Kinne, and Ed realized they needed to bring in an agent from out of town. The agent they selected was G. Tyrus "Ty" Cobb. Cobb was recognized as one of the Bureau's best criminal undercover operatives. He had recently been transferred to the Miami Office from Milwaukee where he worked—under the undercover name Tony Conte—in a highly successful bust of mob boss Frank Balistrieri.

The plan was to introduce Ty into Coldwater as Vincent "Vinnie" Russo, Tony Rossi's best childhood buddy from "the orphanage back in Pittsburgh." They'd grown up together and kept in touch over the years. They were like brothers. In fact, they looked like brothers; Ty and Ed shared the same thickly muscled build, dark coloring, and medium height. Ty was forty-four, two years older than Ed.

Vinnie wanted to come down to Florida and "take a look, see what Tony's into." Ed and Ty made up stories about the old days, like the times they ran away from the orphanage and those bleak Christmases when "they didn't get no gifts."

Ed involved Ty in the King's Court renovations. He told the crew that Vinnie was going to be his partner in the club. Ty hung out at The Club and Harv's. Gradually, he made himself popular with JoJo, Acquafredda, Joe Pullicino, Trascher, and the rest of the boys. Ty even began to attend the garbagemen's association meetings, keeping a low profile, gaining the members' respect and confidence with his few but well-chosen words.

Ty had slipped easily into the mob social circle. He was

excellent at his craft: patient, strong, quiet, likable, but tough. He knew the rules of the underworld and the twisted logic of the career criminal. In a few months, Vinnie Russo had become Tony Rossi's second-in-command, and would be able to take his place if and when Ed left.

By the time Ty established himself, Ed came to realize that there was more mileage left to Coldwater, possibly much more. Coldwater was the biggest undercover operation the FBI had mounted to date. It was Ed Robb's baby, he was there from the beginning, his imprint was all over it. He knew this might turn out to be the highlight of his undercover career. As competent as Ty Cobb was, Ed made the decision to stay. Vinnie Russo would not get the shot to step into Tony's undercover shoes and take over. It was just too soon. Ed couldn't let Tony Rossi go, not yet.

CHAPTER NINE
Turning Tony Loose

Mobsters often embody contradictory traits. They can be cunning, even ingenious, but they routinely concoct schemes that a ten-year-old could tell them simply would not work. The mob can be fanatically loyal, right up to the lethal second when they betray their loyalty. They are often gentle, funny, and tragically sad, and in the next moment may shrug coldly and not "give a fuck" about anything. Mafiosi take pride in their codes of honor but are blind to the harm they do.

JoJo Fitapelli was a classic. His Lucchese loyalty could sometimes be a thing of beauty. It could also be the stuff of high comedy and danger. One evening in early September of 1979, Ed, JoJo, Acquafredda, Bernie, and Mazzenga met for dinner with Jimmy East at Malio's in Tampa. The conversation, recorded by the Nagra taped to Ed's thigh, covered The King's Court and the garbage association, then turned to Johnny Cascio. The thug from Chicago, who was fast becoming friends with agent Salmieri, had been "mentioning Santo's name" again, dropping it around town as if The Old Man's name were his business card. Jimmy East mentioned that somebody ought to "give Cascio a kick in his fuckin' head."

Two nights later, in the hallway at The Club, JoJo encountered Cascio and Salmieri. With no warning, JoJo clubbed Cascio in the head with his fist. The two tangled and JoJo fell down a flight of stairs, breaking his arm in two places. He got up swinging anyway, until Salmieri broke up the fight. JoJo told Salmieri that he was just showing "respect" to Jimmy East by doing to Cascio what he requested.

Jimmy Acquafredda was another standard-issue Mafia mutt. He was an incredibly bad businessman who kept up appearances through bravado and costly habits. Almost every deal he touched went sour, despite the fact that he seized upon whatever short-cuts he could find or invent. As a true felon, he never figured he needed to work harder or smarter, or even change careers. He simply decided he hadn't cheated enough.

Acquafredda was under a lot of pressure from the Pinellas Sheriff's Office for pistol-whipping Sylvester Hutchins. He had been charged with assault and a trial date was set. Hutchins agreed to testify.

At the same time, the city of Oldsmar put out a request for bids for the city's sanitation contract. Five members of the West Coast Cartmen's Association, including Acquafredda, met and decided to rig the bid so that Hutchins' company would win the contract. Acquafredda wanted the business for his own company but he was voted down because of the criminal case pending against him. The association decided to offer Hutchins an olive branch, to make the peace and perhaps convince him to drop the charges against Acquafredda. Also, they wanted to show Hutchins what the association could do for him to encourage him to join up.

Acquafredda went to Hutchins to give him the news that he would win the Oldsmar contract. He gave him the figure to submit to the City Council to guarantee the winning bid. Then Acquafredda went a step further. He told Hutchins they should let bygones be bygones. What was done was done. And even though the association had decided to award Hutchins the Oldsmar contract, Acquafredda insisted that his company and not Hutchins' should be the one to do the actual job.

"You owe me," Acquafredda told Hutchins, "for getting me in trouble with the cops."

"OK, sure," Hutchins replied, then went straight to the Sheriff's Office.

At the Oldsmar City Council meeting, Hutchins secretly

wore a wire. Ed knew he was wired because Kinne found out from the Sheriff's Office. At the meeting, Ed told Acquafredda to stay away from Hutchins; he's bad medicine, he said. Ed didn't want the local authorities to build their own case against Acquafredda or the association; they would only compromise the federal investigation.

That night, the Oldsmar City Council granted the sanitation contract to the lowest bidder. It was not Hutchins but Imperial Carting, one of the members who had agreed to rig the bids. Acquafredda had made a greedy mistake. Thinking he would keep the Oldsmar business—under his secret arrangement with Hutchins—he inflated the bid a few thousand dollars more. The number crept above Imperial's bid. He and Hutchins both lost the contract.

Acquafredda was furious. The next day, he called a meeting of the association. He was forced to admit that he had made a separate deal with Hutchins but insisted that, in fairness, Imperial should turn the contract over to him. The association assigned a Grievance Committee to look into all the facts. The following week, the Committee let stand the award of the Oldsmar contract to Imperial Carting. Acquafredda was speechless. He couldn't believe the outcome; the Committee had held against him even though he had bribed every one of the members.

With Acquafredda's influence in the crew so clearly ebbing, Ed picked the moment to confront him with Jimmy East's decision to make Tony Rossi the boss of Pinellas and Pasco. Ed cornered Acquafredda one evening at The Club soon after the Imperial Carting fiasco.

"Lookit, Jim," Ed said with calm and empathy, "you got too much heat on you. You know that. So do us all a favor. Wait 'til you cool off, then come around. We'll be there for you, but for a while, don't fucking come around. And another thing, we're opening this club, The King's Court. You're a member, you're a partner, but don't come around there neither. Oh, and one more thing. Little Jimmy wants you to give me the gambling equipment out of Trascher's garage so we can set it up in The King's

Court. But hey, you're gonna share, as soon as you cool down. Oh, Jim, and the cop you own, that Donahue? You don't own him no more. Little Jimmy wants you to hand him over to me."

Acquafredda's face went the color and hardness of a boiled lobster. Ed stood his ground. Jimmy Acquafredda served no more purpose: All the Coldwater cases against him were made and he wasn't leading the investigation into any new realms. The time had come to step over him, strip him of his powers, and lay the mantle of "boss" across the shoulders of Tony Rossi.

"Hey, Jim," Ed concluded the interview, "look at the facts. You're the one who fucked up beating this guy Hutchins. 'Cause of you we had to shut down the casino. 'Cause of you Hutchins didn't even get the Oldsmar contract. Little Jimmy says I'm the boss. You got a problem with that, we'll go have lunch with him, OK?"

He turned away, then snapped his fingers as if he'd just remembered something else important.

"You tell Donahue to come see me before we open."

After this confrontation, Ed heard no more disgruntled noises from Acquafredda. The Gambino mobster took his demotion from master to mutt with polite resignation. He, like JoJo, realized that Tony Rossi possessed the stuff to make a better boss of Pasco and Pinellas than he would be. The casino was going to reopen once the King's Court renovation was complete. Tony had brought in two more crew members, Chico Navarro and Vinnie Russo, who were working a lot of angles themselves. The garbage association was moving forward. Even Jimmy East was taking an active interest in their affairs. They were all going to make money off Tony Rossi. So, OK, he could be the boss.

* * *

Ed turned Tony Rossi loose. His gangster alter ego stretched out to fill the role of boss of Pasco and Pinellas Counties. Tony became authoritarian and idiosyncratic. He refused to ride in the back of a car; he had to be in the front. He refused to ride in an elevator. He behaved as if he had no memory for insignificant things like addresses, names, or phone numbers. He'd snap over his shoulder, "JoJo, remember that, will ya?" His drink was Jack Daniel's and it was an invitation to a scene to offer him anything other than a Marlboro. He nurtured his reputation for a volatile temper.

Ed squired Tony Rossi past the bounds of sensible behavior to distinguish himself from the predictable patterns of a cop. Typically, cops walk into a room, sit with their backs to the wall, and watch everything. Tony moved through crowds, looking at no one and sitting wherever. Cops were talkative; Tony, without being surly, became aloof now that he was the boss. Cops acted tough; Tony was quietly and confidently dangerous.

* * *

Perhaps the sharpest human contradiction among the Coldwater characters was Sheriff's Captain Joe Donahue. Donahue had been a law enforcement officer in Pasco County since 1962. He claimed to have been a police detective in New York City during the 1950s. By 1967, he had worked his way up to Chief of the Port Richey Police Department and ten years later joined John Short's staff after Short's election to Sheriff of Pasco in 1977. Donahue was given a captain's rank and made a supervisor in the Sheriff's special unit investigating the growth of organized crime in Pasco County.

Jimmy Acquafredda stopped by The King's Court the afternoon of October 4, 1979, to tell Ed that Donahue was going to be there in a few minutes to discuss gambling and other activities. Ed replied that he would not initiate these topics with Donahue but would pursue them if the cop brought them up. When Donahue's cruiser pulled into the parking lot, Ed and Acquafredda met him outside. Jimmy introduced them. Ed shook the cop's hand and took him on a tour of the club.

"I want this to be a first-class operation," Ed said, sweeping his hand across his emerging domain through the sound of carpenters' banging. Acquafredda trailed behind several steps. "A place where you'd be proud to be a member. In fact, I'm gonna give you a membership, Joe. All the finest people in Pasco and Pinellas are gonna want to come here."

Ed made no mention of illegal activities at The King's Court as he guided Donahue. But while in the "game room," the room that Ed intended to use for high-stakes card games, Donahue volunteered several recommendations to make the room safer for gambling purposes. He suggested double-pane glass on the windows and heavy drapes to make the room more soundproof. Donahue carried himself like a lawman, erect and conservative. He spoke little and often issued orders instead of conversation. Ed got the impression that Joe Donahue thought he was slick, a man who was one up on everybody, both the criminals and the establishment, moving with respect in both worlds.

Ed took Donahue and Acquafredda into the office. The FBI sound teams had already wired the office with hidden microphones and a video camera. Ed switched these on with the secret toggle behind the door.

"OK, Joe. No bullshit." Ed put his hands on the table, palms up, as if presenting an unseen gift, "what can I do for you and what can you do for me?"

"Alright, Tony. I'm a high-up with the organized crime unit in Pasco County. I've got relationships with the FBI and other police agencies. I'm so well thought of by the FBI that they wouldn't make a move without telling me. I got my fingers on everything. Anytime there's a wiretap in Pasco, I know about it."

Acquafredda jumped in. "Are there any wiretaps on my phone?"

"No." Donahue said there was only one wiretap at the time, and that was in East Pasco.

Donahue emphasized that, while he was not the head of the Organized Crime Unit in the Sheriff's Department, he would be aware of any investigations that the Unit conducted and he would give Ed early warning of anything involving his operation. The cop also asked Ed to tell him in advance of any illegal activity that was planned at The King's Court so he could "protect it." He added that, so far, the federal authorities had shown no interest in Tony Rossi or his club.

"OK," Ed said, creeping in for the kill. He pulled an envelope from his desk, fingering it where Donahue could see it.

"We're gonna be running gambling out of The King's Court. You agree you're gonna cover it?"

"Yeah." Donahue said he would bring his wife and kids by the Court. He mentioned that he would also keep tabs on Jimmy Falzone, owner of The Club. Falzone had been complaining that Tony Rossi was opening a rival nightspot just up Rte. 19 from him. Donahue suspected there might be trouble.

The Captain put out his hand. Ed opened the envelope and counted the two hundred dollars aloud so that the concealed camera and microphones could witness the cash, with its serial numbers recorded, pass into Donahue's palm.

CHAPTER TEN
Open for Business

The West Coast Cartmen's Association soon reverted to its former status as a joke. None of the members wanted to pay dues, and no new members had been introduced in a month. Several of the garbage collectors openly questioned the mob qualifications for the association's leadership, forcing Ed to ask Jimmy East to make a phone call. East called a connection in New York who then made it clear over the phone to several association members that the Mafia was well represented in the association.

Ed sensed the frustration growing among the association members. He feared they would soon lash out if the mob couldn't produce a monopoly. Despite his pleas for restraint and constant reminders of the trouble resulting from the Hutchins beating, the mood among the members turned surly and insistent.

One of the main obstacles to a monopoly was Kenneth Faircloth, owner-operator of Faircloth Sanitation Co. in Largo. Faircloth was a big man, a no-nonsense type from Tennessee. To the city-slick mobsters from New York, Faircloth was a hayseed. They spoke regularly of "bouncing" Faircloth for refusing to cooperate. To calm everybody down, Tony Rossi and his sidekick Vinnie Russo offered to pay Faircloth a recruitment visit.

On November 28, Ed and Ty met with Faircloth at his Largo office. Their approach was mannerly and nonthreatening. Ed advised the Tennessean that the West Coast Cartmen's Association could be a big help, especially in getting cheaper deals on dumpsters, tires, and insurance. When Faircloth balked, Ed added frankly that he was fearful for the man's safety, as several of the

101

members had threatened force because of his refusal to cooperate. Ty gave Faircloth a break on the monthly dues; he could join for only $1,200, plus $35 per truck. The meeting ended on a hopeful note. Faircloth thanked Ed and Ty and said he would contact them soon with his decision.

That night, Ed and Ty met JoJo at Mr. Pete's Riverboat Restaurant in New Port Richey. JoJo was delighted that the visit with Faircloth had gone so well. JoJo mentioned that Vito Signorelli, an association member, had also called Faircloth and was certain he was going to join.

In the meantime, Ken Faircloth phoned a friend of his, Joe American, operator of American Garbage Disposal in Tarpon Springs. He told Joe he was furious at "that Guinea bastard" Tony Rossi for threatening him into joining the association. Faircloth told Joe he was going to get a contract out on Rossi and "blow him up in his fucking Mark V."

Joe American was one of several other garbage collectors Ed had been courting to join the association. Joe called and asked Ed what he had done to piss Faircloth off so badly.

"Nothin', Joe. Just talked to him."

Now Ed had a problem. The association was surely going to injure Faircloth if he didn't join. In return, Faircloth was so angry at Tony Rossi that he might actually try to do Ed harm. Faircloth was one of those resolute, backwoods men Ed had known during his days as a young Special Agent working the Tennessee hills: Those men didn't threaten anyone unless they meant it. Certainly, Ed couldn't allow violence to befall Faircloth. He would blow his cover before letting that happen. Faircloth would have to join the association or Tony Rossi and Coldwater were both in jeopardy. Ed devised a plan that he shared with Kinne.

That week, Kenneth Faircloth was approached by the Pinellas police—rather than the Pasco Sheriff's Office, since Donahue might have gotten wind of it—to join the garbage association and report back to them about the meetings. The cops asked him to keep his temper in check. Their brand of revenge—

nailing the whole association rather than just Rossi—would be better, they suggested. The Pinellas police even offered to pay Faircloth's association dues—knowing they would be reimbursed by the FBI.

At the next meeting, Ed watched Faircloth saunter into the room seeming glad to be there. He held lengthy conversations with each member and was a spur to the evening's business discussions. Ed was amused at Faircloth's good-old-boy enthusiasm, knowing how hard the big man was working to remember every word spoken that night to repeat later to the police.

Tony came off looking like a genius. He had won over the toughest operator of them all. The association members had finally seen some headway and were placated. Ed also breathed a sigh of relief watching Faircloth work the room, knowing that the Tennessean was getting his revenge by smiling and shaking hands instead of sliding a stick of dynamite into the muffler of Tony Rossi's Mark V.

* * *

The King's Court opened for business the week before Thanksgiving. The banners of eight different nations, purchased by JoJo, flapped on poles at each of the corners of the octagonal building to give it the look of a castle keep.

Anticipation ran high in several circles. Local gangsters saw the Court as a haven, a place where they would be treated with dignity and privacy, a preserve for their gambling and scheming. Vincent "Jimmy East" Ciraulo viewed the new business as an extra income stream and an extension of the Lucchese family influence in South Florida. JoJo Fitapelli enjoyed his status as closest associate of Tony Rossi, the owner of the club. Captain Joe Donahue figured on an easy extra grand a month in protection payments. On the other side, the FBI, which had sunk a lot of time and resources into The King's Court, was waiting for the payoff in the form of new cases.

The King's Court was a private bottle club. The members,

who paid $25 to join, supplied their own alcohol, which was labeled with members' names and kept in lockers behind the bar. The club supplied only the mixers and the environment, thus avoiding the need to obtain a liquor license. The mixers, however, brought in almost as much as liquor would have, with a glass of water costing $2.50 and soda $7.50.

The front door, at the end of a short wooden drawbridge, had a peephole and a buzzer for security. Inside the Court were a large lounge decorated in medieval motif, heavy tables covered in a rough, black Formica to suggest stone, padded chairs, a piano and cigarette machines, a game room containing a poker table and slot machines, coatroom, and Ed's office. In the middle of the lounge was the Round Table, the only circular table in the club, permanently reserved for Tony Rossi and his invited guests. The game room would also serve as the meeting hall for the garbage association meetings. JoJo, as executive director of the association, shared Ed's office and telephone, for which he was charged $150 a month.

Ed hired a staff to operate the club. Fat Art, the manager, was a guy Ed knew from hanging out in New Port Richey. Art had been a pilot for Eastern Airlines until he grew too fat to fly. He was now more than four hundred pounds. Ed kidded him about not going behind the bar; if Art died back there, he said, they'd have to tear the bar away to get him out. Art was smart, a decent guy who kept his mouth shut and his eyes open. The head barmaid and assistant manager was Nancy, a sharp lady who was so thin Ed claimed she only had one side to her. Skinny Nancy brought in a few friends of hers to handle the coat check and waitress duties.

Unknown to its patrons or employees, the King's Court, in addition to being the newest place on Rte. 19 to drink, dance, schmooze, plot, and bicker, also was a very large recording and transmission chamber. Mike Lunsford, a Special Agent in the Tampa Field Office, was in charge of surveillance and coordinating the technical side of Coldwater. Lunsford's sound and video crew had installed hidden cameras and microphones in false walls and strategic locations throughout the club. A bug was concealed in the wagon-wheel chandelier above the Round Table; a remote-control 35-mm camera, buried high in the corner of the lounge, also was focused on the table. Above the door in the game room hung a wooden sign that read "The King's Courtroom." The sign, carved by Jim Kinne, featured several decorative holes between the words; recessed in one of the holes was a camera lens no larger than the cap to a pen. A second video camera recorded activity in the office while a third covered the bar.

The only telephone in the building that was bugged was Tony's private phone at the Round Table. The federal court in Tampa had not allowed the FBI's Title III request for wiretaps on all the club's extensions, stating that there was no guarantee that a law enforcement agent—who would consent to being recorded—would be the only person using the phones. However, because the telephones were owned by Tony Rossi, records of toll calls would be available to the FBI. This limitation—that a consenting individual be a part of all recordings—also applied to the secret video cameras in The King's Court: The moment the agent left the room, the video would become inadmissible as evidence.

When The King's Court opened, Ed moved from his Pelican Point condo to a one-bedroom apartment at Holiday Park, across Rte. 19 from the club, in the third row of buildings. The FBI rented an apartment in the second row. From here, Mike Lunsford and his crew would monitor audio and video transmissions from the club, with two agents always on duty.

At the Court, beside a door leading to the liquor lockers, was a switch Ed could hit to alert the surveillance agents waiting in the apartment, like an alarm, that something important was about to happen and to turn on the transmitters, cameras, and recorders. All the mikes in The King's Court were wired by coaxial cable and run under Rte. 19 to the FBI's apartment. The three video cameras sent their images via microwave frequency. Lunsford installed an antenna outside the apartment to gather in the transmissions from the club one half mile away.

During the summer, a giant palm tree and a mimosa just off the balcony bloomed, and the extra foliage blocked the signals. One night, Lunsford trimmed the branches back to clear the way. The next morning, he observed two elderly ladies come out of their neighboring apartment.

"You know, Mildred," Lunsford heard one say, "something's been eating on those trees."

One Sunday morning just after The King's Court opened, Lunsford and agent Ron Wooldridge were at the club repairing a microphone cable. They were surprised when JoJo, who had keys, got out of a taxi and entered the building. The agents hid in a storage closet for two hours as JoJo rummaged around, talking to himself. At one point, JoJo tried to open the closet door. Lunsford, a short but athletic man, heard him coming and grabbed the doorknob from the inside and propped his foot against the wall. JoJo tugged hard to get in but Lunsford's grip was firm.

"Goddamit, who locked this fuckin' door?" JoJo shouted.

Wooldridge held his radio high should JoJo manage to open the door. His impromptu plan was to crack JoJo over the head and leave him inside the closet as if he had been ambushed by burglars hiding in the building. But JoJo gave up and left.

As in any surveillance, not everything that Lunsford and his crew observed during Coldwater was of use. Most of it, in fact, was useless because it lacked criminal content or recorded incomprehensible statements, or even such absurdities as the three occasions when they witnessed JoJo having sex with The King's Court vacuum cleaner. The vacuum was thereafter awarded an affectionate nickname by the droll Kinne: "Lady Kenmore." Kinne drew and distributed cartoons of the mobster courting Lady Kenmore in a bar, buying it a drink, and taking it to bed.

Now that The King's Court was operational, Ed, Kinne, and Jack Case decided to add another undercover agent to the Coldwater undercover team of Ed, Steve Salmieri, and Ty Cobb. Richard Holland, a young agent, had been a pretty good college tennis player. Operating as Dick Stauder, Holland was named The King's Court tennis pro to run the tennis courts, give lessons during the day, and cultivate his own share of the criminal contacts now swarming about the place. Not only would Holland's presence add to the club's legitimacy, he would expand the Bureau's covert coverage into the daylight hours, as Ed, Steve, and Ty were rarely at the club before nightfall.

Before Holland could begin teaching tennis, the courts had to be refurbished. They had become overgrown with elephant grass. Rather than hire a private company to clean and resurface the courts, several agents in the Tampa Field Office volunteered to do the work, to get themselves out in the sunshine for some exercise as well as help keep the costs down for the Bureau. These men were all office agents, untrained in undercover techniques. The afternoon they completed the work on the courts, Ed pulled into the gas station across the street from the club.

The attendant approached Tony Rossi, by now a recognizable mobster in the community. The man informed Ed that the guys who had been working on his tennis courts had stopped in that morning and filled up with gas.

"So?" Ed asked.

"They used a government credit card, Mr. Rossi."

Ed thanked the attendant and slipped him a fifty.

"Forget about it," he said.

As he drove to the club, he wondered: What's going to get me killed? How many agents were telling their wives or girlfriends about the case? How many were using insecure phones or talking too much to their own snitches about Coldwater? Who's going to slip up, and how, and when?

* * *

Jim Kinne was a talented man. Beyond the immense respect his FBI colleagues held for his abilities as an agent, he was also renowned as a wag for his wry poems, cartoons, and biting wit. Now that Coldwater had expanded to include several more undercover agents, support agents, and additional targets, Kinne gave each principal player a nickname. The challenge Kinne set for himself was that each label was to be of a nautical nature, in keeping with the operation's code name Coldwater. Aside from simple amusement value, the nicknames also served to identify each subject or agent during surveillance, without naming that person over the air should the broadcasts be monitored by the mob.

The first nickname was given to the original Coldwater target, Jimmy Acquafredda. In a prior case in the early 1970s, Kinne had investigated the gambling operations of Henry Trafficante, Santo's brother. One of the defendants, Sam Vaglica, owned a Tampa saloon, the Neptune Tavern, out of which he ran his sports book for Trafficante. Suspended over the bar was a wire cage containing a wooden fish. Attached to the cage was a sign, "Mullet of the Week"; with room on the sign to insert the name of that week's big betting loser. Kinne tagged Acquafredda with "the Mullet," a loser, good only for bait.

Kinne's own nickname was given to him by Coldwater's informant. When Ed told the snitch of Acquafredda's title, the snitch laughed and said, "If Jimmy's the Mullet, then Kinne must be the Shark!"

JoJo Fitapelli was crowned the Crab for the arm he'd broken in the fight with Johnny Cascio. Tony Daniels, the investigation's supervisor, was granted two names. His nautical brand was Lobster because he was constantly in hot water. Behind his back the agents called him the Mushroom because he claimed he was kept in the dark and covered with manure. Jack Case, the case agent, was the Clam. He was the quietest of all the Coldwater agents. Mike Lunsford, the technical and surveillance guy, carried the name Sonar. Bill Garner, a gangly man with an unrelenting friendly manner, was the agent in charge of documentation. Garner kept the Coldwater books, paid the bills, arranged all fake histories and identifications, handled correspondence with FBI headquarters, paid off the agents' several credit cards, and signed the undercover agents' paychecks. Kinne nailed him with Filefish.

Ed didn't get a nautical nickname. Early on, Tony Daniels had pegged him with Magilla, as in the Gorilla, for his broad shouldered, long-armed lope, curly dark hair, and flat, sideways nose. Kinne tagged Ty Cobb with Godzilla because he looked a lot like Magilla. When questioned on the nautical nature of this nickname, Shark responded correctly and with Irish indignation that, in several films, the giant Godzilla did in fact do battle underwater as well as on dry land.

* * *

The shadow cast by Tony Rossi across the local underworld scene was growing larger. He was the owner of The King's Court and the boss of Pasco and Pinellas. He was the guy everybody in two counties called on with stolen goods, a scheme, a connection, a problem, or an opportunity. The King's Court became a watering hole for all the local "half-ass wise guys," crews, and party girls. Ed sat in the center of it all, inviting special guests to the Round Table, then into his office or the meeting room for private discussions, where the recordings were clearer without the ambient clankings and voices from the bar.

Throughout the balmy winter, from December of 1979 until March of 1980, Ed explored dozens of avenues to increase the criminal stature of The King's Court and its crew. He wanted such an array of illicit activity buzzing about Tony Rossi and the club that the ultimate boss Santo Trafficante, or at least one of his minions like Jimmy East or the lawyer Henry Gonzalez, would be drawn in. Trafficante was the apex of organized crime in Florida; every decision Ed, Kinne, and Jack Case made was aimed at getting an introduction to bring The Old Man into the Coldwater net.

Ed set himself the task of displaying just how good an earner Tony Rossi could be. One of his first moves was to have the FBI send him several million dollars worth of counterfeit bearer bonds, confiscated from another sting. These were negotiable instruments and extremely valuable. Ed put them in a safe deposit box at a local bank. He made a big show of the deposit, knowing that a few of the female tellers were dating some of the local mobsters.

Ed cast about for buyers. He asked twenty cents on the dollar for the value of the bonds. This was known in the Bureau as a "reverse"; undercover agents rarely sell, they typically buy. When none of the local suspects showed any interest (the bonds were probably too rich for their tastes,) he loaded the bonds into his briefcase and took them ten miles south down Rte. 19 to Tarpon Springs. Ed had begun to expand his presence into other local mob communities, particularly among the Greeks. He had become friendly with the three brothers who owned Pappas' Restaurant in Tarpon Springs. Ed could walk past a long line of waiting patrons at the renowned restaurant and be ushered to a table opened just for him. The Pappas brothers were not FBI targets though they were suspected of being on the mob periphery. One Pappas brother, Lukie, showed some interest in the bonds but didn't buy. Ed took note that, for whatever reason, Lukie did not call the cops later to report the gangster Tony Rossi and his millions of dollars in counterfeit bonds. Ed was just fishing. This time, he came up empty. But his contacts and experience with the Greeks would come into play later.

On another occasion, the Bureau sent the Coldwater agents an assortment of confiscated diamonds, cheap watches, and gems. The jewelry, presented as stolen goods, was attributed to Chico Navarro, agent Steve Salmieri who posed as a cat burglar. Ed set up a meeting between Chico, JoJo, and Bernie Agostino to fence the goods. They met for lunch at Malio's. During the meal, Bernie left the table for a few minutes. When he returned, he said a meeting was set for 3:00 p.m. that afternoon to be attended only by Bernie and Chico. The pair left Malio's for A. Tifany & Sons, Inc., operated by Jay Weisman. At the jewelry store, Chico showed Weisman the jewels but Weisman was not impressed. He told Chico to come back if he "got anything good."

Chico and Bernie rejoined Ed and JoJo at Malio's. Bernie reported that there would be no sale. Chico volunteered the idea that Weisman looked like a "good score"; he had a lot of money and plenty of jewelry at his establishment. They ought to consider "tipping" him.

Bernie went crazy. "Are you nuts? You'll get us all whacked." Bernie explained that Weisman was "with Trafficante." Chico backed off, but he had exposed another connection to Trafficante.

In early January, JoJo brought Freddie Cataudella and Pete Solmo to The King's Court. Both were in their late forties. JoJo and Cataudella had been childhood friends in New York. Solmo muled cocaine between Miami and Alaska for the pipeline workers while Cataudella muled between Miami and Chicago. The bearded Solmo claimed that his son had gotten him involved in the narcotics business. The boy was high up in a Medellin drug cartel; Solmo was proud that his son was making it in the big time and was such a "stand-up guy."

Cataudella and Solmo wanted to be Ed's drug connection. Solmo told Ed that he and Cataudella had access to cocaine being shipped into Miami "by the ton" and that he had "three salesmen" working full-time. Ed's crew had been getting increasing inquiries about drugs from the patrons of The King's Court. Though the narcotics trade was dangerous and distasteful, and despite Jimmy East's warnings regarding "junk and whoores," Ed saw it as an inevitability as well as another way to prove to those who were watching his worth as an earner.

Every mob crew had its "junk man." Ed's knowledge of narcotics was limited so he asked Kinne and Case to bring in another agent, a specialist in the street drug trade. Steve Salmieri recommended a young rookie in the Orlando Office who had been a narcotics cop in Ft. Lauderdale. Salmieri assured Ed and the others that the young agent was good, he knew drugs and the street. Ed didn't like the idea of having a rookie agent in his stable. How, he wondered, could a new agent, who hadn't yet mastered the structured environment of the FBI, expect to succeed on the unstructured, shifting, and perilous ground of a Mafia deep undercover sting? How could a man who had not firmly established his identity as a federal agent then layer a new criminal identity on top of it? Would his base hold or crumble? Salmieri's stamp of approval was enough for Ed to let him join the Coldwater covert team, but his reluctance was soon validated. The young agent commuted from Orlando whenever he was needed to work Solmo and Cataudella, but he never fit in with the cast of characters of Coldwater. Within two months, he left the investigation, not because of a lack of talent or courage but because the peculiar strains of deep undercover work got to him, as Ed was afraid they would. By March, Ed was making the case against Solmo and Cataudella by himself.

In Pasco and Pinellas, Tony Rossi had been installed on the tier of mob power just below Jimmy East. Whenever he entered The King's Court now, sliding through the crowd to shake hands and point at pals, Julio the piano player shook loose a few bars of the theme from The Godfather.

Every night, Ed held court at the Round Table or in the office. People waited to importune him with whatever they felt would have a greater chance of success if Tony Rossi first said grace over it. A woman asked his assistance in stopping her husband from running around on her, another complained that her husband was not paying his alimony. A young girl had been beaten by her boyfriend. These women and dozens more could go back to their men and say, "Hey, I talked to Tony Rossi about you." If the men didn't adjust, Ed might call them up to say, "Look, do the right thing here, alright? Don't make me get involved." When he was presented with offerings, Ed either ignored them or passed them off to one of his crew. He didn't want to get involved with anyone who could not help carry him to the next level, who might cause him to shift his focus from Trafficante.

In January, Johnny Cascio approached Ed slowly, the right way. He started coming around The King's Court, spending money, hanging out, getting back into everyone's good graces. Ed insisted that Cascio apologize to JoJo for the fight at Harv's. Then Cascio brought up a plan that involved the participation of his Chicago family connections. Ed's ears picked up at this. He arranged a sitdown in his office for the next night.

At the sitdown, attended by Bernie Agostino, JoJo, and Ed, Cascio related his hopes of opening another bottle club in the area. Money and assistance would come from Cascio's compare Michael Spilotro, a made Mafioso in the Chicago Outfit. Since Tony Rossi was the boss of Pasco and Pinellas, his blessings were needed. Cascio said his club would not compete with The King's Court. Cascio wanted the new place to be "hard rock," appealing to the younger set. He would run bingo games as well as a gambling operation similar to Tony's but for smaller stakes. The high-rollers would remain the prerogative of The King's Court.

Ed agreed to put Cascio in business and provide protection through Donahue. Ed would put up a $10,000 stake to be matched by Cascio. They'd be partners, with Ed getting 50 percent of the take, which he would then share with his Lucchese sponsor Jimmy East. Kinne, Case, and Ed were pleased with the opportunity to bring Chicago money in and widen the scope of Coldwater. Ed went to a sitdown with Jimmy East at Malio's and was given the green light for Cascio's club. East said, OK, but watch him. East didn't relish the idea of Chicago's influence seeping into his Florida domain. He still disliked Cascio for dropping Trafficante's name around town.

Ed negotiated a lease for a closed-down club in Port Richey named the Ridge Runner, owned by an Italian optometrist from New York. Ed planned to install Chico Navarro as his emissary in Cascio's operations. This would give Salmieri a direct line to Spilotro and his Chicago family.

Bernie Agostino was impatient. He wanted the gambling activity up and running at The King's Court as soon as possible. He intended to be involved in operating and financing the games. Bernie told Acquafredda to produce the gambling equipment and to provide Ed and JoJo with all the assistance they needed. In the last week of January, Ed met with Donahue and informed him they were starting a high-stakes poker game at the club. The cop was to alert Ed if he heard anything. Ed would use the code name "Alex" whenever he called the Sheriff's Office to look for Donahue. Also that week, Ed gave Acquafredda $600 for the purchase of the blackjack tables, crap tables, cards, dice, chips, stools, and two lamps. These were installed in the game room of The King's Court.

In early February, Cascio attended a sitdown at The King's Court with Ed, Solmo, Cataudella, JoJo, and Frankie Foggia (who continued to hound Ed for help with his plot to extort the ex-Boy Scout official). In addition to drug transactions, Cascio's club was discussed, and Solmo and Cataudella were enlisted as partners, with Cascio as the manager.

Cascio hadn't come up with his $10,000 stake. Instead of sending the money, Chicago sent Mike Condic and Tony "Nags" Panzica to check out Cascio, his plans, and his Florida connections. Condic and Panzica arrived at The King's Court and met with Ed and JoJo in the office. Condic introduced Panzica as "the best lock man" in the business and referred to himself as the "best safe burglar" in the country. Condic dropped the name of Cascio's uncle, "Philly Beans"—who was Philip Tolomeo, a former Chicago cop with strong organized crime connections in Chicago and Milwaukee—as a close friend of his. Condic also let it be known that he was affiliated with Ron DeAngelis, an electronics expert and a suspect in the 1975 murder of mob boss Sam Giancana.

Ed knew Mike Condic. The old burglar kept a mobile home in New Port Richey. He had been a regular at Acquafredda's casino. Panzica lived in Boca Raton. The two broken-down wise guys hadn't seen each other in years; they waxed nostalgic at the reunion in Ed's office. Back in Chicago, in their salad days, both men had belonged at one time to Paul "The Waiter" Ricca. Panzica had manufactured silencers for the mob. The two reminisced about how fast Tony Nags could do this or how smooth Mike could do that. They fell into gales of laughter remembering the time they burglarized the cash box at Ebbitt's Field during a World Series game.

Ed listened for a while, then interrupted to get to the meat of their visit. Condic and Panzica revealed that they had been sent by Chicago interests to interview Tony Rossi, take a look at The King's Court operation, then provide Chicago with information to decide if Cascio should be allowed to work with Rossi. This was proper, as Ed was an asset of the New York Luccheses, claimed by Jimmy East, and Cascio was connected to a different crime family based in Chicago. The rules were clear on this point: No two families could be partners without permission from the top.

Three days later, Condic and Panzica got back to Ed with a report. "The kid Cascio," Condic said, "has fallen out of favor with the Chicago Outfit," but he was "alright" and could be trusted. If Cascio was not earning, Ed should do with Cascio whatever he felt needed to be done. Condic gave the go-ahead for Cascio either to work for Ed at The King's Court or to manage the second club, but he would not be allowed to be a club owner in Lucchese territory. Cascio would be directed by his uncle Philly Beans to do, to the letter, whatever Tony Rossi told him to do.

Panzica asked Ed to instruct Cascio to get down to Boca Raton for a sitdown at Nate's Port of Call restaurant. There, Panzica would personally give Cascio his instructions. Ed thanked the two old burglars. He added, "The kid's a pain in the ass."

Panzica nodded. "I know."

Johnny Cascio was upset. He disliked the idea of being checked out by Chicago, especially by his uncle Philly Beans. Didn't Chicago trust him? Also, working for Tony Rossi meant he was under the Lucchese JoJo Fitapelli, a man he despised.

Ed asked Ty Cobb to go to the meeting in Boca Raton. Ty, as Vinnie Russo, would attend the sitdown as a representative of Tony Rossi's interests. The idea was to get Ty hooked in with the Chicago crews operating in Boca.

With the gambling equipment finally installed in The King's Court meeting room, Bernie Agostino started up a regular poker game. JoJo and Frankie Foggia ran sandwiches to the players, for which Ed gave them $50 each per game. Another local mope, Tommy Petrizzi, got $100 for dealing and keeping order. Tommy dragged 5 percent for the house from each pot. Ed didn't like the games and tried to keep their frequency down. From a law enforcement angle, there was nothing to be gained by allowing the gambling to continue on the premises, while the risks of being robbed by a rival crew or screwing some poor citizen out of his mortgage remained high. Still, Tony Rossi had to be a good earner—good earners gain the mob's trust and have license to do almost anything they want—and The King's Court needed to establish itself firmly as the local center for mob activity.

Johnny Cascio broadcast his unhappiness over the high-level decision to deny him his own club. His obnoxious behavior, normally only an irritation, now made him dangerous. He constantly wanted to fight those who questioned him or shrugged him off. Ed knew it was only a matter of time before Cascio flew off the handle and a fight broke out at The King's Court. Cascio's volatile mouth and his careless name-dropping also were threatening to get him whacked. The last thing any FBI undercover sting needs is the occasion for local law authorities to open an investigation. Kinne, Case, and Ed decided to ban Cascio from the club. It would cost them Cascio's link to Chicago but it would remove a real threat to Coldwater. One evening at a poker game, Ed tossed him out. Cascio vowed revenge and went up the street to The Club, owned by fellow Chicagoan Jimmy Falzone. Good, Ed thought. Let Falzone have him. I couldn't wish him on a nicer guy.

Falzone, a local tough guy still angered by the opening of The King's Court so close to his Club, had jumped into his pickup truck on opening night for The Kings Court's and run over Ed's signs. Days later, Ed went to Falzone on a peace mission. "Jimmy," he asked, "what's the problem? I don't want no competition with you. I don't want your clientele, just the high-class business." This remark sent Falzone into a rage. Later, at a sit-down with Jimmy East, Ed asked the older man's advice.

"You go up to that club of his," East steepled his fingers as he spoke, his advocacy of violence cool and matter-of-fact, "take a baseball bat and wreck everything in sight. Make like you're goin' for him. Tell him that from now on he's your partner. He's gotta open his books to you, show you everything. You tell him who said so."

Ed replied to his Lucchese mentor that there was still too much heat from Acquafredda's beating of Hutchins. "Me and Donahue," Ed said, "we'll do it quiet. We'll get Falzone's ass busted on something. We'll do it right, with no noise."

Jimmy East was satisfied. "Alright. After things settle down, I'll send someone to see this guy personal. OK, Tony?"

Ed sent go-betweens to Falzone to tell him that he had saved Falzone's ass with Jimmy East and the rest of the punks who wanted him slapped around. Falzone should stay calm and stay healthy.

Ed had averted violence by threatening worse and making the threat stick. He had the necessary forces around him: the imprimatur of Jimmy East, a growing crew of loyal mobsters and mopes, the protection of Captain Donahue, the garbage association members just itching to hit or burn something, and a reputation as a gangster around whom money and activity swirled. He used all these people and powers against one another like separate, leashed packs of dogs, to avoid confrontations, to keep the balance of peace.

Occasionally Ed had to shatter the peace in order to maintain it. Johnny Cascio became a target because he was acting dishonorably and everyone knew it. Ed encountered Cascio outside a drugstore in a mall. Cascio approached and started sucking up to him, to let bygones be bygones. Ed rejected the overture.

"Look, you fuck!" he shouted. "You know the rules! You made a lot of mistakes, dropping The Old Man's name and not following orders. You made trouble in my club. Jimmy East told me to put you in the hospital but I didn't do it. You got off easy. The next time I see you, I don't even want you fucking looking at me. You got that? Don't ever fucking look at me again!"

117

Two weeks later, Ed sat in a New Port Richey bar alone, sipping his Jack on the rocks. Across the horseshoe-shaped bar sat Johnny Cascio. Ed caught Cascio glancing at him. He looked around the smoky lounge to make sure the story would be chronicled and re-told by the proper witnesses and went berserk.

"I told you to never fuckin' look at me, you scumball! You're determined to catch a beating, aren't you? What is it with you, you little prick? You stupid, low-life, lazy . . ." Ed went on and on, berating Cascio in the worst terms possible for an Italian-American mobster to hear in public. But Cascio did nothing. He hung his head and took it.

Weeks later, Ed allowed Cascio back into The King's Court, a cowed and quiet young man. Ed had broken his spirit, and from that point on Cascio did what he was told to the letter.

* * *

A few days before Christmas, Vincenzo "Jimmy East" Ciraulo traveled to his home in New York City for the holidays. He was arrested on January 22, 1980, by the New York FBI Office on the outstanding loan-sharking warrant.

The Tampa Field Office had begged New York not to arrest Ciraulo. He was Coldwater's main link to both the Luccheses and Trafficante. He was the base of Tony Rossi's power in Pasco and Pinellas Counties. If the New York Field Office had allowed the fugitive Ciraulo to continue in Florida, he would inevitably be swept up and arrested with the rest of the gangsters when the Tampa Office closed Coldwater down. But once Ciraulo was arrested in Florida, the New York Office's outstanding warrant would have to wait. New York, apparently, did not want to wait. Ed, Kinne, Case, Daniels, all the agents behind Coldwater, felt betrayed by what they considered inter-office squabbling and petty territorialism. The arrest of Jimmy East was such a blow to their operation it made them consider shutting down and settling for the ample number of cases already made.

Throughout February and early March, Coldwater was

mired in the doldrums. The Chicago connection had dead-ended with Cascio's fall from grace. With Ciraulo taken off the streets, the most direct route to Trafficante was blocked. Cases against the original targets were all well in hand, needing no further evidence. Still, The King's Court was open for business and there were plenty of crooks left in the area to tumble into the investigation's net. The Coldwater agents never slacked off, even though it seemed the operation was approaching its natural end. Ed kept plugging. He purchased an illegal slot machine from Bob Curry of St. Petersburg, a connection of Bernie's brother, Sal Agostino. Sal told Ed that, through Curry, he had access to a whole warehouse of slot machines in West Virginia. Ed continued to work drug dealers Pete Solmo and Freddie Cataudella to see where they would lead.

One night, a flashy cat from Miami, Angelo Bertolotti, slipped into the club with a blonde on his arm, jewelry hanging on his tanned skin like Christmas ornaments. Ed knew he was somebody from somewhere. He invited the slick newcomer to take a seat at the Round Table as his special guest, then recorded Bertolotti as he confided to Tony Rossi that he was "hiding out." While he was in The King's Court, FBI surveillance agents checked the tags on his girlfriend's car. They hit a match in a computer at the National Crime Information Center. Bertolotti was wanted in Miami on an outstanding warrant for failing to appear for confinement after being given five years in the federal pen on extortion charges. The FBI followed him from The King's Court and arrested him at his motel where he was found with a loaded 12-gauge shotgun.

But none of this was taking the investigation closer to Santo Trafficante. A year earlier, at the outset of Coldwater, Trafficante was thought to be untouchable. The sixty-six-year-old gang boss had never seen the inside of an American jail cell, despite being the uncontested king of Florida's organized crime network for twenty years.

The principal Coldwater agents, Ed, Cobb, Salmieri, Holland, Daniels, Kinne, Case, Lunsford, and Garner, held weekly strategy sessions to review prospects for the operation over the coming six-month period. The central question had become whether they could still hope to get to The Old Man. The King's Court had connected Jay Weisman with Trafficante; the West Coast Cartmen's Association had a hook into Henry Gonzalez, The Old Man's lawyer. JoJo, the mutt, was still a Lucchese and a link to Trafficante, despite Jimmy East's absence.

Ty Cobb was the one who came up with the plan, the gambit that would turn Coldwater into one of the most famous and successful undercover criminal operations in the annals of the FBI. Florida was largely open territory and anyone could come in with a new line of work as long as Trafficante, whose crew from Cuban days still enforced his will, gave his approval. That was how the Luccheses had come down from New York with Jimmy East, who had in turn green-lighted the Gambino Jimmy Acquafredda. But with Jimmy East gone and not replaced, there was a vacuum into which another family could presume to enter. Ty's plan was simple: bring in another family to compete for The King's Court and thus create a confrontation with its Lucchese proprietors. There was only Trafficante. He would have to step in and mediate. That was the rule.

Ty recommended just the New York crime family Coldwater needed, the Bonannos, though it would mean his leaving the case for good. Ty Cobb knew the Bonannos well, and they knew him as Tony Conte, the undercover agent who'd busted Frank Balistrieri in Milwaukee.

Tony Daniels approved the plan. A new chapter in Coldwater was about to open.

CHAPTER ELEVEN
The Soldier and His Pal

Lefty Ruggiero's job was to pull the trigger when his New York Bonanno bosses gave the word. Mafia murder—a "contract"—is the mob's ultimate way to pay certain debts of honor and duty. That's how Benjamin "Lefty Two Guns" Ruggiero saw it, and that's how he maintained his status as a soldier of his famiglia.

Lefty was born in Little Italy in Manhattan. He lived only blocks from his birthplace in a one-bedroom apartment with his wife Louise. Had Lefty ever found himself on a psychiatrist's couch, he would have been diagnosed as a classic paranoid schizophrenic with visions of grandeur. Lefty Ruggiero was mercurial, alternating between anger and a spooky, docile calm like a caged panther. For Lefty, violence was a form of communication, like talking, or gesturing with his thin hands and polished fingernails. He threatened strangers, friends, and loved ones as readily as he professed his unyielding love and loyalty. Lefty had the whole mob package—the bizarre stew of brutality mixed with the sociopath's ability to schmooze. His entire identity was wrapped around his Mafia affiliation; Lefty asserted his power and importance because he was a Bonanno, a made man, and because he had "one thousand guys" backing him up. He knew the mob rules and he lived, and killed, by them.

Lefty owned a small, storefront social club in Little Italy, a hangout for local Bonannos to drink and place a bet. He ran the sports book for Nicky Marangello, the Bonanno underboss. Lefty had to split his take with his capo, Mike Sabella, who owned an Italian restaurant on Mulberry Street, named CaSa

Bella. One of Lefty's friends, another Bonanno soldier, was Anthony Mirra, a dangerous, knife-toting Manhattan wise guy. Mirra was a regular at Lefty's club. One day in late summer of 1977, Mirra brought along a buddy, Donnie Brasco.

Lefty and Brasco struck up a friendship. They were similar mob types, lazy, unschooled, trash talking, scheming do-nothings with vile language and threats salting most of their conversations. Donnie was tough, a square-shouldered six-footer with a confident air and ready fists. Donnie had been around; he knew the rules. He began to run with Lefty, helping him with his book-making, running errands for him around town, picking up a pack of English Ovals for him at the corner, hanging out at Lefty's little club. Soon, Lefty put in a claim on Brasco with his captain Mike Sabella and with Tony Mirra, the man who had introduced Donnie to Lefty. Brasco now "belonged" to Lefty Ruggiero. He became Lefty's constant companion, answerable to him. Donnie carved off half the take from all of his own scores and handed it over to Lefty; in return, Lefty turned on for Brasco "all the green lights."

Donnie Brasco was FBI undercover agent Joseph Pistone.

* * *

Tony Daniels had never met Joe Pistone but he heard a lot about him, as did everyone involved with covert operations in the FBI. Pistone, like Ed Robb, was one of the original Special Agents to volunteer for criminal undercover work who had shown an aptitude for it. Pistone had just finished a successful undercover operation in Milwaukee, called Operation Timber. He'd teamed with agent Ty Cobb to infiltrate the organized crime family in Chicago that ran Milwaukee.

In the summer of 1978, the Milwaukee Field Office realized that it had a mob problem. It seemed there was a muscle war raging in Milwaukee. Balistrieri was firming up his grip, ridding himself of enemies. There had been a steady rise in controlled gambling in the city as well as several bombings of gangland figures. Bombing was an idiosyncrasy of the Midwest Mafia. Other families, especially the major New York mobs, preferred single bullet, or knife assassinations. In New York, it was considered amateurish to blow up cars.

The FBI's plan was to insert Ty Cobb, under the name of Tony Conte, into Milwaukee to set up a vending machine business. This would put him in direct competition with one of Balistrieri's most lucrative empires. When Balistrieri came down on Ty to push him out or extort him for protection, the FBI would bring the hammer down.

But Balistrieri didn't go for the bait. He let Tony Conte stay in business but put the word on the street that no one was to take his machines. Operation Timber sat, stagnant.

The Milwaukee Field Office brought in Joe Pistone and his Bonanno partner Lefty Ruggiero from New York to see if Lefty could arrange a sitdown with Balistrieri. Though Lefty was a psychopath, he was still a wise guy and a trusted Bonanno. As Lefty put it, he was "well known down on Mulberry Street."

Ty flew into New York to meet with Joe and Lefty. He brought money for Lefty, the key to Lefty's soul. Joe vouched for Ty as a guy he'd done business with ten years before in Baltimore. Lefty accepted Ty at face value and, through the Bonannos, reached out to Balistrieri to arrange a sitdown in Milwaukee.

In Balistrieri's offices, Lefty introduced Ty and Joe to the boss. Balistrieri laughed when he shook Ty's hand.

"So you're the guy we been lookin' for." Balistrieri had put a contract out to clip Tony Conte. In fact, two shooters from Kansas City were staking out his motel at that moment. Balistrieri called them off.

With Lefty vouching for him, Ty got in with Balistrieri. His vending business flourished, and the FBI obtained several Title III wiretaps and put together a solid case against Balistrieri. But six months into Operation Timber, something went wrong. Balistrieri, who had warmed up to Ty, suddenly went cold after returning from a trip to Los Angeles. Then the FBI learned from a wiretap that Balistrieri suspected Ty Cobb of being "the G," a government agent, and was planning to have him killed.

Ty left Milwaukee immediately, leaving Donnie Brasco behind to spread the story that Conte had been whacked or run off. Balistrieri called the New York Bonannos, who—through Lefty—had vouched for Conte. The word filtered down to Mike Sabella, then to Lefty, that Brasco had brought an agent into their camp. Pistone was in real danger; he had committed the most severe breach of mob security. But he had laid his groundwork well. Lefty was reluctant to believe that Donnie, his best friend, his best earner, was also the G. Lefty went to bat for Donnie with the Bonannos and his capo Mike Sabella. Lefty won out.

Sabella stayed angry at Joe, but because Joe wasn't a made guy he wasn't held responsible for his mistake with Ty. After all, his vouching had been qualified; Joe had said he and Conte "had done some business ten years ago in Baltimore." He might have been an agent then too, who knew? When the dust had settled, Donnie Brasco was still hooked up, still Lefty's boy.

In July of 1979, Carmine Galante, the Bonanno family boss, was shotgunned in a Brooklyn restaurant. His blood-spattered body, cigar clamped in his teeth, was on the front page of every New York paper. Galante, just two months out of a federal prison, was replaced by Phillip "Rusty" Rastelli, himself serving a prison term in Lewisburg, Pennsylvania, for extortion. The two Bonanno captains, Mike Sabella and Nicky Marangello, were also in line to be clipped with Galante, but both made deals instead to concede power, saving their lives. The two former captains were now regular soldiers, Lefty's rank. Lefty was worried about his status in the new Bonanno order, especially because he had been a member of Sabella's crew. The day after Galante's hit, Lefty was claimed by a new Bonanno captain, Dominick "Sonny Black" Napolitano of the Brooklyn crew.

If Lefty was now owned by Sonny Black, that meant Donnie Brasco was too. Pistone only knew Sonny by reputation; the mobster had been in prison for hijacking most of the time Joe was working Lefty. He'd heard that Sonny was tough but fair. And Lefty liked him, which told Joe that Sonny Black must be a lot more than tough. He was probably very dangerous.

Joe's relationship with Lefty had grown so close that Lefty gave him the commission of finding scores for the two of them. Joe traveled around the country as Donnie Brasco digging up deals for Lefty. The opportunities he located were, in reality, FBI stings. Lefty used his Mafia connections and talent for coercion to lend credibility to these stings with local mobsters. Within the Bureau, the two became a sort of Lefty & Donnie Traveling Vouching Show.

Lefty was cunning, with a sixth sense for danger and bullshit. If he didn't like the smell of a deal, he'd nix it. He turned down an FBI jewelry operation in Los Angeles and a chop shop on Long Island. An investigation of Miami banks laundering Colombian drug money went down in flames because Lefty and Joe were too intimidating, and frightened the target away.

In Ft. Lauderdale, Joe arranged with the captain of a private, Chinese-made luxury yacht, named The Left Hand, to entertain Lefty and some of his New York associates on board. Lefty was agog; the boat was splendid. Donnie Brasco must have some powerful connections to gain access to such a thing.

Donnie's connections were to the FBI. The Left Hand was part of ABSCAM, an FBI undercover operation to catch U.S. Congressmen taking bribes from rich Arabs. Lefty and his party were invited on board during a break in the investigation's schedule. A year later, when ABSCAM broke, Lefty saw a picture of the yacht in a magazine. He asked his pal Donnie about it. Pistone played dumb: "Who knew?" Joe added that, if it had in fact been a federal boat at the time, he and Lefty and their friends must have been pretty smart. They had spent the day on the yacht and hadn't given the FBI anything. "We had a great party and we walked away from it, didn't we, Left?" Presented again with clear evidence that he should be suspicious of Donnie Brasco, Lefty was in denial. He loved Donnie, the one person in his life who showered affection on him, brought him money and deals, did his bidding, carried his luggage, and treated him like a king.

Some in the FBI wanted to shut Lefty and Joe down. The Bureau had sunk tens of thousands of dollars into the relationship, including a $10,000 investment in a fish and chips business for Lefty's daughter in New York, which Lefty and Joe were supposed to operate together. Lefty's daughter ran the restaurant with no known illegal acts whatsoever. But the Bureau decided to give the Lefty-Donnie Show one last go-round when Tony Daniels invited them to Florida and to Coldwater.

* * *

Ed Robb believed he was the best undercover agent in the FBI. Joe Pistone thought the same of himself. Tony Daniels knew he had to keep these two on short leashes if they were going to work together.

The first meeting between the two took place in February 1980, when Pistone flew to Tampa to take a look at Coldwater. Like both a professional undercover agent and a Mafia point man, he needed to assure himself of the quality of the operation, the information, the setup, the FBI backup crew, the supervisors, The King's Court. He was just like Lefty, sniffing around any caper before getting involved.

Ed Robb and Joe Pistone sat down to dinner with Jack Case, Jim Kinne, and Tony Daniels. During the discussion, Pistone cursed, swaggered, and acted every bit the gangster from New York.

Daniels ordered Ed and Joe to spend the next day together, to hash out their respective responsibilities. He made it clear to both of them that Lefty's involvement was pivotal. If Coldwater was going anywhere, Lefty Ruggiero was going to take it there. Without him, the case stood little chance of reaching Trafficante now that the New York Office had taken Jimmy East off the street. If Lefty would claim Ed and The King's Court for the Bonannos, it might create the desired confrontation with the Luccheses that would require a sitdown adjudicated by The Old

Man. If Ed and Joe couldn't work together, both of their separate operations would be shut down within a month.

The two agents had heard of each other, knew that the other was talented and capable, a star in his own right. They also knew they needed one another. They agreed that each had his role to play in the investigation and they would divide responsibilities along those lines. Joe was Lefty's keeper and the conduit to the mob families in New York. All decisions regarding how to handle Lefty and contacts with the Bonannos were to be made by Joe. Ed was the boss of Pinellas and Pasco Counties. He owned The King's Court and the cop Donahue. He was an officer in the garbagemen's association and the head of an expansive crew. Ed would take the lead in these areas. The two agreed to respect each other's turf and to watch the other's back.

They defined the characters they would play: Joe would blow into town with Lefty from New York. In the absence of Jimmy East, they were going to take over. Tony Rossi would be their mark. Pistone arrived in Tampa as the underworld tough Donnie Brasco for the first time on March 3, 1980. Ed picked him up at the airport and took him to The King's Court where he introduced the crew to his "buddy Donnie from the old Pittsburgh days." Pistone played the hulking mobster from Manhattan to the hilt. He was crude and inconsiderate, aloof and mean, a brooding counterpoint to the calm, steady, boss Tony Rossi at the center of the action. None of Ed's crew liked him, but Brasco wasn't intended to be popular.

"He's my New York connection," Ed explained to those who questioned him. "I'm sick of you mopes. I ain't getting anywhere dealing with you bunch of broken-down losers. I told you I knew people. Donnie's with Lefty Two Guns out of Mulberry Street in Manhattan. It's time I got some real support down here to make this King's Court idea take off, franchise it all over Florida like we talked about."

JoJo was unnerved by the new presence in their midst. "You can't have two fractions working here, Tone. You can't bring in a guy from another crew. That's gonna cause problems. You know you're with us." JoJo meant the Luccheses. This was exactly the reaction the FBI wanted. Ed and Pistone let JoJo get good and steamed. After three weeks of his loyal Lucchese protests, the time looked right to bring in Lefty.

On March 26, Ed and Joe picked up Lefty at the Tampa airport. Ed was prepared to behave humbly, to act in awe of the big-time button from Mulberry Street, the killer Lefty Ruggiero.

Lefty started bitching the moment he walked up the breezeway. According to proper Mafia form, he addressed all his comments to his buddy Donnie. This other guy, Tony Rossi, he hadn't proven he was worth talking to.

"Hey, Donnie, what the fuck did you get me that seat for? You know I hate sitting in the fucking back of the plane like a fucking cattle. I want to be in the front. You know that."

"Hey, Left," Joe backpedaled, "it was the only seat."

"I don't give a fuck. Don't ever do that to me again."

Joe took Lefty's baggage from the carousel. Ed drove them to Tarpon Springs and Pappas' Restaurant, still without being spoken to. At Pappas', Ed walked them past a long line of waiting patrons. The maitre d', Johnny, greeted them. "Hey, Mr. Rossi, you want your regular table? Come right in." Lefty was impressed. The table overlooked a marina. Once seated, Lefty turned to Joe.

"Donnie, tell Tony to tell me what the situation is."

Ed told Lefty of his activities over the previous twelve months in Pasco and Pinellas Counties. He described the gambling setups with Acquafredda and Agostino and the garbagemen's association. Jimmy East, a captain in the Lucchese family, had granted him permission to operate The King's Court and given him control over all criminal enterprise in his territory.

"But I'm disgusted with these guys," Ed told Lefty. "I'm getting nothin' out of them. They say they're from New York but they don't do shit. They're a bunch of broken-down mutts. Jimmy East went home for Christmas and hasn't even come back. I want to get some things done down here, maybe move over into Orlando. But I don't want these guys because they don't produce."

Now Lefty addressed Tony Rossi. "Anybody else invest money in your club?"

"No. It's all my own money."

Lefty explained that since no other wise guys had taken a stake in Tony's operation, there was nothing to stop them from forming a partnership. This was a rule: Once a wise guy invests, no other wise guy can muscle in. Lefty believed he could help Tony break into central Florida. He'd be willing to take a look at The King's Court.

After dinner, Ed drove them to the club. The lounge was busy. They sat at the Round Table. The waitress took their order.

"Spritzer, honey." Lefty smiled.

Jimmy Acquafredda sat at the bar with his girlfriend. Ed pointed him out as one of the losers. Lefty jerked a thumb at Acquafredda. "You tell him to come over to the table here and sit down. Tell him you want him to meet a dear friend of yours, a wise guy from New York City."

At his first glimpse of Lefty Ruggiero, Acquafredda looked as if he'd seen his own gravestone. His face turned ashen and his gait, normally the swagger of a bantam, went limp, as if on a walk to the chopping block. He didn't know why Lefty was there, but he still owed the New York Gambinos the $60,000 they sent down with him to set up the garbagemen's association. If the Gambinos had gotten the go-ahead from the Commission— the heads of the five New York crime families—to clip him, they would likely hand the job off to another family, to an evil-looking, knife blade of a man like Lefty. It would have been typical for a triggerman to come to the club, meet his target, and have a drink with him before the whack. Acquafredda looked as if he wanted to run out the door, but his feet carried him to the Round Table.

Acquafredda was humble. He and Lefty talked about mutual acquaintances from New York, like Jimmy The Dome and the new Bonanno boss, Rusty Rastelli. Lefty told Acquafredda he was in town to visit his old friend Tony. He said he had just put a "bundle of money" into the club and was now a partner. He'd be coming down every once in a while to check on things. He also claimed to have a sixteen-member crew in the Miami-Ft. Lauderdale area and they would be frequenting the club from time to time.

"If Tony has any problems with the club here, we're gonna be standing with him. We're gonna send whatever help he needs to get done what he needs to get done." Lefty couldn't go back now. He had vouched for Ed with another mobster.

"Any problems with the club," he concluded his interview with Acquafredda, "you can contact me in New York. Ask for Lefty on Mulberry Street or Madison Street. Everybody knows me."

Acquafredda returned to the bar. Next, Ed identified JoJo at the front door manning the peephole and the buzzer. Lefty asked to have him brought to the table. Ed returned with JoJo. Lefty told him the same things he told Acquafredda, about being Ed's partner and his investment in the club. JoJo mentioned his cousin, Anthony DeMeglia, a Lucchese button in Jersey. "Antny," JoJo said, was planning to come down the following week to look The King's Court over.

"You tell your cousin Anthony that he's welcome here as a guest anytime. But since I'm Tony's partner, there's no reason for your cousin to come down unless it's for a vacation." Lefty was telling JoJo that he would not accept another partner or competition from the Luccheses. The King's Court now belonged to the Bonannos. The word would get back to New Jersey fast.

Ed squired Lefty around the club. A poker game had started in the meeting room, run by Petrizzi and Foggia. JoJo worked the door while agent Steve Salmieri, as Chico Navarro, kept track of the house's 5 percent cut. Later that evening, Lefty began negotiations over what he would be paid by Ed for his services. He told Pistone to take Ed outside to discuss the matter. This was Lefty's way of insulating himself from overhearing any criminal discussions.

Lefty claimed to need $5,000 to put the deal together in New York. He needed to spread it around, he said, to make appointments. Also, he had to split the take with his captain, Dominick "Sonny Black" Napolitano.

Outside, Ed and Joe agreed to give Lefty only two grand. They would stick to that amount no matter how Lefty railed.

Back at the Round Table, Pistone told Lefty that Tony didn't have that kind of money; he only had $2,000 he could put up right now.

"OK," Lefty nodded, "you give me the four."

"Lefty," Ed pleaded, "I only got the two."

"Good. Excellent. You bring me the four and we'll turn on the green lights. Donnie, ask him how much he makes a week off that poker game in the back?"

Again, Ed and Joe went away from the table to discuss business. When they returned, they told Lefty the games realized a house take of about $500 a week, only a fraction of the games' real take, which was in turn only a fraction of the club's total earnings. They didn't want Lefty to bite into the existing business too deeply but they did want him to see the potential for far greater profits. It worked. Lefty agreed to accept half that amount. The money was to be mailed to him in Brooklyn every Wednesday, so he'd have it by Friday.

Ed didn't want to look like a mutt in Lefty's eyes, despite the agreement between him and Pistone that he would play the role of the mark. He asked what Lefty was going to do for him in exchange for all that money. Lefty's face shriveled into a pucker in his attempt to remain calm. "The fuck do you think? I'm gonna open all the doors and turn on all the green lights. I'm gonna call the right people for you to move into Orlando. You got any problems, we'll be down here with fucking hand grenades. You can now tell people we're partners. Anybody gives you a problem, it's them that got problems. That's what I'm gonna do for you. I'm gonna give you peace of mind."

Lefty was impressed by the size of the club's grounds. Whatever he thought of the miserable weekly take, he could see a better future. He wanted to expand the operation to include an Olympic-sized pool, hot tubs, cabanas, and racquetball courts to make The King's Court more exclusive and high class. They would market the design all over Florida.

"Tony," he said, "call up an 'archi-texture," get one out here to draw up the plans."

"Yeah, Lefty, first thing in the morning." It was after 11:00 p.m.

"Naw, get one now. Tell him you're Tony, owner of The King's Court. T'row him a steak and a hunnert dollar bill and he'll draw up the fuckin' plan." Lefty wanted the drawings to take back to New York to show his connections there how sweet this Florida deal was going to be.

Ed picked up the phone at the Round Table and dialed the safe house. Jim Kinne answered.

"Hey, Jim," Ed said, "I need an architect's rendering by morning of some plans. Can you help me out?"

In the background, Lefty shouted, "All you need is a fuckin' sketch!"

Kinne laughed in the receiver. "Christ, Magilla. You crazy bastard." The next morning, the sketches were delivered to the club. Kinne, always clever with a pen, had done a marvelous job. He signed the designs "Jim Sharkey, Architect."

After midnight, Ed drove Lefty and Joe to the Best Western Tahitian Motor Lodge, a few miles from the club on Rte. 19. Pistone was in Lefty's room the next morning when Lefty said he had to call Sonny. Lefty told Sonny he liked what he'd seen. "Everything here is all right, Sonny. I'm satisfied with the situation here."

Ed picked Joe and Lefty up for breakfast. At the restaurant, Ed handed over The Shark's drawings and paid Lefty $2,000. He assured the mobster that an additional $1,000 would be wired via Western Union by the following Saturday.

After breakfast, the three returned to The King's Court for another tour. While walking the grounds, Pistone asked Lefty if there would be any problems with Trafficante. Lefty told them not to worry about The Old Man, just concentrate on building up the business in Holiday.

That afternoon, Lefty flew back to New York. Joe Pistone had done his job well; he had delivered Ruggiero to Coldwater, where Ed and his team of agents hooked and landed him.

Now it was Lefty's turn to deliver Sonny Black.

CHAPTER TWELVE
Sonny

Lefty phoned and said he'd be back in Florida in a week. Sonny was sending him down to sign a partnership agreement with Tony Rossi.

Pistone picked Lefty up at the Tampa airport on April 7 and brought him to The King's Court, where Lefty dictated, for Ed to draft by hand, a partnership agreement between E. Anthony Rossi and Thomas Sbano, the name of Lefty's son. The agreement specified that Rossi and his partner Sbano had each invested $15,000 in the club and that all profits were to be divided fifty-fifty. The document was backdated one month to preclude any claims by competing families. They went to a notary, where Ed signed as Rossi and Lefty signed as Sbano. The notary was chosen with care: He didn't ask either man for identification.

That afternoon, Lefty phoned a friend in Miami, Johnny "Spaghetti" Tagliarini. Lefty claimed that Johnny Spaghetti was a member of his Florida crew and a big shot in the Bonannos. After the FBI checked him out, it was determined that Tagliarini was just a retired customs agent, a guy from the old Brooklyn neighborhood. Lefty invited him up to Holiday for a visit, telling Ed and Joe that Johnny Spaghetti was on his way to Holiday to look the operation over.

When Tagliarini arrived, Lefty told Ed to give his friend a couple hundred bucks for his gas and to play the dogs that night at Derby Lane greyhound track. Ed refused. Why should I? he asked. What had Lefty done for him so far? Lefty went into his well-worn routine: He opened with bluster and intimidation.

134

Then he leveled out, like a plane emerging from turbulence, into a steady whine.

"Tony, you're fuckin' impatient! You can't wait for all I'm gonna do for you. I'm gonna give you peace of mind, provided you're honorable and you're a stand-up guy, and here you fuck with me for a couple hundred bucks. You wanna fight all the time. You're fuckin' Irish. You're Tony Irish, is who you are! Yeah, you're from Pennsylvania, you're a fuckin' hoosier. All you wanna do is fight!" Lefty patted Ed's shoulder. "Look, that's all water over the bridge. Tony, I love you. I'm gonna make you the boss, no one is gonna be bigger than you in all of Florida. But we gotta get over the hump. OK?"

Ed gave Johnny Spaghetti $40 and handed Lefty his $250 weekly cut. Lefty emptied his pockets that night on the dogs.

Lefty spent most of the next day mewling about the additional $2,000 he insisted he needed to assure Ed of "peace of mind." Ed suspected that Lefty's greed for cash was in no small part because he was a compulsive gambler who was probably always one step ahead of getting himself whacked in New York. Ed responded that he couldn't put his hands on that amount of cash immediately but he'd see what he could do. Lefty persisted.

At dinner at Malio's the evening of April 10th, a compromise was struck: Lefty would allow Ed to send him $150 per week instead of the usual $250 cut for the next twenty weeks in return for the $2,000 payment now. That night, in Lefty's room at the Tahitian Motor Lodge, Ed peeled off the two grand from the wad in his pocket (whenever Lefty came to town, Ed carried plenty of cash) and gave him the money.

Lefty Ruggiero flew back to New York the next day primed to do business with Operation Coldwater.

* * *

Lefty called on April 13th to say he had shown Sonny the plans to enlarge The King's Court. Sonny was so pleased with the progress in Holiday that he, his girlfriend Judy Brown, and

Lefty were coming down three days later.

While waiting for Sonny, Ed met Donahue at Sambo's Restaurant in New Port Richey. Ed said he had temporarily closed down the gambling at the club because several unrecognized people had arrived recently asking questions about the games. Donahue responded that he knew of no current gambling investigations by the Sheriff's Office but he would look into it. During their conversation, Donahue asked if Ed knew a man named Bill Sakelson. Donahue said that Sakelson owned a marina and was in an excellent position to bring narcotics into Florida aboard shrimp boats. Perhaps, Donahue suggested, Sakelson and Ed might be able to help each other earn. Ed was interested. Set it up, he said.

*   *   *

Of the five New York crime families (Bonanno, Lucchese, Gambino, Colombo, and Genovese), the Bonanno tradition was the most violent. The family's roots extended back to the 1930s, to Albert Anastasia, Prohibition, and the original Murder, Inc., reputed to be the first mob hit men for hire.

From his cell in a federal penitentiary, the new Bonanno boss Rusty Rastelli had tabbed Dominick "Sonny Black" Napolitano as his street boss. Sonny, known as the "skipper," was the strongest of the captains. The street boss of the Bonannos would run the family's businesses, enforce its decisions, and order the whacks. He would have to be ruthless and cold-blooded.

Ed and Joe met Sonny, Judy, and Lefty at the Tampa airport on April 16. Just as Lefty had done earlier, Sonny addressed himself almost solely to Pistone at first. This was proper under the mob rules: Lefty had only vouched for his pal Donnie Brasco with Sonny, not Tony Rossi. Sonny would have insulted Lefty by dealing with Rossi first, even though Rossi and The King's Court were the reasons he'd come to Florida. Ed drove them to Malio's. He and his party were ushered in and served with deference. Sonny continued to reserve most of his conversation for Pistone.

Sonny Black, fifty, was one of those men whose physical appearance was a tip-off, like a fingerprint, of his character. Sonny was dark and hard, top to bottom. Though only 5′ 7″, he was one hundred seventy pounds of solid menace with coal eyes and a penetrating stare. His arms and torso were thick and powerful and he sported a tattoo of a panther on his right biceps. Sonny dyed his hair jet black, earning him his nickname. The man seemed to cast a shadow in all directions as he moved.

Sonny's style was more refined than Lefty's. Where Ruggiero was a bully, a griper, and a schizoid louse, Sonny emanated confidence and strength. He kept a low profile, without flamboyance or loud clothes. He was clever when he spoke; his words were lean and direct. He meant what he said and listeners were well advised to pay attention. In his brusque way, he was considerate of others, even doting on his girl Judy. He was loyal to his friends and alert for betrayal, but he made it very clear what he expected from those around him. Saying "no" to Sonny would be very different from saying "no" to the soldier Lefty.

After dinner, back at The King's Court, Ed and Joe walked Sonny around the club. Ed left the two of them to attend to business, making sure everything ran smoothly for Sonny's eyes. During their talk in Ed's absence, Sonny asked Joe what he wanted to do in Tampa.

"Maybe some bookmaking and shylocking," Pistone replied.

Sonny was pleased to hear this because gambling was still a good moneymaker. He told Pistone that he'd heard good things about him from Lefty. He assured Joe he'd be backed by "our people in New York." Sonny asked what Joe would need to set up operations.

"Maybe twenty-five grand."

Sonny asked, "What's the vig down here?" referring to the weekly interest points on shylock loans. Pistone didn't know; he told Sonny he'd find out.

The two discussed expansion into Orlando. Sonny said that

everything was in place in Orlando and they could move in there whenever they were ready.

"Donnie," Sonny advised, "we can all earn. When you're doing business with friends, we all share everything equally and not try to cheat one another."

He instructed Pistone to get the bookmaking operation set for the upcoming football season, figure out the vig rate, and get the shylocking going soon, too.

"I got an army behind me in New York," Sonny said, concluding the talk. "Nobody can bother us as long as we conduct ourselves in the proper manner."

The next morning, Ed and Joe picked Sonny and Lefty up at the Tahitian Motor Lodge and brought them to The King's Court. The club was closed during the day. The four continued their discussion of the club's expansion.

Lefty and Joe took a walk around the grounds and Sonny stayed behind. He took Ed into his confidence.

"Tony, you with anybody?" he asked. This was big. Sonny was moving in.

"No, I had some talks before with a wise guy Jimmy East but they didn't go nowhere. I ain't seen him since before Christmas. No, Sonny, I'm not with anybody right now."

"Don't worry about Jimmy East. There's no problem there."

"Good."

"You seem like a stand-up guy. You look like you earn. I like your operation. I want you with me. This is our place now, alright?"

Sonny Black, the Bonanno street boss, had now claimed Ed and The King's Court. He was stepping in over Lefty as partner. Ed and Joe now belonged to the most powerful crew in the family.

How would this affect Lefty, Ed wondered, to have Donnie Brasco and Tony Rossi snapped up by Sonny Black on the captain's first visit? Would he blow up and create a rift with Sonny? Even if he threw a tantrum, would that damage the investigation? Probably not: Lefty's only use was to get to Sonny Black. If he left in a huff and took Joe with him, Coldwater would sail on by.

In any event, Ed was pleased: Sonny was far better company than the creep Lefty and, most importantly, as street boss, Dominick "Sonny Black" Napolitano was one step closer to, perhaps even just one rung below, the ultimate target of Coldwater, Santo Trafficante. Ed would let the chips fall with Lefty where they may.

* * *

That afternoon, Sonny, Judy, Lefty, Ed, and Joe lounged around the pool at the Tahitian Motor Lodge. Sonny continued his dialogue on his plans to increase illegal activities in Pasco County. He now treated Ed with courtesy and respect. He included Ed in all the schemes he had made privately with Pistone, the bookmaking and shylocking, and asked Ed's opinions and advice.

"Tony, what's the vig down here?"

Ed responded quickly. "Four to five points, depending on the customer and the amount of the loan."

Sonny said he would make the shylock money available. He was going to send members of his New York crew down to help set up the sports book and loan shark operations. Ed made a recommendation. "Sonny, why don't we limit the shylocking to $500 a head. A manageable amount. We get more customers that way."

Sonny liked the idea. Tony had a head on his shoulders. For Ed, this guideline would limit the damage Sonny's shylocking money might do to citizens by restricting how deeply the mob could get its hooks into Joe Public.

Another idea popped up. Sonny wanted Ed and Joe to look into obtaining a sandwich truck route to visit job sites in the area. The truck would be an ideal vehicle for running the loan-sharking and bookmaking. Sonny promised to get the truck in New York and ship it down to Florida. Sonny also figured that Las Vegas Nights at The King's Court could be big moneymakers. The events would be fronted by a charity of their creation.

"Once we have a Vegas Night, then it becomes ours," Sonny explained. "Nobody else can have it."

He instructed Ed to put together a list of charities, one of which would be designated to receive the proceeds. Of course, the selected charity would only see a tiny fraction of the money. "Get something for crippled people," Sonny recommended. That way, the state cops would lay off, making the Vegas Nights easier for Donahue to protect. Sonny assured Ed he would send the casino equipment down from New York in the near future.

Sonny wanted Ed to isolate himself more from the criminal activities emanating from The King's Court. "Let someone else step out front," he said. "Don't be a show-off. Be nice and considerate. Be a businessman. Let someone else be the tough guy, let them take the blame if it's coming."

Sonny was riffing. He reclined on the chaise lounge in the Gulf Coast spring sun, surrounded by his girlfriend Judy, his trusted Bonanno triggerman Lefty, his newly claimed club owner Tony, and the loyal tough-guy Donnie. All of them nodded at his every word as if this white-skinned, tattooed thug beside the motel pool were a Hollywood mogul making stars with each pass of his hand. Sonny let his criminal mind spin, throwing off plots and scams, sensing his strength and the opportunities for it here in what must have seemed to him the Promised Land.

*   *   *

Ed and Joe took Sonny, Lefty, and Judy to the airport the afternoon of April 18. While waiting to board their flight to New York, Sonny reiterated his wishes for them to get busy on the bookmaking and loan-sharking. Cheeks were kissed and Sonny said he'd be in touch.

Later that day, Joe also left. It had become his habit to leave Florida for his home in the southwest as soon as Lefty's plane banked northward. He stayed in touch with Lefty every day by using call forwarding from his apartment in Holiday (he had moved into Ty Cobb's former apartment at Holiday Park) to a protected, recorded line, a "hello phone," in his home. After his chats with Lefty, Joe made daily telephone accounts to Jim Kinne of Lefty's news and when he was expected back in Holiday.

A constant question for undercover agents is whether and when to wear a wire. Joe stated that he alone would decide whether he would wear a transmitter or recorder. Joe had several reasons. First, his Mafia buddies were a touchy-feely, hugging bunch and a metal lump under his clothes ran the risk of discovery. His cover would be blown and he'd be whacked in a Mafia minute. Also, the quality of the recordings or transmissions was frequently unrecognizable because of radio interference, background noises, inarticulate speech, even stomach rumblings. Often the batteries wore down, long before any significant criminal conversation could be captured, their energy spent capturing hours of blathering. The risk, Joe believed, was rarely worth the results.

His concern was also based, in part, on the out-of-date devices that were given to the FBI agents. Any recording equipment they used would be open to scrutiny on the witness stand, so that the state-of-the-art electronics used by CIA agents, who never emerged from their cover, were off-limits to the FBI. In 1980, the FBI's two recording workhorses were the Nagra tape recorder, bulky and often unreliable, and the T4 transmitter. The T4, while small, half the size of a deck of cards, and powerful, featured a thin wire loop antenna that often came detached, making the transmitter useless. Once, Joe grew so frustrated with a malfunctioning T4 that he shattered it against a wall.

Ed began to feel as if he were carrying more than his share of the load, especially when Joe, who had nothing to do in Florida on weekends, went home, leaving Ed behind at the club. Sometimes, taxed to his limits by Lefty's bitching, Sonny's demands, JoJo's daffiness, late nights, bad food, booze, and cigarettes, his mood took on the dark and vengeful tones of the true mobster. Ed stomped around the safe house apartment, shouting about whacking people, fucking them up. During one such explosion, Jim Kinne threw his lead agent into a chair, whipped out his own FBI badge and shoved it close to Ed's face, filling his vision. "Who are you?" Kinne shouted. "Who are you? Remember!"

* * *

On April 27, 1980, Lefty flew to Miami, hoping to make contact with Frankie Albano, Trafficante's nephew, for a sitdown. He also wanted to "school" Ed in the ways of the Bonannos. Ed was to be "introduced around," to get his name and face on the family circuit. This was all part of the peace of mind Ed had been promised in return for his money and partnership.

Lefty was accompanied by Louise, his second wife, a girl from the old neighborhood. Louise, a kind-hearted woman in her late twenties, put up with a lot from Lefty, just like everyone else around him. She knew what business he was in. She had grown up around wise guys, and was impressed by them. Louise was a secretary in New York. Joe got on well with her. He was the best man at their wedding.

Ed and Joe flew to Miami. They were picked up at the airport by Johnny Spaghetti and taken to the Deauville Hotel in Miami Beach. The Deauville had been owned by Meyer Lansky, Trafficante's old compare from the Havana days. Ed and Joe met Lefty and a retired New York Homicide Detective named Al Smith. Lefty also introduced Ed to Nick Coluntuna, the manager of the Deauville. Coluntuna told Ed that Frank Sinatra and Sammie Davis Jr. stayed in the hotel's penthouse whenever they were in Miami. When Lefty arrived in town, that's where he stayed.

After lunch, Lefty and Ed wandered into the Deauville's gift shop. Lefty picked up several hundred dollars worth of gifts for his four kids and his grandchildren, plus towels and pool gear. He told Ed to pay for it all. When Ed objected, Lefty grinned.

"Tony Irish, what are you worried about? Take it out of next week's pay, for Christ's sake."

Lefty had already sucked up several weeks' pay in advance. Ed kept his mouth shut. He could smell Trafficante, Albano, Meyer Lansky, the New York Bonannos, all of them inching closer. This was not the time to nickel and dime. Let it go, pay for the stuff. He would scream at Kinne later back at the safe house to get it out of his system. Ed dug out his pocket roll and laid the money on the counter.

Lefty told everyone to change into their swimming suits for an afternoon dip in the Deauville's pool. Ed wanted to record the poolside conversations. Because of airport security, he had not risked carrying his Nagra or a T4 transmitter on the plane or in his luggage. While Joe and Lefty arranged their chaise lounges "to take the sun," as Lefty said, Ed slipped off to the men's room where Kinne gave him a T4. He placed the transmitter inside his jock strap beneath his boxer-style trunks. He couldn't jump in the water with the device in his shorts, but fortunately Lefty wanted to drink and talk so nobody got wet.

While Ed was at the pool bar, Kinne walked past, heading for the men's room. Ed excused himself from Lefty and followed. In the men's room, Kinne handed Ed another T4. The antenna on the one in his trunks had broken; Kinne and Daniels, sitting in the parking lot monitoring the transmission, had lost the signal.

When they left the pool, Lefty chased Joe and Ed upstairs to dress for dinner. While Joe showered, before Ed could change out of his swimsuit, Lefty dropped by the room.

"Hey, Tony," he nagged, "get ready for dinner."

"I gotta take a shower. Donnie's in there."

"You don't need a fuckin' shower. You're clean enough. We're gonna be late. We got reservations, so change."

"Alright, Left, I'll change."

Lefty didn't turn and go. He stood his ground. He seemed to want Ed to strip and start putting on his clothes while he watched, to make sure it got done.

Ed couldn't take off his swimsuit with Lefty watching. The

T4 was still in his jock.

"Lefty, what? You wanna watch me change?"

Lefty started to climb all over Ed. "Tony, you're walkin' on thin water with me here. I told you to fuckin' put on your clothes. What are you waitin' for?"

Ed had to think fast. He banged on the bathroom door.

"Donnie!" he screamed, pounding away, "Donnie, come out! I gotta take a shit! Donnie!"

Joe cut off the water. He opened the door. "What?"

Ed shoved him aside and hustled into the steamy bathroom.

*   *   *

Lefty came back by the room to collect Ed and Joe for dinner. He appeared agitated; it seemed he had big plans for the evening. While Joe finished dressing, Ed answered a knock on the door. In the hall stood a beautiful Egyptian girl, whose dark hair set off her green eyes and red lips to make them glow like traffic lights at night. Ed had met her that afternoon in the pool-side bar and invited her to join them for dinner that evening. He figured Lefty would be impressed.

The woman walked into the room wearing a revealing dress. Lefty stood in front of her, barring her path into the room and to Ed.

"Get missing," he said evenly as if she, like everyone else, awaited whatever instructions Lefty had for them. "You look like a whore."

The woman looked to Ed. She said nothing.

"Get missing," Lefty repeated. "You ain't coming with us."

Ed shrugged. "Get missing, the man said."

After she had gone, Lefty "schooled" Ed about respect for women. He refused to have Louise in the company of a hooker. This was another of the mob rules: Women get treated with esteem, at least while you're with them in public. No cursing in their presence, Lefty explained, shaking his finger in Ed's face, no crude stuff. Behind their backs, that's another set of rules entirely.

They had dinner that night at Joe Puma's Little Italy Restaurant. Joe Puma belonged to the Bonanno Miami crew. Lefty and company strode past the line of waiting citizens. They were seated immediately and got the personal treatment from Joe Puma and his staff. During the meal, Lefty introduced Ed to Puma and beckoned to their table several other local players, including the junk man Johnny Irish, plus Steve Marucca and Dick Marino, two wise guys in the Miami crew.

Marino, a dealer for mob card games, was a connection to Trafficante's nephew, Frankie Albano. At Lefty's behest, Marino excused himself and made a phone call. He returned to the table to inform Lefty that Frankie was out of town. Lefty thanked Marino and turned to Ed for money for Marino.

"We gotta take care of these guys that are taking care of us."

Ed shook his head and Lefty started in, repeating his promises to hook Ed up with everybody important, like Albano and Meyer Lansky's son-in-law Joe Lombardo. Peace of mind, connections, schooling, backing, the green lights, all this and more in return for Ed's love, loyalty, and money. "And all you gotta do is walk the toe line, Tony. Now take care of the bill." Lefty headed for the bar.

After dinner, Ed, Lefty, and Pistone discussed the upcoming Las Vegas Night to be held at The King's Court. Lefty and Sonny planned to send down two blackjack tables and a gambling wheel within a week. Lefty would report back to Sonny that they needed a $25,000 bank for the Las Vegas Night, plus another $25,000 to start the shylocking operation. He and Sonny planned to bring in a professional gambler to run the crap table. The next day, back in Tampa, Ed made plans to hold the Las Vegas Night at the club on Friday, May 9. In a recorded phone call, Lefty told Pistone that preparations were being made for the gambling event and that he was "making moves" in Miami on their behalf.

On April 29, Captain Donahue paid a visit to the club. In the office, Ed told Donahue he would soon be shylocking money and wanted to know what the attitude of the local police would be. Donahue said that shylocking was new to the area and the cops wouldn't really know what to do about it. Ed said it would be New York money on the street and that he would be lending it out at four or five points. He also revealed his plans for a football book during the coming season. Donahue said there would be no problem. Ed told him of the coming Las Vegas Night. He made sure Donahue understood that he wanted everything to be cool on May 9 because he had people flying in from New York. Ed expected to be operating three blackjack tables, a crap table, and a roulette wheel. He added that there would be good money in it for Donahue.

Ed discussed security measures. He asked if he had the right to deny a deputy entry to the club. The cop said no, but the deputy couldn't search inside any locked rooms without a warrant. Donahue promised he would stay on duty the night of the 9th. He assured his patron Tony Rossi that everything would be under control so long as Pinellas-Pasco County State Attorney Russell didn't get wind of their plans.

"He gets a bug up his ass every once in a while," Donahue said. "He's down on everyone and he's a prick when he wants to be."

"Just take care of it," Ed muttered while he made Donahue take the $200 in cash out of the envelope and count it aloud for the cameras.

*   *   *

On May 8, Ed and Joe drove to the Tampa airport to retrieve Lefty and professional gambler Mimmie Matchicote. Mimmie was in his late fifties, two hundred pounds of cocky, trash-talking goombah. He was another of the denizens of Lefty's old neighborhood.

That evening, an airfreight company delivered the gambling equipment to The King's Court. The shipment included playing cards, dice, a roulette wheel, and three blackjack shoes. The shipper on the air bill was listed as The Italian-American War

146

Veterans Club, 415 Graham Ave., Brooklyn, New York. This was Sonny Black's social club in Brooklyn. Ed had a sign made up stating that The Italian-American War Veterans would be the beneficiaries of the proceeds from the Las Vegas Night.

Sonny arrived the next day to help supervise the first Vegas Night and to deliver a lump of cash to bankroll the evening. He hadn't brought along the $25,000 he had promised but did tell Ed he had $10,000 if it was needed. Soon, he'd be able to supply even larger sums of family money to start up the shylocking and sports book operations. Sonny said the family wanted a vig of one and one half points per week for any money they loaned. Whatever was left over after Ed put the money on the street at four to five points would be "split by us."

Sonny also gave Ed the official disposition of the family's rulings on him, The King's Court, and the conflict of claims between the Bonannos and Luccheses. There had been a sitdown with the Luccheses in New Jersey, attended by Trafficante and Steve "Stevie Beef" Cannone, the Bonanno family consiglieri. The issue had been settled peacefully; there would be no war. The Luccheses could keep the garbagemen's association, which would be allowed to meet in the club but had to pay Ed rent. JoJo Fitapelli could work for Ed but could not be a partner in the club. The Gambinos, Jimmy Acquafredda's family, were shut out entirely. The Bonannos got the plum, The King's Court.

The plan Ty Cobb and Tony Daniels had concocted had worked perfectly; the only trouble was that the sitdown took place in New Jersey and went unrecorded.

There had been another, separate sitdown in New York, Sonny said, this one occasioned by a beef put in by Pistone's old pal Tony Mirra. Once the scent of easy money out of Florida had begun to perfume the breeze on Mulberry Street, Mirra claimed that, since he'd been the one to introduce Donnie Brasco to Lefty, any interest Donnie had in The King's Court belonged therefore to him, not Lefty. Mirra didn't know that Brasco had no stake whatsoever in the club or its operations. Nonetheless, the complaint was heard. Ordinarily, Sonny, the Bonanno street boss, would have heard the complaint. This time, because of his personal involvement, it was adjudicated by another family captain. Nonetheless, after listening to Mirra's claims, Sonny stepped forward and settled it all. He claimed The King's Court and Tony Rossi for himself. Why? Because he'd met Tony Rossi through Fat Sonny years ago in Miami, he said. Tony Rossi was his. The King's Court, the cop, Pasco and Pinellas Counties were his too, and that was that. Sonny instructed Ed to remember that story: Should anyone ever ask, his answer would be that they had been introduced long ago by Fat Sonny down in Miami.

The decision was made: Donnie Brasco remained the property of Lefty Ruggiero. But from that day on, Tony Rossi belonged only to Dominick "Sonny Black" Napolitano. "Meanwhile," Sonny said, "just go along with Lefty. Humor him. Buy him shit, what the fuck."

That evening, Ed walked tall among the gamblers at the Las Vegas Night. He stood at the center of the gambling hubbub to survey his busy kingdom. He watched the commotion of money, dice, and cards flickering and slipping around him like moths about a porch light, and felt accomplished. His career was on the rise; the crime bosses knew his name and prized his abilities.

The Las Vegas Night came off without a hitch, playing late into the morning hours. Lots of regulars came to play. Mimmie Matchicote and Dick Marino ran the craps table. JoJo manned the door. Frankie Foggia and a Greek kid from Charleston, Billy Tsachilis, dealt blackjack. Tennis pro Dick Stauder (agent Dick Holland) operated the roulette wheel. Sonny and Joe Pullicino were pit bosses, Lefty and Donnie hung out. Agent Steve Salmieri picked up money from the tables and ferried it to Ed in exchange for chips.

The next morning, Ed settled up the take. The house had cleared just $1,704 after paying salaries to the dealers and barmaids. Sonny was a little disappointed but upbeat and patient. When Ed offered him his share, Sonny said, "Keep it, Tony. We'll make it grow."

* * *

The next afternoon, John "Boobie" Cerasani arrived. He was Sonny's closest friend in the family. Boobie was an imposing figure with a strong, athletic build. Across his chest was a large tattoo of two songbirds. Boobie had a calculating manner; he was a chess player who had served a lot of time in prison. Boobie was smart, a watcher with a mean streak. He was an armored car specialist whose legitimate business was as owner of Arturo's Coffee Shop on Mulberry and Canal Streets in New York. Boobie wasn't just Sonny's trusted right-hand man; he was Sonny's right fist.

Accompanying Boobie was Sonny's girlfriend, Judy Brown. Judy, like Lefty's wife Louise, was a younger girl, pleasant and fluffy, with the loyalty of a pet. She was, like most of the mob's women, unconcerned with what her man did.

On the ride in from the Tampa airport, Boobie told Ed and Joe he'd come to town for a meeting with Rafael Puig, a Cuban living in Miami. Puig, he said, wanted to meet Boobie's lawyer about getting released from a lifetime probation following his conviction on drug charges. At the Tahitian Motor Lodge, lounging around the pool, Puig walked up. Sonny and Boobie took him to Sonny's room for a short sitdown. When they emerged, Boobie and Puig took a walk. Sonny sidled up next to Ed's chaise lounge and confided that they were discussing a big coke deal "for the New York family." Ralph Puig. Boobie Cerasani. Two more names and faces for The Shark, Jim Kinne, and Jack Case to chew on.

The next day, Boobie flew home. Sonny and Judy stayed by the pool in Tampa while Ed and Joe accompanied Lefty back to Miami. This was both a business and pleasure trip for Lefty. His principal mission in Miami was to bestow upon Steve Marucca, at the direction of Rusty Rastelli, the title of capo. While in town, Lefty also hoped to take a stab at setting up a sitdown with Lansky's son-in-law Joe Lombardo. Along the way, Lefty intended to continue his "schooling" of Ed, introducing him to additional crew members in Florida. Once he had done his official chores, Lefty had some private time planned in Miami.

Waiting for him at the Deauville Hotel were his mother, wife, his daughter Josephine, and grandson Allie Boy.

On the plane from Tampa to Miami, seated in the first-class. nonsmoking section, Lefty nattered in a good mood. He lit up an English Oval, waving it as he chatted. A woman asked him politely to put the cigarette out.

"Shut up," he snarled.

A stewardess asked him next. He ignored her, wouldn't even look at her, and finished his smoke. After the short flight, Lefty was incredulous that these people had their nerve to ask anything of him. The woman, the stewardess, the world in general, were just "citizens," people whose concerns did not touch him. He considered himself unbound by their gravity, their chains of conduct, a free-floating bird of prey. Lefty's only society was the Mafia.

In Miami, Lefty played the family man: grandpop, father, husband, and son on "vay-kaysh" in Florida. Ed stood aside and watched; a curious kinship with this psychopathic killer tickled in his chest. Lefty lived a double life, too. In the Deauville's gift shop, Lefty picked up a black squirt gun in the shape of a tommy gun. He bought it for Allie Boy.

"Now you can be a tough guy like your granddad," he said, presenting the toy to the child. "You can be a shooter when you grow up, just like me." Walking out of the gift shop, Lefty confided to Ed that he'd had to whack the boy's father, his own son-in-law, for doing drugs.

The sitdown with Lombardo didn't materialize. Lefty was just showing off to keep Ed on the hook for more of the FBI's money.

The next morning, Ed got on a plane with Joe to go back to Tampa. For two days, Sonny filled their ears with talk of the various criminal enterprises he intended to bring into Florida with Bonanno money and power. He wanted Ed to contact other clubs around Tampa about hosting Las Vegas Nights that Ed would run for the family. He asked if Ed had someone he trusted enough to be sent to New York and schooled in running crap games. Sonny again prodded Pistone to make progress setting up the sports book and shylocking operations. He told them both, emphatically, that he, not Lefty Ruggiero, was their boss. "You report to me," he said. When Joe complained privately to Sonny that Lefty bled Ed for plane tickets, meals, and gifts, even beyond the weekly $250 payments, Sonny said to put a stop to it.

He asked if Joe or Ed had any cocaine connections in Florida to assist with the big deal being put together by Boobie and Puig. Sonny said that he had invested $400,000 in the deal, expecting a million in return. The transaction would have gone down already except that a factory owner who was to deliver the drugs had reneged. Sonny claimed to have burned down one of the man's factories, saying he would keep torching them until the load was handed over. Sonny wanted to start up a numbers racket in Holiday; again, he would provide the financing.

Sonny and Judy flew out on May 13th. Joe flew home that afternoon. Ed stayed behind to meet with Donahue about people Donahue claimed he wanted to invest in a pari-mutuel dog track in Pasco. He asked Ed to contact his own people to determine if they also would be interested. They talked about getting bribes down with several public officials to ensure passage of the proper licensing for the track. Donahue was confident they could get the needed permission from "higher ups" in the state government. More importantly, Donahue's people knew that to operate any gambling in Florida, even legitimate gambling, you needed the permission of Santo Trafficante. Donahue wanted to know if perhaps Tony could "reach out" to the Florida mob boss.

Ed gave Donahue $1,000 for protecting the Las Vegas Night. He told him to keep half and give half to Sheriff Short for his upcoming re-election campaign. Then Ed had his first sitdown with Bill Sakelson, Donahue's friend. Sakelson could supply Ed with a cocaine source for a fee up front. Ed told Sakelson that his New York connections were looking for a coke supply and he'd set up a meeting.

On May 26, Sonny, Lefty, and Boobie returned to Holiday. Joe arrived in time to join Ed at the airport to pick them up.

Throughout the afternoon, Sonny held court from his plastic lounger beside the Tahitian Motor Lodge pool, like an Arab prince reclining in his tent. He brought in visitors and associates to pay homage, to plot and seek his grace or partnership for their own schemes. He met with a "big-time operator in stolen and fraudulent securities" named James Corr. He sat down with Robert Capozio, a Bonanno from Orlando who owned a fleet of cars ready to mule coke from Florida to New York. When Sonny left on May 26, he promised he'd be back in a week or so with Stefano Cannone, the Bonanno consiglieri, for a sitdown with Trafficante.

Sonny Black saw big business in the air for the Bonannos in Florida. Soaring beside him, like the pelicans in formation over the Gulf, would be Tony Rossi and Donnie Brasco.

* * *

The next day, May 27, Sonny phoned Ed from New York. He asked if Ed knew anything about paintings and artwork. Sonny's crew had burglarized a warehouse in Brooklyn where the dying Shah of Iran had stored some of his artwork. One of the paintings was a Picasso. He needed a fence.

"Chico has some contacts," Ed said, referring to agent Salmieri. "I'll ask him if he's interested and get back to you."

Three days later, Salmieri and an agent out of the Chicago Office posing as a crooked art dealer were picked up by Sonny at La Guardia and driven to an apartment on Staten Island. There, they met Boobie Cerasani. Chico and Boobie took Polaroids of the paintings and several gold artifacts. Boobie worked the camera in the warm apartment without wearing his shirt. One of the photographs taken by Boobie turned up later as evidence to link him to the robbery. The snapshot bore a reflection from the painting's protective glass pane of Boobie's bare chest, displaying in a ghostly image his tattoo of two songbirds. The Shah of Iran had terminal cancer. He begged the world's leaders to grant him asylum, a place to receive treatment and finally die. The United States had refused his requests. His sister, Princess Ashraf Pahlevi, nonetheless maintained an opulent apartment on Beekman Place. Sonny's plan was to hit the Shahrina's home. He had read that the Shah, living in Egypt at the time, had placed a large part of his collection in his sister's New York apartment. Sonny claimed to have Dennis Mulligan, a former New York City detective in charge of Princess Ashraf's security guards, in his pocket. The burglary would be a "piece of cake." By Sonny's reckoning, it figured to be close to a billion dollar score.

On June 2, Sonny called to tell Ed and Joe that, in the next few days, he'd give them notice to "come running." He'd already sold a few of the pieces from the warehouse robbery. There was nothing the FBI could do; they couldn't stop Sonny without revealing and endangering Ed and Joe.

No more was spoken of the planned Beekman Place hit until Sonny came to Holiday on June 4. In the coffee shop at the Tahitian, he told Ed and Joe what had happened. The night before, he'd driven his burglary crew to the Shahrina's apartment and waited in the car. Minutes after they were let in, he heard a shot. Spooked, he took off for his club in Brooklyn. After several hours, the burglars showed up. One of them, Ray Wean, who later became an FBI informant, had shot himself in the hand while tussling with one of the few honest and unsuspecting security guards. The job fell apart.

It looked as if Sonny would keep Jim Kinne and Mike Lunsford's surveillance teams very busy. The Bonanno street boss was quickly turning Coldwater into hot water.

CHAPTER THIRTEEN
A Full Plate

In November of 1979, still fresh from Jimmy East's gift of power and several months before Joe Pistone tugged on Lefty's leash to turn him toward Tampa, Tony Rossi happened upon another nasty nest of thieves. His investigation of them would inevitably run parallel to The King's Court.

Tony Rossi had become a celebrated figure among the Greeks who gathered in Tarpon Springs. Like the Italians, though on a smaller scale, the Greeks had their own clandestine mob. It too was rooted in criminal enterprise, rigid loyalty, and a skewed brand of honor with similar levels of status and profit sharing. As in La Cosa Nostra, the principal form of security was an elaborate system of referral and vouching.

Tony Rossi came prevouched. He was the Lucchese kingpin of Pasco and Pinellas, the owner of The King's Court, the secretary of the Gambino-backed garbagemen's association, and a rising Mafia star in Florida. No question, Tony was real.

Ed was introduced to Nick Tsachilis, a Greek businessman from Charleston, South Carolina, who was visiting friends in Tarpon Springs. Tsachilis owned and operated the Corinthian Room, a Charleston nightspot. He knew Ed was connected and wanted to talk. Ed bought a few rounds and went into his "Look, I don't want to discuss business" act. While the cigarettes choked the ashtray and the waitress ferried fresh whiskey, he listened reluctantly to Nick's problems and proposals. Little by little, almost painfully, he resolved his manner into a smile. "OK," he said, "I'll take a look at your operation," and cemented their new

154

relationship with a last round of Jack on the rocks.

In the Charleston FBI Office, Agent Bill Coggins had been trying for years to make cases against corrupt local and state officials. The Bureau suspected Tsachilis of running gambling out of his Corinthian Room. When Jim Kinne called to inform Coggins of Ed's undercover hookup with Tsachilis in Tarpon Springs, Coggins wanted the relationship pursued. Ed visited Nick Tsachilis in Charleston in late January. His first night there, Nick took him to the Corinthian Room.

Nick's clients were mostly Navy. Topless dancers in G-strings shimmied to disco on the small stage. The sailors, those still sober enough to emote, whistled and howled. After each turn on stage, the girls became waitresses, accepting credit cards and ringing up a few dollars extra, knowing the men were too perplexed by flesh and alcohol to notice or object.

Occasionally, a scantily clad waitress offered a tipsy patron a bottle of cheap champagne, usually Asti Spumonte, and the opportunity to drink it with her in private for $100. The girls ushered their guests into a shadowed room off the main saloon, known as the Champagne Room. There, in a secluded booth, the patron got sexual satisfaction to go with his cheap champagne.

Ed sat at Nick's table playing gin with some of Tsachilis's buddies. In a back room, Nick also ran blackjack and poker games. He hinted to Ed several times that the games were pro-tected. Ed told Tsachilis he liked Charleston; it looked like a good town to open a club similar to The King's Court. Ed planned to run a sports book out of his club, put some shylock money on the Charleston streets, and operate some high-stakes casino gambling that wouldn't compete with the Corinthian Room's games. As always, Ed desired only the high-class patronage.

Ed needed assurances there would be no hassles with the law. He promised to make Tsachilis a partner in the sports book but not in the club. Nick responded that, yeah, he had the con-nections.

* * *

The Columbia, South Carolina, Field Office applied to FBI Headquarters for a Group 1 operation to uncover political corruption in Charleston. The Bureau's Undercover Review Board approved the request.

Because of Tony Rossi's involvement in both Tampa and Charleston, the two investigations would inevitably have to be shut down at the same time. In February of 1980, months before Lefty and Sonny Black arrived at The King's Court, Coldwater seemed to be on its last leg. The plan in Charleston was to get Ed in quickly, make the cases, then close up shop in both cities. Because it wasn't expected to last very long, the Charleston sting was code-named Operation Fast Hit.

But just as it happened in Coldwater, the vines of vice uncovered by the FBI in Charleston went deeper and higher than expected. Once Lefty and Sonny were introduced into the Tampa case, the pressure to conclude Fast Hit eased and allowed the operation to take on a wider scope. Fast Hit survived side by side with Coldwater for another year and a half.

* * *

By pure coincidence, the FBI notified Ed that a familiar face from Coldwater, Bernie Agostino, ran an Italian Restaurant in Charleston, near the airport. Ed paid Bernie a visit. The moment he walked into Bernie's place, it became old home night.

What are you doin' here? Fuck you, what are you doin' here? Hey, how's everybody down in Tampa? Everybody's good. Bernie, I'm trying to do a deal here. Maybe you can help me. OK, Tone, you got it. Good to fuckin' see you.

Over the following months, Ed flew in from Tampa often, usually between visits from Lefty and Sonny. He hung out in the bars with Bernie, including the sleazy Corinthian Room. He played gin and poker with Tsachilis and his pals. Tsachilis's Greek crew and Bernie's Italian goombahs all accepted him as a big businessman, a connected guy from Tampa.

Ed intended only to get Fast Hit off and running, then bring in another agent as Tony Rossi's hand-picked partner to run the Charleston operation for him. Thereafter, Tony would fly in once in a while to check up on things. Ed had become too deeply involved in Coldwater to expect to be the lead agent in two separate Group 1 investigations four hundred miles apart.

The undercover agent selected to replace Ed in Fast Hit was Charley Gianturco, from the New York Office. Eight years earlier, Charley's brother Nicky had been one of the original cadre of UCA volunteers along with Ed and Joe Pistone. Charley was a wonderful athlete, an accomplished handball player, and a law school graduate who'd been—as he often bragged—"dead last" in his class. He was a dark, pleasant kid with a natural street swagger and an eager grin. He, like Pistone, always seemed in mob character, on and off the job. His nickname within the FBI was Charley Chains for all the gold he sported. To the targets of Operation Fast Hit, he would be known as Charley Sacco.

Ed introduced Charley to Nick Tsachilis as his partner. He asked that Nick help Charley find a location for their new club. Whenever he could, Ed came from Tampa to hang out with Charley and help build the young agent's status with the crooks there. Charley worked hard to get in tight with all the right players. Bernie and Nick liked the kid; Charley stood up.

It was Charley who dislodged the name that broke Operation Fast Hit wide open. Nick Tsachilis introduced him to Ray Scarboro in late summer of 1980. Scarboro, fifty-five, was a club owner from nearby Moncks Corner in Berkeley County. Scarboro had purchased an unincorporated island surrounded by the city of Goose Creek in 1964. The island, known as the Goose Creek Strip, was home to a tackle shop, an adult bookstore, a pizza restaurant, and a nightclub.

Over drinks, Charley mentioned to Scarboro that he represented some large interests out of Tampa, money men looking to open a nightclub in the area. Scarboro said that his property in Goose Creek would be an ideal location for a nightclub.

Scarboro drove Charley to the Strip for a look at the site. The agent liked what he saw, then played his hidden card. He told Scarboro that his "interests" in Tampa were actually a New York crime family.

Scarboro wasn't scared off. He wanted to know more. Charley invited him to Tampa to meet his people and see their operation there, The King's Court.

Two weeks later, Scarboro arrived in Holiday. Ed gave him the treatment. He rolled out The King's Court, the dog track, the best tables at Malio's and Pappas', the gambling, the shylocking, the sports book; he pulled out all the lure of being a criminal like a sofa bed to lay Scarboro and his eager greed down comfortably. He sold Scarboro on the proposition of opening a club and similar illegal enterprises in Goose Creek.

"But," he said, closing in, "I'm not putting up a hundred grand for no club in Goose Creek unless I got protection. I got a cop here in Pasco. What have I got up in Goose Creek, Ray?"

Tony Rossi smiled. Ray Scarboro smiled back.

"Let me look into it, Tony."

*   *   *

On June 4, Ed rushed home to Charlottesville. His daughter Amy had broken her thighbone running hurdles, and she was in the hospital. He arrived at night. Gretchen hurried her husband to his daughter's bedside. That night, and the next day, he tried to be supportive. He knew there must be something he could do for his family, though it would not come to him what it was. He soon saw that everything was firmly under Gretchen's control. He understood that his daughter's injury would heal without him. The other wounds in his family, the ones he caused, could not be healed just yet.

The afternoon of June 6, he flew back to Tampa.

*   *   *

Sonny Black arrived in Tampa the day Ed had rushed home to Virginia. The next day, while Ed sat in the hospital holding his daughter's hand, Sonny holed up in his room at the Tahitian Motor Lodge waiting for the phone call to tell him a sitdown with Santo Trafficante was set. That evening, Sonny called Joe Pistone, who'd flown in the day before Sonny arrived. Sonny asked Joe to drive him to Pappas'. The Old Man had telephoned and said he felt like eating Greek that night.

Joe drove Ed's car, which was wired with a Nagra in the trunk. He entered the bar with Sonny and stayed for a round at the bar until Sonny dismissed him. On his way back to the car, Pistone passed Trafficante walking through the parking lot. Santo was a solemn-looking old man with thick glasses, his shoulders hunched with age. He wore the pastel golf attire favored by the elderly of Florida. Joe, observing proper mob etiquette, did not acknowledge him.

An FBI surveillance team covered the meeting, snapping photos of Sonny, Trafficante, and an associate, Vincent LoScalzo. During the meal, the daughter of Trafficante's lawyer Henry Gonzalez and her husband came to the table and spoke briefly.

Surveillance agents were seated in the restaurant but were too far away to overhear any significant conversation between Sonny and the Florida mob boss. Nonetheless, the sitdown had occurred. Coldwater had climbed to within a single step of Trafficante. The Old Man teetered on the edge; one good nudge and he'd tumble right into the FBI's waiting net.

Later that night, Sonny called Joe to pick him up. On the way to The King's Court, and in further conversations in the club, Sonny told Joe the results of the sitdown. Trafficante had given Sonny permission to operate in any part of Florida as long as Trafficante was allotted a percentage of the profits. It fell to Sonny now to do the right things, to operate in such a manner that The Old Man did not close the doors on the Bonannos.

"You got something," Trafficante had told him. "We'll all work together."

The morning of June 7, Ed met with Sonny in the Tahitian's breakfast shop. Sonny told him of his sitdown with Trafficante. The Old Man, "the most powerful guy in Florida," had agreed to make available to them all the strength and support they needed to conduct business in the state. Sonny confided that the sitdown in Tarpon Springs was actually the second meeting between the two: They'd been introduced the week before in New York by Stevie Cannone.

"It's a dynamite alliance," Sonny said.

He directed Ed to begin work immediately on plans for the dog track with the cop's political connections. Sonny also wanted to install vending and game machines in Pasco County, from which Trafficante would get a 40 percent cut.

Sonny and Trafficante were interested in establishing large-scale bingo games. The Old Man was big into bingo throughout most of Florida but he didn't have anything going in Pasco or Orlando. Within the next few days, Sonny expected to be contacted by a member of Trafficante's crew to furnish the details of the bingo operation. Sonny would hand the guy off to Ed.

Sonny wanted to stage another Las Vegas Night at The King's Court. Also, the time had come to contact Ed's "shrimp boat guy," Bill Sakelson, to put together a cocaine deal. Sonny promised to send Ed an expert to test the drugs to ensure quality.

Ed was instructed to make a heroin contact in Florida; coke had become "passé" in New York. Ed told Sonny he had a heroin connection already in his pocket, referring to Theophilis Nicholis, one of the Tarpon Springs Greeks. Theo claimed to be hooked into the Medellin cartel through his uncle, a mid-level official in the Colombian government. A month before, Theo had approached Ed about going fifty-fifty on a Merlin aircraft, a plane with the range to fly nonstop to Colombia and back. Theo also had a guy named Rick in his pocket, a supervisor for Eastern Airlines at the Miami airport. Rick was in charge of offloading commercial baggage; he could move the drugs directly from the planes to circumvent customs. Ed wasn't about to make the FBI partners in a drug airplane but he would give Theo some business. He could make a case against Theo, Rick, and Sonny with just samples of heroin. Once the narcotics were in the country, he'd arrange a buy between Theo and agents to keep them off the street.

Finally, Sonny told Ed that if things kept going as well as they had been, he—Tony Rossi—would someday be the family boss of Florida. Who knew how many guys Sonny Black had said this to? It didn't matter. Ed was flattered.

* * *

Sonny wanted the sports book in place before the 1980 football season kicked off in August. The FBI believed it was important to keep the bookmaking in the hands of an agent: The names and numbers that would emerge from controlling such a widespread gambling operation would be invaluable intelligence throughout south Florida. But who would run it? Ed's plate was heaped too full already, with Fast Hit warming up plus all the dizzying angles in Coldwater he worked. He would soon become involved in Trafficante's bingo operations. Once in a while, he had a real home and family of his own to visit.

Pistone recommended another undercover agent whose work he was familiar with: Eddie McLaughlin, a savvy ex-street cop from Philadelphia. Pistone and he had been First Office Agents together in Alexandria, Virginia. McLaughlin, now in his late thirties, had done some undercover work as a bookmaker in a Baltimore sting. Kinne and Daniels decided to bring McLaughlin in. Joe vouched for him with Sonny as his longtime friend from Baltimore, Eddie Shannon. Sonny accepted the new guy on Joe's word.

Eddie Shannon's bookmaking operation was set up in a rented storeroom in an out-of-the-way strip mall. The sports book would not be run out of The King's Court; the FBI didn't want the club jeopardized in the event Donahue slipped up and the betting operation got taken down by local cops. Tapped phone lines were run into the storefront. The regular card games were also moved from the club to Eddie Shannon's storeroom. Sonny sent Ed an official charter from his private Italian-American War Veterans Club in Brooklyn so they could make the Holiday game room nonprofit. Gaming was legal in Florida as long as a registered charity, in this case the IAWV, received the proceeds. This would make Shannon's operation easier.

The mob's reason for running a sports book is, of course, to earn money. It's also a valuable tool for creating new criminal contacts within the community and establishing a front porch for corruption through loan-sharking. If a loser can't pay his debt, the bookie will lend him the money at a 4 to 5 percent vig. The average gambler figures he'll win it back the next week, which he often does not. He may double his bets again, his faith in his luck still strong, and before he knows it, he's in fearful trouble with La Cosa Nostra, which—unlike Satan, who only collects your soul—takes repayment in any number of ways. If the loser happens to be a policeman, a judge, a lawyer, even a simple building inspector, the mob enters and controls him like an evil possession from the netherworld.

Running a sports book is not as simple as placing bets, paying off winners, and collecting from losers. Bookmaking is a specialized criminal skill. To pull it off convincingly, an undercover agent must have had training either on the street or in the FBI's gambling school. For a typical football game, say, between the Giants and the Saints, the street will adopt a spread, usually from Las Vegas bookmakers. The bookie will accept bets on both teams. He can't lose, whichever way the game turns out, as long as he has his bets balanced, meaning he has the same money down on the Giants as he does on the Saints. If he's heavy on one team, he'll "lay off" bets, or place the right amount of bets himself with another bookie to balance his accounts. Some bookies take bets only from other bookmakers.

In addition to a sports book, Sonny wanted Shannon to run a numbers game. The numbers racket is essentially an illegal lottery. Usually, the winning ticket consists of three numbers. These three numbers can come from any of a myriad of sources established by the bookie. They can be the last three digits of the New York Stock Exchange closing volume from the day before, or the AMEX volume, or the Chicago grain market. The numbers have been the last digits of the third-place finishers in the third, fourth, and fifth races at Calder or the daily handle at Hialeah. To win, the numbers must be picked in their order of appearance but they can be bought boxed (in any combination). Just as the bookie does with sports bookmaking, if he gets more action on three numbers than he can carry, he'll lay off action by placing bets with those three digits in the legal lottery. Bookies are always glad to see legal lotteries come into their states so they can lay off to the state-run lottery.

Why would a citizen play an illegal lottery instead of the legal one? No taxes and a better payoff explain a part of it. Some people simply like to associate with criminals. It's more exciting for them, just as some folks will go to a nip joint for a drink instead of a legit bar, for the thrill.

The next morning, June 8, Ed met with Captain Donahue at The King's Court. He filled the cop in on Sonny's wishes: the vending and gaming machines, another Las Vegas Night, bingo, and the dog track. Donahue planned to leave for vacation on July 15 so he asked if the next casino night could be in the first week of July. He advised Ed to secure a nonprofit sponsor for the bingo games: Donahue seemed familiar with the mechanics of protecting bingo. The cop volunteered to find a sponsor. Ed told Donahue that he had "very big people" behind their efforts to build a dog track and hotel, "the biggest guy there is in Florida, you know who I'm talking about?" Donahue said, "Yeah." Donahue repeated that his political connection, a woman named Joann Saunders, could handle any problems with public officials. He assured Ed she could produce.

That afternoon, in the lounge of The King's Court, Ed reported to Sonny on his meeting with Donahue. Again, Sonny gave him the green light for all the plans, promising to send whatever personnel and money might be needed.

The following day Trafficante's bingo guy, Benny Husick,

dropped by the Tahitian for a sitdown with Sonny. After thirty minutes in Sonny's room, Husick left without being introduced to Lefty, Ed, or Joe. Sonny reported on the meeting to his crew gathered at poolside.

Everything was set for the bingo operation. Husick knew everything about bingo. He'd been instructed by "the man" to line up two sponsors and secure an air-conditioned building between 8,000 and 10,000 square feet. Sonny and the Bonannos would supply the location and half the money; Trafficante would chip in the equipment, the staff, the know-how, and the other half of the money. Sonny told Ed and Joe to start the search for a location immediately. An abandoned supermarket would be perfect.

In the following months, Benny Husick became Ed's connection to Trafficante for anything to do with gambling. Benny was another mobster in the old-timer mold of Jimmy East and Trafficante. He was affable, high energy, like a Jewish uncle. He wore the slicked grey hair, gold, silk, and sharkskin trappings of the well-to-do connected guy. But Benny was no smoothie. He was an ex-prize fighter, a talkative, street-smart Miami bookie who knew how to make friends and keep them between himself and his enemies. "Tony," he'd say, always solicitous, "how you doin? You alright? You gettin' enough sleep?" Benny's rap sheet included charges of armed robbery and counterfeiting, with convictions for grand larceny, assault, and burglary.

Ed subscribed to Benny's betting line for the football book. Either he or Eddie Shannon would dial the Miami area number and ask for "Benny White. Tommy calling." The voice on the other end would respond in rapid-fire fashion with the line: Giants and 5, Rams and 1, Chargers and 6, so on and goodbye. Shannon used a combination of Benny and a Greek bookmaking operation in Charleston, one of the targets of Fast Hit, to lay off bets whenever he came up heavy one way or another.

All phone calls between bettors and bookies emanating from the sting were recorded.

*   *   *

Ed met with Donahue on June 13 in front of the cameras in The King's Court office. They first discussed the bingo operation. Ed said that even though "professionals" would be running the bingo games and they knew many of the loopholes in the state bingo statute, they'd still need support from Donahue. Ed described the type of building he required. Donahue replied that he'd be on the lookout for such a place.

On the topic of the proposed dog track, Donahue reminded Ed to file the proper papers by July 1. He estimated it would take a year to obtain the necessary licenses.

Donahue advised Ed that his boss, Pasco County Sheriff John Short, "wants a piece" of the dog track action but would not be able to be actively involved in securing it until after the coming election in November.

After the meeting, Ed sensed that Donahue worked diligently behind the scenes to follow Tony Rossi's instructions. The old cop was crooked as a bent nail but he was dependable.

*   *   *

On June 20, Bill Sakelson made a phone call from The King's Court to his drug connections in Chicago. He spoke with "Johnny" and asked where he could get in touch with "Louie." The number Sakelson dialed in Chicago was listed to John Balzano, a known fence suspected by the FBI of drug-trafficking.

At times, Ed felt as if he were running a criminal employment agency out of The King's Court, matching crooks and connections, talents with jobs. Every crook he met knew fifty, a hundred other crooks. Tony Rossi sat in the center, stitching them together into a sort of criminal quilt.

*   *   *

On June 29, JoJo came to The King's Court to speak with

Ed. He asked if Ed had plans to run a numbers game. JoJo had some experience with numbers and wanted to earn. Ed said he had to talk with his people in New York before he could involve anyone else. JoJo also asked if he might hire on as a manager of the club. Ed said that because JoJo didn't have his own car, he wouldn't be able to get around enough to do the job.

Ed didn't need JoJo hanging around. The cases against him were made long ago and JoJo Fitapelli was unlikely to do anything worse than he already had. There was no need to keep him close and under scrutiny. In his own, clownish way, JoJo was harmless, an alright guy. Ed wanted him out of the club, safe from further temptation. What JoJo was going to get when the investigation finally concluded would be enough.

* * *

On June 30, Sonny, Judy, and Boobie came down for the July 4th holiday. At the Tahitian Motor Lodge, Sonny gave Pistone $5,000 in $100 bills, money he described as coming from the "organization." This was a stake to get Ed and Joe started on the shylocking. Sonny told them to hang onto the vig until the amount built itself up to sixty g's. He instructed Joe to send $200 a month to Steve Cannone to pay back the family. The two agents recorded the serial numbers and turned the money over to Kinne.

Of course, they couldn't put the money on the street. Whenever Sonny asked for a progress report, Ed gave Joe a number for Sonny's ears that was supposedly in the kitty. If Sonny asked for some of the cash, they gave it to the gangster out of his own till.

Ed drove Benny Husick and Sonny to Port Richey on July 3 to inspect a potential site for their bingo operation. The Ridge Runner was a former nightclub. After a half-hour inside the building, Benny declared it unsuitable for their purposes. The ceilings were too low for the monitors and the space was limited. Benny told Ed that he had a 3:00 p.m. meeting with The Old

Man that afternoon. He wanted Ed and Joe to meet him in Tampa the next day to show them one of Trafficante's bingo halls so they could see the kind of operation they needed to assemble in Pasco.

Ed, Joe, and Sonny met Benny at the Britton Plaza Bingo Hall in Tampa on July 4, 1980. Benny showed them around the grounds. They met the manager, and Benny pointed and instructed like an old drill sergeant revisiting the barracks. He explained all the facets of running a proper bingo game for the mob and about setting up a charity as the front.

"The best ones are the ones with the most pathetic people involved," he said, "like war veterans and crippled children. You put them at the door in wheelchairs taking tickets so if the cops raid you they have to climb over them. Get as many of them as you can and when the bust gets written in the paper the next day it looks better for you."

Husick and Sonny had another sitdown with Trafficante that afternoon at a Howard Johnson's in St. Petersburg. Sonny told Ed and Joe to go wait in a Jack in the Box, he'd be back for them. Husick drove Sonny off to the meeting.

An hour later, Sonny reappeared, elated. Trafficante again had assured him that "we can do anything we want in Florida," so long as The Old Man got a piece of it. Sonny told Ed and Joe they had to "get things going, since The Old Man expects things to happen." Sonny was confident; when Santo retired or died, he was the heir apparent to take over Florida; Trafficante had expressed many times his dissatisfaction with the people he had around him now. Sonny was so pumped he claimed he was going to give up fifteen soldiers in New York and assign them to other capos so he could "concentrate on the big stuff in the Florida operation."

Ed searched for a room big enough to seat five hundred people, a large open space to set up tables and chairs, hang TV monitors, and pack them in. Ed would set up a subchapter S corporation to supply the equipment, callers, tables, and chairs, and the charity handicapped would be at the door handing out cards and handling the concession for $100 each a night. Benny figured that, with only two hundred players, they could clear up to $2,000 per session. The charity was slated to get all the proceeds after expenses. But Ed's people would be the ones counting, and the expenses could get incredibly high. The cash payments to the wheelchairs at the door should keep them from ratting.

The next week, Ed found a vacant store in New Port Richey. Before he could arrange a lease, the owner of the building got wind that Ed represented mob interests. The guy phoned Ed and said, "No way, I'm not leasing to you." Jim Kinne visited the owner and told him the FBI had these mobsters under surveillance, so why don't you go ahead and lease to them so we can keep an eye on them? The man said, "No thanks, they're the bad guys, you're the good guys and I'm the guy caught in between." This, opined Kinne, was not a stand-up citizen.

The FBI was not enthusiastic about becoming involved in Sonny's bingo dreams. Bingo wasn't needed to make cases against Sonny, and Benny Husick already faced a bookmaking charge and conspiracy. The Bureau only wanted to play it through to increase Ed's status as an earner, to get him at the table with Trafficante. Bingo was a part of the undercover backdrop, the scenery of authenticity. No criminal could believe that Tony Rossi was an undercover cop, considering all the trouble he went to every day just to turn a buck for the family.

Sonny kept asking for progress reports on the bingo. Ed went through the motions, making sure that he had a hell of a time finding the proper site. What can I do, Sonny? I'm looking every fucking day, I can't find nothin'.

Sonny stayed on his back about the bingo, probably for the same reason Ed stayed on everyone else's back: to get next to Trafficante. The Old Man seemed fixated on getting a game going in Pasco. Sonny did what he had done ever since Ed first met him. He told someone else to get on it fast.

Bingo. Great, Ed thought, one more item to be tossed in the air and juggled. Ed counted his responsibilities at night, alone in his condo, at rest for a rare moment. The King's Court, The War

Vets Club, loan-sharking, bookmaking, Las Vegas Nights, the garbagemen's association, Fast Hit in Charleston, Sonny, Lefty, Boobie, Johnny Cascio, JoJo, Jimmy Acquafredda, Donahue, the dog track, drugs, Sakelson, Theo Nicholis, Trafficante, Benny, all the undercover agents making their own cases, the support agents he reported to daily. As Tony Rossi, Ed led a full life. It was demanding and complex, like any other life, except that it was false, he was false. Rossi's life was led in tandem with another one, Ed Robb's real one, peopled by Gretchen and his kids, his family, his home, the Bureau, his identity. These two worlds pulled in opposite directions.

How many of us can exercise any grace or control over one life, he asked the ice in his quiet Jack Daniel's, much less two?

* * *

In August, Sonny stepped up his demands for narcotics from Florida. Sonny and Lefty had to be convinced there was activity, but Ed could never let the transactions actually go down. Nor could he allow a bust that might compromise Coldwater. So Ed, Joe, and the other undercover agents had to make a show of stirring up connections for smoke, coke, and heroin. The mobsters got into a pant, anticipating a deal, and were always willing to finance it. The agents would then have to thwart it somehow, running a secret interference between the buyers and sellers to make sure they never hooked up, while making it look like the lack of results was not their fault.

Bill Sakelson set up an August 3 meeting at The King's Court with Mario Rocomaro and Pedro, two sources for cocaine at $35,000 a kilo. Mario said he had thirty kilos available at the moment, plus a quarter-ton of Colombian marijuana at $260 per pound. Mario gave Ed two samples of coke, which he claimed were 90 percent pure. Ed told them his people in New York would test the drugs and let him know if they were interested. Mario and Pedro offered to deliver the drugs directly to New York after the first deal. Ed thanked them and reminded them of the necessity of caution when discussing narcotics. When they had gone, he smiled at the camera.

The next morning, Ed flew to Charleston. Nick Tsachilis and his boy Billy took him around town. Nick introduced Ed to his bookie partner Emmanuel Stavrinakis. Emmanuel and Ed agreed to lay off bets with each other. They'd settle up every $10,000, with Nick as courier between Charleston and Florida. Ed met another close friend of Tsachilis's, a former partner named Henry Smith. Smith was the self-acclaimed "Night Mayor of Charleston."

Pedro. Mario. Emmanuel. Henry the Night Mayor. More names, more faces, seined out of a nefarious ocean. Ed was both the fisherman and the bait. He snared these men, then tossed them and their fates to "Shark" Kinne, Mike "Sonar" Lunsford, Jack "the Clam" Case, and their watching, listening, surveillance teams.

Ed wondered when the net would break under the strain of the catch.

*   *   *

Sonny and Lefty arrived in Tampa on August 7. The next morning, Ed and Joe met them in the Tahitian's coffee shop. Again, they discussed plans for bookmaking, bingo, and the dog track. Sonny told them The Old Man planned a visit that afternoon.

At 3:00, Trafficante and Benny Husick arrived and went to Sonny's room. Lefty sat outside, sunning himself like a lizard. After a few minutes, Benny, Sonny, and The Old Man came out and walked to the coffee shop. Ed and Joe followed. The two were instructed by Sonny to sit at a table by themselves while he, Benny, and Trafficante sat a mere two tables away. Ed and Joe tuned their ears in but heard only snatches of conversation about bingo and the dogs.

Benny drove with Ed and Joe to look at another potential bingo site in New Port Richey. When they returned to the Tahitian, Sonny and Trafficante remained locked in animated conversation. Sonny motioned Ed and Joe to sit at the counter. After thirty minutes, Sonny told Ed to make reservations at a Dunedin restaurant for 6:00. While Ed talked on the phone, Sonny motioned Pistone to his room. Inside, Donnie Brasco met and shook hands with Santo Trafficante. The Coldwater agents were inching closer.

That night, after dinner, Sonny, Lefty, Ed, and Joe met in Sonny's room. Sonny reiterated The Old Man's excitement about the new blood their crew represented in Florida. Santo had "five hundred men in Florida" but they were getting old. Sonny handed Ed a slip of paper bearing three names and phone numbers given to him by Trafficante: an architect and two lawyers to help pursue the dog track license. He warned Ed to discuss nothing "funny" with one of the lawyers, Joseph Donahey in Clearwater, and the architect, John F. Ranon of Tampa, as they were straight professionals.

The second attorney, Henry Gonzalez, was The Old Man's lawyer. "If you gotta talk family business, go see him." Sonny said that Gonzalez would be expecting him to call. The fees would be handled by Trafficante.

Sonny said he'd send down $500 for the first month's rent for Eddie Shannon's bookmaking parlor, plus another $1,600 for the security deposit on the bingo site in New Port Richey they'd visited that afternoon with Benny. In connection with the bingo hall, he instructed Ed to secure a $25,000 loan from a bank to purchase the supplies and equipment. The loan would be paid back with "family money."

Sonny retreated on his plans for narcotics. The price was too high and, besides, he said, "we've got too many other good things going to bother with high-priced narcotics at this time."

Finally, he relayed Trafficante's advice that they keep the word Italian out of their activities in Pasco County.

CHAPTER FOURTEEN
Making the Cases

Coldwater became like a movie set of a Western town: Behind the facades of solid activity and structure loomed the wide-open emptiness of reality. Ed and his fellow agents worked very hard throughout the late summer and autumn of 1980 to make it appear to the mob that they were really getting things done.

In late August, Ed met with Joseph Donahey, the straight lawyer in Clearwater, to set up the bingo corporation, Rental Halls of Holiday. He also sat down with the architect, Ranon, to go over plans and costs for the proposed dog track. Both professionals had been contacted by Henry Gonzalez and told to expect Ed's visit. Ed met twice with Captain Donahue, and Sheriff John Short attended one of the meetings. The Sheriff stayed cool, allowing only that Ed's bingo operation would have no problems with the Pasco cops as long as everything was legal. Sakelson dropped by The King's Court to ask how things with Mario and Pedro were going. Ed put Sakelson on hold, claiming the drugs were priced too high. Sonny, Lefty, and Benny called frequently.

Sonny didn't return to Florida until August 24. He stayed only one day, long enough for Ed and Joe to show him the storefront bookmaking operation under Eddie Shannon and for Sonny to hold a quick sitdown with Trafficante. Joe had an informative—and videotaped—meeting with Benny in Ed's office about the nuances of setting up the bingo parlor. Benny suggested that Joe place a pot at the door and announce each night that the bingo games were held for charity and the employees received no pay. Any donations the patrons put into the pot for the selfless employees would be appreciated. Ed and Joe could then put into the pot cash received from the games and attribute the amounts to contributions, making the money untraceable and untaxable. They would divide the money up among the workers, including themselves.

On September 4, Benny called to give Ed the first line for the college and pro football games for that weekend. He left two phone numbers to be called each day between noon and one, for that day's spread and to lay off bets. Ed and Shannon were reminded to use the name "Tommy White" when calling. That week, Ed paid Donahue another $200. He advised Donahue of the opening of the bookmaking operation, and asked if Donahue was going to steer any bookmaking action their way. The captain said he would. Ed gave him Eddie Shannon's phone number, adding that Donahue should tell Shannon what bettors he brought in so credit could be extended to them. Lefty called Joe several times to complain that the take from the bookmaking wasn't enough. He assured Joe of ample family money to support them in case the operation took a loss at any time. Lefty also bugged Joe about moving ahead on the big Colombian coke deal. Lefty claimed he was setting things up in New York to unload the drugs. He planned to send his son Tommy to Florida to mule the narcotics back to New York City.

To give Joe something to report to Lefty on the drug front, Ed set up a meeting between himself, Eddie Shannon, and Theo Nicholis. At The King's Court on October 7, Theo described for the two agents his incredible, and unbelievable, experience as a pilot: He claimed to have flown 5,860 combat missions, thousands of hours in multi-engine aircraft, over 1,200 combat helicopter missions, and had considerable time as an instructor at the Ft. Rucker Aviation School. He repeated his desire to buy an Aerostar or Merlin aircraft to make the Medellin run, and again invited Ed to invest. He described various airstrips in Colombia where he might land and bring back high-quality cocaine, 88 to 92 percent pure, "right straight from the kitchen," for $28,000 per kilo. Rick Renner, Theo's man at Eastern Airlines, also served as his mechanic and co-pilot. If Ed wanted, he could bring back four kilos of "merchandise" for a sample run. After an hour's talk, Ed agreed they should meet again and put together a deal.

The next day, Frankie Foggia brought into Ed's office a local bartender, Steve, who claimed to know "all the bartenders on the beach." If suitable arrangements could be made, Steve would give all the bartenders Ed's bookmaking phone number. Ed told Steve and Frankie he wanted them to deal directly with Eddie Shannon; he wanted no connection between The King's Court and the betting. Ed called Shannon into the meeting, and the agent and Steve worked out the details of placing the bets and Steve's cut. JoJo told Ed at The King's Court on October 9 that he too had entered the bookmaking business, with Joe Pete Pullicino as his partner. JoJo only wanted to handle the small, $5 to $10 bets. He hoped to lay off the bigger players to Ed's operation. Ed made arrangements for JoJo's cut and instructed him to deal with Shannon.

Sonny and Judy Brown arrived at Tampa airport late on the night of October 10. Ed had made reservations for Sonny at the Tahitian Motor Lodge. The FBI had finally obtained Title III permission from the federal court for telephonic and microphonic coverage of Sonny's room. Ed dropped Judy off at the motel while he and Sonny went to the club for a nightcap. Sonny told Ed to get one hundred pounds of marijuana. He had an outlet in New York for at least that amount per week.

The next morning, Santo Trafficante and brother Fano came for a breakfast meeting with Sonny. The surveillance team in the next room waited by the tape machines, eager to record their first real evidence against The Old Man. If he opened his mouth in Sonny's room about bingo, the dog track, gambling, anything criminal, they'd have him on conspiracy.

With the surveillance team, Mike Lunsford grew skeptical. He knew The Old Man's reputation: Trafficante was the most cautious and clever of all the mob bosses. Lunsford recalled a time years earlier when Trafficante traveled to a sitdown with the New Orleans boss, his close friend Carlo Marcello. The FBI learned that the sitdown was to be in a large meeting room in a building owned by Marcello. The Bureau obtained Title III permission to bug the room. Upon entering, Trafficante said to Marcello, "We can't talk in here." Marcello replied, "Sure we can. It's my fucking building." Unconvinced, and rightly so, Trafficante sat with Marcello in the middle of the large open floor and the two men whispered in each other's ear.

Santo, Fano, and Sonny went into Sonny's room. Through his headphones, Lunsford heard the door open and close. Then he heard a click followed shortly by the unmistakable sounds of a football game. Santo had turned on the television. For the next thirty minutes, Lunsford could hear only football. The Old Man's conversation with Sonny and Fano was an inaudible mumble in the background. Finally, Santo, Fano, and Sonny went to the coffee shop. For an hour, they waved hands and pointed fingers, deep in hushed conversation, out of earshot of any agent.

* * *

For the next two weeks, Ed and Shannon worked Theo Nicholis and his connections to set up a drug smuggling link for grass, coke, and heroin. Nicholis never let up in his quest for a long-range aircraft. "I could make a million by Christmas," he said.

On October 27, Sonny canceled his trip to Holiday that week, and suggested that Ed and Joe fly up to New York and stay with him, to discuss upcoming narcotics deals. He told them to bring along a sample of marijuana. The morning of the 29th, Theo Nicholis's partner Rick Renner handed Eddie Shannon a sample of marijuana at the Miami airport. Shannon gave the sample to surveillance agent Lunsford, who carried it to Ed for the trip to New York.

The instant Ed delivered the marijuana to Sonny, a narcotics case would be made against Rick, Theo, Sonny, and anyone else who'd handled it, all from one sample. Even so, Ed intended to continue searching for a heroin connection for Sonny. Though a marijuana conviction would be good, a case built on heroin would be better. And Shannon was doing a great job; Theo and Rick wanted to introduce him all over Miami and Ft. Lauderdale to their sources for coke, hash, heroin, and Quaaludes.

At Kennedy Airport, Ed and Joe were met by Boobie Cerasani and Nicky Santora, a fat, easy-going member of Sonny's Brooklyn crew. Boobie asked, "Where's the shit?"

They went into the men's room. Ed handed over the sample of marijuana.

"Why did you bring this? I thought you were bringing heroin."

Boobie was upset. He had a guy standing by to test the "horse." There had been a mix-up, Joe explained. He thought Sonny wanted grass. Boobie sent them to an apartment in Little Neck, Long Island, owned by John Palzolla, a friend of Sonny's. At the apartment, Sonny climbed all over Ed and Joe for bringing grass instead of heroin. Nonetheless, he had a few joints rolled from the sample and stuck them in his pocket. He gave the rest of the grass to Nicky Santora to see what he could get for it. The price Ed had negotiated in Florida with Theo Nicholis was $270 a pound.

"That's high," Nicky said. "It's got a lot of seeds in it. Maybe we can get three-fifty to four hundred in the city if the quality's alright."

Sonny made a few phone calls, including one to a woman named Nina. Nina was a "pig," short for guinea pig. Her job was to use the drugs and report to Sonny if they were any good. In this way a middleman like Sonny could later insulate himself from blame if the drugs turned out to be a rip-off. He could point his finger at someone else. "What did I know? She told me the shit was good."

Nina met them downstairs in the condo restaurant. Sonny handed her a joint. She came back an hour later. "Gee," she said, "that wasn't bad." Sonny decided to do a deal with Ed's source.

The next day, Sonny took the party to his Italian-American

War Veterans Club in Brooklyn, then over to a car wash owned by his cousin, Carmine Rufrano. Carmine was a fence. Everybody had a specialty. He sold stolen goods out of the back room at his car wash. On this occasion, Carmine had boxes piled high, a whole truckload of boots.

Ed tried on a few pair. Carmine asked, "Hey, Tony. You want to see a lion?"

"Get the fuck out of here, a lion."

Carmine walked Ed to a warehouse he owned next to the car wash. Inside the warehouse, locked in a dark room, paced a young lion, maybe six months old. When Carmine opened the door, the lion snarled and prowled unhappily. Sonny's crew had stolen the lion while still a cub from an exotic zoo to sell to a private zoo owner in New Jersey. Lefty and a few others had grown fond of the cat and kept it around for a few months. The dark room in the deserted warehouse and the lion's agitated state made it clear that Lefty and his boys were not caring pet people. Each snarl made it equally clear that this was no suitable pet.

"What's its name?" Ed asked.

Carmine shrugged. "Lion."

The animal was getting to be a problem, clawing things up. The cops had come looking for it once. If they'd found it, the fine would have been $10,000. A lion costs a lot to feed.

A few weeks after their visit to New York, Pistone was at The King's Court on the phone with Lefty. "Get today's Post," Lefty told him. "They found our lion."

The front page of the New York newspaper bore the banner: KING OF THE JUNGLE FOUND IN QUEENS! The photograph showed the lion on a leash between two cops. Joe called Lefty back and got the story: The night before, Lefty had loaded the beast into a van and taken it to St. Mary's Cemetery in Flushing, Queens. He'd tied it to a bench and left it.

* * *

Lefty called Joe the morning of November 20, 1980, and

177

told him to rent a car and some rooms. Lefty was bringing four guys down. He wouldn't say why. Three days later, Ed and Joe went to the Tampa airport to meet Lefty and Boobie, who were accompanied by ex-New York policeman Dennis Mulligan and James "Jimmy Legs" Episcopia, so known for his short, pot-bellied torso and his gangling, skinny legs and arms. Jimmy Legs wore a ratty toupee.

Joe drove Lefty, Jimmy Legs, and Mulligan in a rental car. Ed climbed into his Mark V with Boobie, who seemed to be running this expedition. On the way up to Holiday, Boobie asked Ed, "Tony, how many guns do you have?"

This wasn't good. Guns boded danger, probably to innocent bystanders. Ed sized up the reason for Boobie's visit immediately: He and the crew had come to Florida to pull a job. Boobie had a background as an armored car man. The crew needed to have the guns available in Tampa; they couldn't bring weapons with them on the airplane because of airport security.

Ed had to answer. Tony Rossi was a criminal, and what kind of criminal doesn't have access to guns?

"Three."

"Good. Except I don't want any small guns like .25s. I want .38s."

"I've got .32 automatics."

Ed referred to the Walther PPk's used by FBI undercover operatives. These handguns already had the serial numbers filed off so they couldn't be traced. Ed knew he could get them from the Bureau and have the firing pins filed down so the hammer wouldn't reach the cap at the base of the bullet. He was confident that none of these New York crooks would spot the alteration. He couldn't give them live weapons; obviously, Boobie was contemplating something dangerous, but as a connected guy, Tony Rossi had to help out in whatever way Boobie requested.

"Those are OK," Boobie responded. "Otherwise I'll have to send guns down from New York. We aren't going to do anything now. We're just looking things over and running time tests, learning the streets in St. Petersburg. We'll be back next week to do the job if everything works out."

The next morning, surveillance agents followed Boobie, Lefty, Mulligan, and Episcopia to the St. Petersburg area where Boobie's crew cased a bank. Then they lost them.

That evening, on the way to Pappas' Restaurant, Boobie told Ed he didn't want to discuss the details of the score; the fewer people in the know the better. But he might need Ed's apartment to "hole up in." He asked again about the pistols.

Meanwhile, Jim Kinne dealt with the guns. Before Kinne could give Ed the approval, he needed clearance from FBI Headquarters. The Bureau's Legal Department took three days to say "No," they couldn't accept the liability. What if one of the mobsters pointed a gun supplied by the FBI, even an inoperable gun, at a bystander who had a heart attack? Ed was amazed. What, he wondered, if Boobie or that killer Lefty pointed a gun that worked? The bystander would be lucky to have a heart attack.

This was the kind of scrupulous micro-management by Headquarters a street agent or undercover agent had to live with—bureaucrats second-guessing their plans or failing to respond quickly to a request that needed urgent attention. An undercover agent could swing a deal with a felon and Headquarters might hold up approval or money for days, even weeks. In the meantime, the agent would have to stall, make up excuses, and in general look to the criminal like a mope. Ed thought that, if he had to, he should buy the guns on the street and file them down himself.

The next morning, Boobie, Lefty, Mulligan, and Jimmy Legs were tailed to Pinellas Park where they picked up a man, later identified as Paulo Badamo, a bank guard from Brooklyn. The five men drove the rental car around the Landmark Trust Bank in St. Petersburg. Ed figured that Badamo had called Boobie in New York and proposed a bank robbery. After casing the neighborhood, they dropped Badamo off and returned to Holiday.

Lefty told Ed and Joe the crew would return to New York

179

that night. They'd decided against the score. "Things didn't look right." Badamo had apparently forgotten to mention to Boobie on the phone that the bank sat only a block from police head-quarters.

* * *

FBI Director Judge William Webster wanted to meet the undercover agents of Coldwater. Kinne set it up so the Director could meet his undercover agents under secure conditions. The meeting between Judge Webster and Ed, Pistone, and Shannon was arranged for midnight at the Bay Harbor in Tampa, a busy hotel near the airport. The three agents went to the lounge and had a few drinks. They weren't concerned about being seen together; they were just out on the town in a bar that all three of them had visited before, doing nothing suspicious. Then they left the table one at a time for the Director's room.

Upstairs, Webster congratulated them on what he'd heard was a remarkable sting operation. He thanked them for the sac-rifices they were making and risks they were taking under such dangerous conditions. Webster seemed familiar with the case and knew many of the targets' names. Ed, as Coldwater's lead undercover agent, gave Judge Webster a quick debriefing on the progress of the investigation. Webster didn't ask for intensive detail; he wanted to know the essentials and if the agents were getting all the support they needed. He said he wanted to see for himself that his men were all right. The conference lasted less than half an hour. Webster shook their hands and Kinne walked each to the door. The agents felt honored and appreciated the Director's gesture.

* * *

In Charleston, Ray Scarboro came through. Weeks earlier, Ed had asked him to come up with protection for the gambling operation he wanted to set up in Goose Creek. Scarboro called to tell Ed the fix was in with his old buddy, Berkeley County Sheriff James W. Rogers.

Ed replied, "I want to hear it from his own mouth."

"Jimmy's having a barbecue next week. Why don't you come on up for it and y'all can meet."

Ed made the trip. At the cookout, he took Sheriff Rogers around the side of the house to talk privately. Also, a quiet chat away from other voices would improve the quality of the recording on the Nagra working in Ed's boot. Ed laid out the whole story: the people he was with in New York, The King's Court in Florida, and his plans for a Goose Creek night club and gambling operations, perhaps some shylocking.

"Don't worry, Jimmy," he assured the sheriff, "we don't do junk and we don't do whoores."

Rogers assured Ed he could provide protection in Goose Creek, and bragged about his importance. He'd been Sheriff of Berkeley County since 1970, and was president of the South Carolina Sheriff's Association in 1976. He was named "Sheriff of the Year" in 1977. He told Ed how many friends he had, the clout they carried, and how many favors they owed him. His brother was a prominent banker in Goose Creek.

Ed knew that simply recording Rogers' agreement to protect a gambling operation was not enough to secure a conviction. The Sheriff could later say that something about Tony Rossi from Tampa smelled fishy and he wanted to work his way into the mobster's confidence to ferret out the man's Mafia sources and evil intentions in Goose Creek and Berkeley County. The corrupt law enforcement officer, unlike a normal citizen, has to do some overt act to seal his fate. Typically, this happens when he allows a criminal enterprise, such as an illicit Casino Night or big-stakes poker game, to take place in his jurisdiction without a bust after being given notice of its time and place. Certainly, he's a goner if he attends the event; even worse if he accepts money in return for his cooperation.

The day after the barbecue, Ed re-visited Rogers' home, again with the Nagra hidden in his boot. He counted out $2,000 in cash and had Rogers agree the amount was all there.

Soon afterward, Ed rented the upstairs apartment at Scarboro's club, The Follies, on The Strip in Goose Creek. He set up tables for blackjack, craps, and poker and told Scarboro, if all went well, he'd consider buying The Follies for $400,000.

Bernie Agostino worked the games as dealer and manager. Ed didn't bring in the big gaming tables as he had in Tampa. They didn't need a large number of players in Charleston; just a few illegal games operated under the auspices of Sheriff Jimmy Rogers would land the cop in jail. Ed instructed Bernie to restrict the number of players for a while. That way, if Rogers double-crossed them, only a few people would go down.

*   *   *

The minute after Bernie Agostino cleared the chips off the table from the first poker game held upstairs at The Follies without a police raid, racketeering, gambling, and bribery cases were made against Ray Scarboro and Sheriff Rogers.

Fast Hit qualified as a home run though it still had six more months of life and would sweep up several more criminals. Fast Hit was a rare sting because no informant was needed to put the undercover agent in place. Tony Rossi, the Bonanno out of Tampa, came to Charleston complete; the identity and status he carried from Coldwater were the only passport he needed for Fast Hit. The underworld is not unlike the business world in this respect: Once you've got the proper credentials, you can go almost anywhere.

CHAPTER FIFTEEN
Boom and Bust

Ed and Joe flew to New York City on December 17, 1980, for Sonny Black's Christmas party. As the Bonanno street captain, Sonny was obligated to entertain his crew. The party was held at Charley's Motion Lounge in Brooklyn, with pasta, meatballs, sausage, and plenty to drink. Everyone in Sonny's crew showed up. Ed and Joe each gave Sonny $200 for his present.

Sonny pulled Ed and Joe, his Florida boys, aside at the party and continued to press them for drug connections. Boobie had found a suitable coke source in Miami at $47,000 per kilo. But Sonny still needed contacts for heroin and marijuana. After the party, Sonny took Ed and Joe to Crisci's Restaurant. He told them he was coming back to The King's Court soon, and wanted $1,000 out of the bookmaking proceeds to give to Trafficante as a present.

After Sonny's party, as they drove along the river past the Fulton Fish Market in Lefty's Cadillac, Lefty was in one of his morose moods. Lefty was never happy or lighthearted; he was usually dyspeptic, and now and then, without notice or explanation, a dark shroud would envelop him. He would sit quietly, staring at nothing. This time he stared at the East River.

"See that river?" he said softly, more to himself than Ed or Joe. "I've thrown a lot of bodies in there."

Looking down with this Bonanno triggerman into the murky waters, Ed recollected an earlier time when Lefty, in this same dark mood, had confided to Ed that he had forty-two hits to his butcher's bill.

The next night, Sonny, Joe, and Ed dined again at Crisci's. They mused over the world of possibilities opening up in Florida. Sonny was eager for another sitdown with The Old Man. He and a few of his crew planned to come down after the first of the year. Sonny's cousin, Carmine, wanted in as a partner in The King's Court. Carmine would put up the money for improvements at the club to include an addition to the rear featuring a dance floor and a swimming pool.

Walking away from the restaurant, weaving slightly from an abundance of good Italian wine, Sonny put an arm each around Ed and Joe. He was in a Christmas mood. He embarked on a paean of praise for the two. They were independent; they made money for him while other members of his crew simply whined and depended on him to do the earning.

"I love you guys," Sonny said. Then he said the "family books" were opening at the end of the year; he had five guys to nominate. Boobie Cerasani stood first in line, then four others who were relatives of made Bonannos whom Sonny was obliged to name. But the books would be opened again next year and then he would nominate Tony Rossi and Donnie Brasco. In twelve months, if everything worked out, both undercover agents would become wise guys, made members of the Bonanno crime family.

Sonny beamed, "You guys deserve it."

Ed Robb and Joe Pistone had just become the first FBI undercover agents to be in line for membership in a Mafia family.

Not long after that unprecedented event, Ed and Joe were lounging at their usual positions at the Deauville bar in Miami while Lefty enjoyed yet another "vay-kaysh." In an effort to increase his influence with Ed, Lefty had for some time been "schooling" him in the ways of the family. Ed always listened politely, and even seemed to be learning. Now he put it to Lefty. "Lefty," Tony Rossi asked, "I understand how we all like to make money. But what is the actual advantage of being a wise guy?"

Lefty put down his spritzer. He shook his head slowly, and

turned to Ed.

"Are you kidding? Tony, as a wise guy, you can lie, you can cheat, you can steal, you can kill, and it's all legit. You can do any fuckin' thing you want, and nobody can say nothing about it. Who the fuck wouldn't want to be a wise guy?"

* * *

Ed called Benny Husick on January 5, 1981, to tell him the next Las Vegas Night would be held the 17th. Benny would supply the dealers to run the craps tables. That afternoon, Ed met Captain Donahue in The King's Court office and told him that several important people were going to attend the upcoming casino night. He wanted no problems. He said he needed a meeting with Donahue's superior, Sheriff John Short, that his people in New York insisted on it. If Short didn't personally go along with the Las Vegas Night, Ed would not stage it.

Donahue agreed to set up a meeting with his boss and to increase the pressure on those handling the dog track license. Ed tossed Donahue "a little something for Christmas," $200 in cash.

* * *

Knowing that Ed was looking for narcotics connections for the Bonannos, and eager to earn a piece for himself, JoJo Fitapelli brought back the junk men—his childhood chum Freddy Cataudella and the father-son team of Pete and Tom Solmo. The afternoon of January 13, they met in Ed's office to talk business.

"What we really need," Ed said, "is heroin."

"Horse is tough," Tom replied, reluctant to discuss the drug. "How much marijuana do you need?"

"If you give me a sample, I've got people coming from New York who'll let me know."

Tom produced a sample packet of grass. He claimed it was one step below Colombian gold. Pete said that he, Tom, and Freddy were sitting on a couple thousand pounds and had

65,000 pounds more coming in.

"My dad finances everything," Tom said. "I go and work it all out. I know what stuff is good and what's bad. I been down to Colombia many times."

Pete, the proud pop, chimed in. "He does all the dirty work. He's captained boats. He's been a runner, bringing it in small ways, bringing it in by the ton."

The two Solmos and Freddy agreed that they could supply Ed's New York people with up to half a ton of grass per week.

"Use us once," Pete reassured. "You'll see."

The conversation turned to Quaaludes. Tom wanted to deal only in large quantities. "If you want five hundred thousand, I got 'ludes."

Joe and Eddie Shannon arrived at The King's Court and came into the office. Ed introduced Joe as "Donnie, my partner from New York." Eddie was "the action guy around here." The two agents sat in on the meeting. Ed said the Solmos could supply whatever they needed, coke, grass, Quaaludes, but not heroin, which was what Sonny Black really wanted for sale in New York.

Joe jumped in. "Fucking coke is nothin' up there. Forget about it. Everybody is using the horse up there. When you gonna know about the H?"

Tom shook his head. "I don't think I want to. Down there, there's too many deaths. I been in battles down there. I can take you down there and let you jump on the bandwagon."

Joe kept coming, pressing for a connection, chasing the drug buy-and-sell linkage as far as it would go. "If we got an introduction, we could make it worth your while to introduce one of our guys in New York to somebody down there."

"Have to find that out," said Tom.

Pete Solmo agreed, careful with names and places. "I'd have to think about that real hard."

Tom left Ed with a sample of coke. The price was $260 per gram. The next day, Mike Lunsford took the marijuana and cocaine samples to the Pinellas County Sheriff's Office lab. The grass was fine, but the coke tested only 46 percent pure. Ed called JoJo to tell his junk buddies to get their asses back to The King's Court, fast.

Ed and Joe met with JoJo and the Solmos in Ed's office on January 15. Joe got in the drug dealers' faces as soon as they sat down.

"I don't know if you think you're fucking with some jerk-offs. But that sample of coke ain't even fucking 15 percent. It's bullshit. It's been stepped on nineteen fucking times."

Ed wondered where the figure "15 percent" came from, but Joe was making this his play. Pete and Tom were nervous, stuttering their excuses. JoJo's chest sank into his big belly.

"You think we'd pull a shot like that, Don?" Tom pleaded innocently. "You think we'd do that? No way I'm gonna do that intentionally." Tom agreed that the sample might not have been up to the quality he'd expected. "It was just something I grabbed that night." He shrugged; if what Tony and Donnie were saying was true . . .

Ed stayed collected, ever the businessman. "It's not if what we're saying is true. It is true. Why would we tell you different? We were hoping it's 90 percent."

"Then someone is going to fall," Tom said. He'd been with his source for five years, he said, and this was the first time he'd been given poor quality.

"It's not a question of the money," Ed soothed, "it's a question of the honorability. Whoever gave it to you is putting you in a fucking box."

Tom shook his head in disbelief. Pete wanted to drop the whole affair. He asked Ed for the sample back; he wanted to check that the bad sample was in fact the one he'd given them. Pete put out his hand for the packet.

"Now," he said.

Ed looked up. "What's now?"

"Give it back! Alright, don't give it back. Done. I'm really getting pissed off."

Joe advanced on Pete and stuck a finger in his chest.

"You can get pissed off all you want. But don't get the fucking attitude, pal, that we're trying to fuck you with a bullshit sample. Understand what I'm saying?"

Pete stepped back, his tone changed. "You ain't got good stuff there?"

"That's what my man says."

Tom Solmo's head sank in his hands. "In my heart, I can tell you, this is the first time."

Joe didn't want to hear anymore of it. "Hey, this business isn't fucking in your heart. This business is in your pocket, in your head. Not what's in your heart."

Joe swept out of the office, a dramatic departure, well-timed, as if he had to remove himself to stop from whacking one or both of the Solmos and poor JoJo, too, for good measure. A nice performance, Ed thought.

The discussion continued with the junk men cowed and contrite. Tom asked what kind of test had been performed on the coke. Ed didn't know. He agreed to let Pete and Tom have the rest of the sample back the next day so they could test it themselves. Pete apologized again for the poor sample. Ed sent them away, promising he held no grudge against them. And don't worry, he would talk to Donnie for them, calm him down.

*   *   *

Sonny and his cousin Carmine Rufrano arrived from New York on January 14. Ed and Joe met them at the baggage claim area of the Tampa airport. While they waited by the carousel for Sonny and Carmine's bags, a man walked up and clapped Ed on the shoulder. "Ed?" he called out, a traveler happy and surprised to see an old friend in a strange city. "Ed Robb! How the hell are you?" The man was John Lowe, a well-known defense lawyer from Charlottesville.

Ed spun on him and pushed him away. "Get your hands off me, you faggot!"

Lowe knew Ed was in the FBI. He staggered backward from

the shove, then figured out his miscue.

"Sorry, mister. You look like a friend of mine."

"I ain't a friend of yours, pal. Buzz off."

Lowe apologized again and backed away. He hurried to a pay phone to call the FBI Office in Charlottesville.

"My name is John Lowe. I'm a friend of one of your agents, Ed Robb. I just bumped into him at the Tampa airport and called him by his real name. I think I might have gotten him killed."

The Bureau voice responded calmly. "I'm sorry, sir, but we don't have an agent Ed Robb." The FBI Office hung up.

At the airport, Sonny asked Ed, "Who was that?"

"The fuck do I know?" Ed was surly. "Some guy."

"Calm down," Sonny said. He handed Ed a brown paper bag containing $10,000, to be used as the bank for the upcoming Las Vegas Night. Sonny said the money belonged to Carmine. He told Ed, "Don't let this out of your sight."

Ed had made reservations at the Tahitian Motor Lodge. Carmine was put in Room 163 and Sonny in Room 161. Sonny's room and telephone were bugged. The FBI anticipated another meeting with Trafficante.

That afternoon, Ed sat with Pasco County Sheriff John Short at the Sheriff's Office. Again, Short was elusive, guaranteeing Tony Rossi nothing, agreeing with everything that sounded reasonable. Ed had never been able to get close to Short. He tried again to become pals with the top cop, perhaps opening the way for later influence or favors. He explored every avenue available. He even proposed the Police Athletic League as a sponsoring charity for the Las Vegas Nights.

"Sounds great," was all Short volunteered.

Short had an interest in a local travel agency. Ed said he liked to go to the Bahamas and gamble once in a while. He would have Short's agency set up his next trip.

"That'd be fine."

Ed wanted to support Short's next campaign for Sheriff with a contribution.

"Thanks. Appreciate it."

Ed suspected from Short's efforts to keep his distance, answering Tony Rossi's friendly overtures with only perfunctory, safe responses, that he might have been warned off.

* * *

On January 16th, Rocky Batista and Tony Martinelli, Benny Husick's card sharks, arrived at The King's Court and spent that day and the next carefully marking playing cards. Rocky called back to Miami and asked for an associate to come up to Holiday and run the craps table.

The day of the Las Vegas Night, the 17th, Trafficante arrived at the Tahitian. Sonny ushered The Old Man into Room 161, but the only words Mike Lunsford's microphones picked up from Trafficante were, "We can't talk in the room." Sonny followed the mob boss to the motel coffee shop where they spoke privately for an hour.

This time, the FBI had planned a surprise. They had arranged for a dozen or so agents from the Tampa Office to arrive at the Tahitian coffee shop at about the same time Santo and Sonny were to meet. The idea was to have someone close enough to listen from any part of the coffee shop or to force them back to the bugged room. It didn't work. Once in the coffee shop, the cagey old mobster and the Bonanno street captain whispered so quietly nobody could hear them.

After the meeting, Sonny told Joe that everything had gone well with The Old Man. The proceeds from the Las Vegas Night were to be divided into a third for the crew, a third for Benny and Trafficante, and a third for Trafficante's dealers from Miami.

That night, The King's Court doors opened for what would be the last Las Vegas Night. It was a stellar crowd: Benny and the three dealers represented Trafficante; the Bonannos were present in Sonny and Carmine; JoJo the Lucchese; the Greeks from Tarpon Springs; and Acquafredda the Gambino was there with most of the garbage guys. The FBI was well represented too: Ed and Eddie Shannon stayed in the game room to sell chips and handle money; Joe hung out; and Dick Stauder, the manager of the club, was in charge of the waitresses and bartenders.

The games started at 7:00 p.m. By midnight, the action got heavy with over a hundred players and a thousand-dollar profit in the cash box. People were lined up at the back room to buy chips from Ed and Shannon. With all the money on hand, including Carmine's $10,000, Ed was keenly aware of the risk of robbery. He kept his Walther in a briefcase beside him and a Derringer Magnum 2-shot pistol with hollow point bullets in a wallet holster.

Ed had a guy on the front door. To get into the club, a customer had to buzz from the outside and be recognized through the peephole as either a King's Court member or a friend. With the push of an alarm button, the doorman could warn Ed in the back room of a raid, a robbery, or other trouble.

At 1:20 in the morning, the alarm went off.

Joe was in the back room with several patrons buying chips. Instantly, he herded them out while Ed and Shannon slammed and locked the game room door. Mike Lunsford, coordinating the surveillance of the casino night from the safe house, called. The cops were raiding The King's Court.

Outside the front door, visible through the peephole, according to Joe's account, were two Pasco squad cars and two uniformed policemen, one a sergeant. Joe went quickly to the door. He told the doorman not to let the cops in until he said so. He figured Ed had paid Donahue for protection so there shouldn't be a lot to worry about. Nonetheless, Joe went around the lounge and made sure no money was on the gaming tables, only chips. He breezed past the Round Table where Sonny sat with Benny Husick and told them there were two deputies at the door but he would deal with it.

Joe opened the front door.

"Hi, officers. What's the problem?"

The sergeant spoke. "We had a complaint of a disturbance in here and a fight."

"No sir. No disturbance. No problems."

The cops walked in.

"I got an anonymous call," the sergeant continued, "and the caller stated that he'd been at The King's Court and lost a considerable amount of money playing blackjack."

Joe told the officer, Sergeant Greg Devlin, that all the gambling was with chips and that no one had lost any money. "We're running a charity event."

"This person will come to court and testify personally that he lost a lot of money playing blackjack here tonight."

Joe didn't rattle easily. "You can bring him to the club or anyone else you want. Do you see any money being used for gambling?"

The sergeant wanted to see the office. Joe conducted him through the lounge.

Devlin pointed at an antique one-armed bandit.

"I saw through the doorway that you have a slot machine. Does it work?"

Joe stayed impassive. "I don't know. I haven't played it at all."

On the way to the office, the cop observed, "You have some of the finest clientele in Tarpon Springs here tonight."

"Well, people like to contribute to charity and have a good time," Joe said.

Inside the office, Devlin said he recognized the chips on the tables as Las Vegas gaming chips. He asked to use the office phone; he spoke with someone he called "Major," reported his progress, and hung up.

Devlin wanted to meet the manager of the club. Joe went into the lounge and returned with Stauder. Devlin greeted Stauder, then walked out of the office. Joe and Stauder sat tight.

A moment later, Devlin returned to say that he'd put a quarter in the slot machine and it paid him back two quarters. Devlin said he would have to call the State's Attorney's Office for a search warrant.

"You're maintaining a gambling place."

The other cop came into the office and saw licenses on the

wall naming Anthony Rossi as owner.

"Where's Mr. Rossi?"

"I don't know where Mr. Rossi is," Joe said.

Tony Rossi sat behind a locked door in the storage room, placing furious phone calls. He woke Donahue up. "What the fuck is going on? We just got raided!"

Donahue, who'd promised to keep all the patrol cars on the other side of the county this night, didn't have a clue.

"This was not supposed to happen. I'll check into it."

"Goddam right you'll check into it!" Ed slammed down the receiver.

At the safe house, Lunsford also burned up the wires. He called Jim Kinne, at home with the flu. He dialed the Tampa Field Office, where Tony Daniels was no longer the Organized Crime Supervisor. Months earlier, Daniels had been transferred to Washington. His replacement, Bob Balog, wanted nothing to do with Coldwater or its problems, and said so. It was Daniels' case, let Daniels deal with it. Lunsford called the new Tampa Agent in Charge, Roy Klager, who'd replaced Phil McNiff, one of the early driving forces behind Coldwater. Klager told Lunsford that his hands were tied at the moment but Mike should call in the morning and he would see what he could do.

Ed and Shannon sat behind the locked storage room door for an hour. Lunsford phoned to tell them to ride it out. Ed called Donahue three more times, bellowing louder each time. No help. He used duct tape to strap his Derringer and the Walther against the back of the furnace. He wrapped Carmine's ten grand and several thousand dollars of chip money in Christmas paper and stashed it all in a box in the furnace room. He stuck $2,000 of FBI cash in another box under several strings of Christmas lights and put that in the furnace room, too.

Then Eddie Shannon opened the locked door to go out into the lounge to see what was happening. He came back and told Ed he might as well come out, the cops weren't leaving.

Joe and the hostesses moved all the patrons out the rear French doors while Devlin was on the phone obtaining his warrant. When Ed walked into the lounge, he saw a mostly empty room. A few of his employees were gathered at the bar. Sonny Black sat scowling at the Round Table with Donnie Brasco beside him.

Sonny shoved an angry finger at Ed. "You fucking embarrassed me more than anybody ever could! You embarrassed me in front of everybody! The Old Man's people. People from Miami. I should slit your fucking throat right here. You get this fixed up fast. And Tony, you better come up with that fucking ten grand I gave you."

"Sonny, I got it under control. I don't know how this happened."

"You're just like all the others who say they're gonna do the right thing and then you fucking embarrass me!" Sonny glowered like an angry child looking for things to break. "And if we find the cop that fucked us, we'll chop him up."

"Don't worry about it."

Sonny stabbed his finger again. "I ain't worried about it. You better worry about it!"

Sergeant Devlin came out of the office. "Where'd everybody go?"

Joe smiled. "I don't know. I guess they figured it was time to go home."

Several patrol cars arrived as backup for the raid. Pasco cops entered the club and wandered about. Ed feared they might tear the place up, find the cameras and recording devices, and stumble onto the true nature of the operation. There was nothing he could do to prevent it.

Ed walked over to his employees. Shannon and Stauder stood among them. Ed turned to Devlin. "You got warrants for these people's arrest?"

The cop shook his head.

"Good. Then they can go home."

Devlin approached. "Who the fuck are you?"

"I'm Tony Rossi. I own the place."

Devlin agreed to let the bar employees leave but Stauder was stopped at the front door. Devlin turned to Ed, Joe, and Stauder.

"Any of you guys got ID's?"

All three shrugged and shook their heads.

"You're fucking New York Guineas, aren't you? How come you Guineas never carry ID's? You three are going to jail."

Ed had to speak up. This was his club; he was the man.

"What are you talking about? For what?"

"Failure to show identification."

"The fuck. This is private property."

Devlin kept at it. "Where do you live?"

Joe spoke now, placating. "Across the street. Maybe our ID's are in my apartment, officer. All three of us were there this afternoon. Maybe we left them there."

"OK. You're coming with us."

"No," Ed said, knowing he had to stand up in front of Sonny, "we're not."

"Yes, you are."

"Fuck you. You don't have warrants."

Devlin turned to another cop. "Another smart Guinea. Cuff 'em."

Ed, Joe, and Stauder were driven to Joe's apartment. There, the three remained belligerent and uncooperative. They were supposed to be New York Guinea bad guys; they kept up the act, ragging Devlin and his deputies, cursing and swaggering.

Joe made a show of looking for the ID's, but came up empty. The cops took them all back to the club where Sonny smoldered. He had been asked for identification and refused to show any. He was informed that he too was going to be arrested.

Ed, Joe, and Stauder were marched into the club.

"Alright, we're all going downtown." Devlin pointed at Sonny. "Him, too. We take all you Guineas in, you'll understand better how we do things down here."

Sonny Black, the Mafia street captain, had his hands cuffed behind his back. Quietly he asked Joe where his identification was. Joe kept his driver's license in the trunk of his car. Sonny told him to get it so someone could stay on the street to bail them out. Stauder went to his car too and pulled his license from his glove compartment.

Joe was released. Stauder was told to stay at the club. The cops took Sonny downtown on the charge of obstructing a police officer by refusing to identify himself.

Shannon had been waiting outside the club. When Joe came out behind Sonny, he and Shannon jumped into Ed's car to follow the Pasco squad car carrying Sonny to the jailhouse. Sonny's bail was set at $10,000. Joe hustled back to the Tahitian Motor Lodge and got $1,000 in cash from Carmine and returned with a bondsman. Sonny was freed within the hour.

Sonny glowed red hot over the raid. He asked Shannon on the ride from the jailhouse to the Tahitian if he knew where Tony Rossi was from in Pittsburgh. He wanted to go after his family. "Yeah, yeah, Sonny," Shannon said, mouthing anything to calm the gangster down, "we'll work it out."

Back at The King's Court, Ed's handcuffs were removed. Though Sonny was now out of sight, Ed knew he had to keep up the tough act all the way for appearances. He could not identify himself without risking the FBI's three-year investment in Coldwater, and quite probably his own life and those of others. Also, Ed was genuinely angry at this latest episode of the harassment that Tony Rossi was subjected to frequently by the local police and Sheriff's Officers.

At the same time, Devlin knew he had to be even tougher than his adversary. He could not blink in the face of a mobster operating an illegal enterprise in his jurisdiction, much less allow him to challenge his authority. The absurd result was two lawmen—one in uniform, the other in deep disguise—trying to face each other down with threats and insults, each trying to out-macho the other, both men striving to keep up appearances.

Ed stomped around the club, making a huge scene. He thundered repeatedly that the cops had no search warrant and had to leave the premises. The cops said, "No, we've got warrants coming and we'll wait here for them."

Ed shouted they couldn't do that. The cops answered, "Shut

up."

Ed replied, "OK, you haven't got an arrest warrant for me, so I'll go." He made several attempts to walk out his own front door but each time the Pasco cops physically restrained him and tossed him into a chair. They put the cuffs back on him. They called him Guinea cocksucker, Dago son of a bitch.

Lunsford finally got the State's Attorney on the phone. The man said one of his assistants had just signed the arrest warrants for Tony Rossi and Richard Stauder and a search warrant had been issued for The King's Court. These warrants were on their way with Devlin to the club.

At three in the morning, Devlin returned with the warrants.

Ed roared from his chair. "Let me see the warrants! And the supporting affidavits!"

Devlin sneered, "Fuck you."

With the search warrant in hand, the cops tore The King's Court apart. They found and seized the two pistols Ed had taped to the back of the furnace. The $10,000 in cash wrapped in Christmas paper was also found and confiscated, as was the chip money and the FBI's money Ed had hidden in a box under Christmas lights. The cops removed a checkbook and cash from Ed's office desk drawer.

Ed insisted he be allowed to accompany the officers around the club while they conducted the search. Devlin refused, telling him to sit in the chair and be quiet. Ed couldn't do that. He raised hell. It didn't take long for Devlin to tire of Ed's bitching. He bound Ed's feet in leg irons. The cops moved him out of the way to a chair at the Round Table and warned him not to move.

At the safe house, Mike Lunsford and Jack Case watched on the video monitor as Ed Robb glared and snarled like a chained bear.

Helpless, Ed glared at the police turning his club upside down. They removed all the gambling equipment, including chips, cards, tables, and Joe's slot machine. They looked in every corner, even tore into the ceilings. They never found any cameras but if they had, Ed was prepared to play dumb. How the fuck do I know how that got there? You didn't let me see what you were doing. How do I know you didn't plant a camera there?

When they were done, Devlin showed Ed an inventory.

"Fuck you." Ed rattled his restraints. "I'm not signing it."

Ed had successfully gotten under the skin of Sergeant Devlin. The officer privately instructed one of his deputies to give Mr. Rossi a ride downtown, and to charge him with the unofficial law violation of "POP," short for Pissing Off Police. This little mention ensured that mobster Tony Rossi would not relish his stay in what Devlin called "the finest accommodations the citizens of Pasco County could afford."

Dressed in a white Panama suit with wide lapels, a brown silk polka-dotted shirt and brilliant shoes, bound in handcuffs and leg irons, Ed shuffled out The King's Court door, under arrest. He was stuffed into the cage of a Pasco squad car and driven to jail. At the lockup, Ed was fingerprinted and photographed. The cops looked in a book and amused themselves with all the things they claimed they could charge him with before morning. Ed refused to sign the fingerprint card or the inventory; he gave them no cooperation. He was tossed into the drunk tank, a cramped cell with three moaning, smelly inebriates.

The drunk tank was a mess. Vomit and urine stained the floor and air. The clang of the cell door awoke Ed's three cellmates, who now found themselves in the can with a real gangster in a white Panama suit. They cozied up to Tony Rossi to tell him they'd heard of him and whisper to him about all the shit they had for sale. Ed decided that if the bust blew his cover and Coldwater, it would not be because he revealed the operation.

He gathered several sheaves of a scattered newspaper off the floor and spread them over a bunk. He folded his coat under his head for a pillow and lay down. A half-hour later, at 4:30 in the morning, the cops called him out of his cell.

"Hey, Rossi! We got to do your fingerprints again."

"Fuck you. You just did them!"

"We got to do them again. On your feet!"

Ed was pushed and bullied with renewed energy. They tried to get him to sign the inventory and the fingerprint card; he refused and was rewarded with more abuse from his captors.

Christ, he wondered: Where are the good guys? The FBI had proved helpless; the real criminal, Sonny Black, was bailed out, leaving him in jail alone with these alcoholics and badge-wearing maniacs. Ed was in misery.

At five in the morning, the cops came for him again for more fingerprints. Ed braced for another round of mistreatment. This time, they let him make a phone call. He called the safe house.

"Sonar, get me the fuck out of here!"

Mike Lunsford told him of his fruitless efforts, that the new supervisor and the Tampa Agent in Charge said Ed Robb had gotten himself into this and he could damn well get himself out of it. There was nothing Lunsford could do for another couple of hours. Ed had to see it through until Sunday morning. Sorry.

Ed returned to the fetid cell, growling under his breath about gutless bureaucrats. The Tampa Office oversaw a multi-million-dollar federal operation; they could have taken five grand out of the office safe to bail out one of their agents and put it back on Monday morning. Lame fuckers, all of them.

Ed stayed in the jail until 11:00 a.m. when Eddie Shannon arrived with the bail money. Lunsford, Kinne, and Case had raised the emergency five grand by borrowing it from the original Coldwater informant, who'd always liked Ed. Lunsford gave the money to Shannon, who arrived at the jail expecting a very upset undercover agent. He wasn't disappointed.

Ed spent all Sunday at the safe house with Kinne and the agents, and later at The King's Court with his crew. Sonny and Carmine were long gone; they'd left for New York just after breakfast. The club was a shambles from the police search.

Over the next few days, Joe did his best on the phone to keep Sonny calm. But the Bonanno captain was riveted on revenge. Two days after the arrests, Sonny called to tell Ed not to talk to Donahue on the phone but to tell the captain in person there was "a big gift in it for him if he could give us the snitch." But who had snitched? No one had lost his shirt and there were no disturbances. If there had been a call, Ed figured it might have come from Jimmy Falzone, rival owner of The Club. Ed couldn't tell Sonny this since just the suspicion of having made the call that embarrassed Sonny in front of Trafficante's people would end Falzone's life. He decided to stick with the story of an anonymous tip.

Sonny told Ed that Benny Husick had arranged for Henry Gonzalez, Trafficante's lawyer, to defend them both against the Pasco charges. Sonny wanted the ten grand back plus the grand in bail money to pay back Carmine. He wanted it soon and he didn't care how Ed got it.

*　*　*

Monday morning, in Washington, FBI Director William Webster was embarrassed that one of his undercover agents had languished in a drunk tank overnight with no assistance from the local Field Office. At the time, no procedures in the FBI covered what happened: an undercover agent arrested and detained in a local jail. Immediately. Webster issued a directive that the Bureau would not allow an undercover agent to be subjected to local and state law arrest any longer than could be prevented. Whenever an agent was arrested, he was to be extricated from the local system as quickly as possible.

Ed's arraignment before a magistrate had been set for later in the week, but the FBI quietly contacted the Pinellas County State's Attorney, and Tony Rossi's arraignment was postponed indefinitely.

The charges against Sonny also were dropped. The State's Attorney was advised of the FBI operation and cooperated fully. More to the point, Sonny Black belonged to the Feds. He shouldn't be wasting his time answering obstruction of justice charges in a county court.

CHAPTER SIXTEEN
Murder

After the raid, Santo Trafficante kept his distance. What if he had been at the club gambling that night? As it was, his three dealers and Benny, his bingo man, had been hustled out the back way with the rest of the customers. That was embarrassing. How could he trust Sonny Black again? Wasn't one of Sonny's crew supposed to have a Pasco police captain in his pocket? What happened? It didn't matter. The Old Man was too canny to come close to The King's Court again, at least not for a while.

Because Sonny had fallen out of favor with Santo, he in turn knocked Tony Rossi, the man he held responsible, down a rung. Though Sonny didn't stay angry and soon relaxed, he never again completely warmed up to Ed. Meanwhile, Joe did a good job keeping the peace and staying tight with Sonny and Lefty. Two weeks after the raid, Ed and Joe flew to New York. Sonny had instructed Joe to take $10,000 out of the shylock money and bring it up. Ed got the cash from Headquarters, where the money was taken out of an emergency fund. Coldwater's Group 1 budget had been stung by the raid, as well.

At Kennedy Airport, they were met by Sonny and Boobie. Ed and Joe each carried half the cash. They handed it over. Sonny was all business, haranguing them again for narcotics connections, especially heroin. He had outlets in New York waiting. He also said he had just bought a machine to make Quaaludes and wanted them to find sources in Tampa for the powder to make the pills.

* * *

Back in Holiday, Tony Rossi was still on the street even though everybody knew he'd been arrested. The King's Court stayed open despite having been tossed pretty hard by the cops. All the gambling equipment had been confiscated. Ed and Shannon shut down the bookmaking operation but kept the numbers going. The local gangsters figured Tony must have paid somebody off to be back in business so soon after a raid.

Even so, the action at the club tailed off. The criminal enterprises that had swirled around Ed and The King's Court for two years hit a noticeable trough. The club had been tainted, touched by policemen's hands. Visits from Sonny, Lefty, and the Bonanno crew, all regulars at the Tahitian Motor Lodge and the club for a year, became rare. Without Sonny's visits, Trafficante had even less reason to be seen in the area. None of the locals knew if the rumors were true, that during the cops' search of the club they'd installed secret cameras and microphones. No one had a line on the snitch who'd ratted on Tony Rossi and set off the raid. Because no one knew anything, no one risked coming around.

Bureau Headquarters decided to close Coldwater. All the cases against the principal players, with the exception of Trafficante, were made. The cases were not getting stronger, while the danger to the agents remained high. In Ed's case, the risk had skyrocketed. Coldwater would be given six more months to settle all accounts, get the agents out, and sweep up the perpetrators.

All the balls that Ed had long kept in the air—the numbers, gambling, sports book, shylocking, bingo, narcotics, opening a new club, expanding The King's Court—he told Sonny on the phone, were still under way. In fact, he let them slip. With Coldwater winding down, Ed focused on reaching the end of the road. But first, the trail had to lead once more through Charleston and Operation Fast Hit.

*   *   *

Nick Tsachilis did what his friend Tony Rossi asked and introduced Tony's partner, Charley Chains Sacco, around town. Charley was Tony's local guy; he would be in charge of the club Tony was looking at on Goose Creek and would handle all the mob's gambling and other criminal enterprises in the area. Charley needed connections. Tsachilis wanted to stay tight with Tony, so he took the apprentice under his wing.

Charley, knowing that Ed needed a heroin supplier for Sonny Black, told Tsachilis he wanted to make some narcotics connections in Charleston. Tsachilis introduced Charley to Gus Flamos, a junk man who claimed to have big narcotics hooks. Flamos claimed he could get his hands on all the heroin Charley could sell. Charley told Flamos that his boss Tony Rossi had outlets and connections in New York. Flamos took the bait, and Charley Chains set up a meeting for him with Tony Rossi and Tony's New York guy, Donnie Brasco.

Whenever Ed visited Charleston, Charley rented him a condo at the Isle of Palms Beach and Racquet Club. Gus Flamos arrived at the club in the afternoon and walked across the sand in street clothes. Rossi and Brasco lay sunning on towels. Flamos introduced himself. Ed told him to sit down and talk. It was safe, Ed assured him; they were out on the beach. The Nagra recorder was buried in the sand under Ed's towel.

Flamos said he was from Harlem. He'd been around, been hooked up before, and still had some pretty high-powered connections. But because he was Greek, he couldn't rise very far in the Italian Mafia, no matter how good an earner he was.

"What can you get for us?" Ed asked.

"Anything."

Joe was direct. "Heroin."

"I got a contact in Katmandu."

Joe acted skeptical, as if Katmandu were not a real place but just a pretty name for a place. "Do I look like a fucking goofball or what? Katmandu?"

Flamos said he could buy good-quality heroin at $50,000 a kilo, bring it in through Canada, and turn it into $300,000 on the street. He wanted Ed to finance the deal plus give him five grand in traveling money to get to Katmandu. Ed agreed but wanted collateral before he'd give Flamos a cent.

"What have you got?" Ed asked the dealer.

Flamos recounted his assets: a stash of marijuana, hash, and hash oil he valued at $150,000.

"OK, I'll take it. You put it all up, I'll give you the fifty grand. And if you don't come back, I got your shit."

Flamos agreed to come back in a week with the drugs to be used as collateral. Ed gave him the address of a warehouse to put the goods in. Flamos was to call when he'd stashed them. Ed would have the drugs tested, then give Flamos the money. During the week, Charley rented a U-Stor-It in Charleston. When Flamos called, Ed told him to meet Charley Chains and Eddie Shannon at a Howard Johnson's for the hand-off.

Flamos arrived at the restaurant driving a new Cadillac. Half the drugs were packed in the trunk. The other half were in a van driven by Flamos's son. Eddie Shannon took the car, the van, and the kid to the warehouse while Charley drove Flamos to Ed's Isle of Palms condo. Ed greeted Flamos and they sat down to wait for Eddie Shannon's call.

The phone rang. Ed answered, nodded, and hung up.

"Looks like the shit is OK," he said, reaching into his coat for an envelope. Flamos stood to accept it, eager to leave for Katmandu. Then Ed sprung his plan on the junk man. Though they still wanted badly to put some heroin in Sonny Black's hands, they were not going to finance a trip to Asia to get it.

Flamos counted the cash, then counted it again.

"The fuck's going on here? This is only five grand!"

"That's what you get," Ed said. "You don't want it, give it back and you're out everything because the shit stays with us."

Flamos stomped and blustered. He'd been burned.

"Oh, man, this ain't gonna go down with my people." This was standard bad-guy procedure, to threaten retaliation from one's "people." Protection was, after all, the chief reason for having "people."

Ed stood firm. He had just gotten $150,000 worth of narcotics off the street at a cost to the Bureau of five grand.

"What are you gonna do?" Ed said. "Go ahead, go to your people in Harlem, go see whoever the fuck you gotta see. They're gonna contact Lefty on Mulberry Street. Lefty's gonna say we gave you the fifty grand and you must've glommed the other forty-five. Who they gonna believe?"

Ed said. "Look, Gus, what are you gonna do? Go to the cops? Call my people? You know who the fuck you're dealing with? I got your cars, I got your shit, and right now I got your kid. Take the money and go to Katmandu, you fuck."

Tony Rossi was a bad guy, bad beyond Gus Flamos's league. Flamos stomped out, the money burning like embers in his hand.

* * *

Dr. Vincent A. Sundry was a newcomer to The King's Court. He was brought to the club the night of March 3 by Nick, a regular and a local Greek who claimed to have been at one time the manager of The Vogues, a popular singing group from the 1950s. Nick introduced Dr. Sundry to Tony Rossi.

Sundry was an osteopath with offices in Tarpon Springs. From the opening handshake, he steered his conversation with Ed toward the Mafia and criminal doings. Ed took him back into the office where Sundry made it clear in front of Mike Lunsford's cameras that he wanted to do a drug deal.

Sundry said he had dealt in narcotics before; he'd even been busted once. Currently, he claimed access to sixteen kilos of heroin stashed in Wichita that were worth $62,000 per kilo. He said the drugs were in the hands of an FBI agent who brought down a narcotics operation in Kansas. The confiscated heroin had turned up missing from the Bureau office in Wichita and the agent had access to it for the right price. Sundry said he'd just returned from Kansas; if he'd known of Ed's interest in advance, he would have brought a sample.

Ed told the doctor he had the connections in New York to move sixteen kilos of heroin, and more. He wanted a sample. Sundry set March 11 as the date for delivery, then left the club. Ed gave the license number from the doctor's car to Kinne, who traced it. Years before, Sundry had indeed been involved in a drug bust in Kansas. He'd beaten the rap by striking a deal with the Drug Enforcement Agency to turn informant. The FBI knew that Sundry's story of a million dollars in heroin missing from evidence in Wichita was a fabrication.

Who was Dr. Vincent Sundry? He had come on strong in Ed's office with what later turned out to be a fairy tale. Why? Ed and Shannon, agents with a quarter century of street experience between them, tried to put the pieces together only to find several different puzzles. They decided to play it out with Sundry but with caution, to see where he was taking them.

On the delivery date, Joe and Lefty sat in a room at the Deauville Hotel in Miami, waiting for Ed to notify them that he had arrived with the heroin sample. Lefty always figured ways to mooch a "vay-kaysh" down in Florida at Ed's expense. There was no reason for Lefty to be in Miami; Ed, Joe, or Shannon could have muled the sample to New York or Lefty could have waited for it in Tampa. But Lefty was comfortable in Miami, hanging out with Joe. He had a guy standing by to test the heroin; meanwhile, Sonny waited in New York with a buyer in his pocket.

Sundry did not show, leaving Joe and Lefty in their hotel room for three days to pace and call Ed every few hours. Embarrassed, Lefty flew back to New York to face an impatient Sonny Black. Joe went home.

Ed pursued Sundry for weeks. He called and went by the doctor's offices in Tarpon Springs, leaving messages that "Tony Rossi wants to see him." He told Sundry's Greek connections the same thing, until the doctor finally called on April 15.

"You got twenty-four hours to bring me a fucking sample of heroin, you son of a bitch. My people in New York are telling me already to throw you a fucking beating."

That night, Sundry appeared at The King's Court. He appeared ashen and jittery, not at all the hardened, experienced junk man he claimed to be. He told Ed he'd brought the sample; it was outside the club's front door in the shrubs. Ed shook his head. Why did he do that? Sundry had a drink at the bar while Eddie Shannon went outside to fetch the sample. Shannon felt around in the bushes in the pitch dark and found the packet. When Ed saw the sample, he knew something was wrong. It was too big, perhaps three ounces, worth over $60,000 if it had been pure horse. A typical sample of heroin was no larger than a toenail.

The next day, Ed took the sample to the safe house for testing at the Sheriff's lab. It came back 100 percent pure milk sugar. Ed called Sundry and drilled him a new ear. The doctor swore he'd been duped himself; he knew nothing about milk sugar. He had just accepted the sample from his source and delivered it, that's all. He sounded panicked, deathly afraid. Had Ed, Joe, and Shannon been real mobsters, Sundry would've been correct to be so scared. His life could have been over. Ed let him off with a warning:

"Next time you play around with somebody, don't play around with the big boys."

Sundry stayed away from the club after that. But the mystery about him lingered. Why had he put himself in such jeopardy? Why such a large sample, why fake shit? Why drop it in the shrubs?

Ed, Joe, and Shannon mulled it over. The answer came to Ed. Sundry must have been setting them up for a fall. The doctor had been busted before; perhaps some other state or federal agency, maybe the DEA, was turning the screws on him to trap Ed and The King's Court. Or the doctor might have been one of the growing trend of freelance snitches, hoping to manufacture some evidence he could peddle. Maybe even another crew, jealous of Ed's turf, lurked behind Sundry. The whole deal was sloppy, reeking of inexperience. Sundry made a lousy undercover agent. He was probably a dreadful snitch too, explaining why he still had work to do for whoever was running him.

Ed never found out who or what stood behind Sundry's plan but he wasn't surprised at the attempt. The King's Court bore a reputation as an axis for criminal activity in Florida. Busting Tony Rossi and his crew would have been a feather in the cap of any law enforcement agency. If criminals were on the other end of the doctor's leash, bringing down The King's Court would have opened up a lot of avenues for new blood. And if Dr. Sundry was just a freelancer, testing his hand "with the big boys," he'd get himself whacked if he ever tried it again with real mobsters.

* * *

In Florida, Coldwater drew to a close. At the same time, in New York City, a war began between two factions of the Bonanno family over who would control the Italian and Sicilian illegal immigrants, known as "zips," in and around New York City. The zips had connections for importing heroin, which flowed from the Middle East through Italy, then into the United States. The issue was simple: Whoever controlled the zips controlled the city's heroin. The immigrants wanted power of their own inside the Bonanno family, and would align themselves with anyone who would give it to them. To award power, you must first have it. So the war was on.

On one side of the conflict was jailed family boss Rusty Rastelli and the captains loyal to him—Joe Massino, Sonny Black, and a couple of acting captains including Lefty—along with consiglieri Steve Cannone. Opposing Rastelli's cadre were captains Caesar Bonventre, Phillip "Philly Lucky" Giaccone, Dominick "Big Trin" Trinchera, and Alphonse "Sonny Red" Indelicato, with Indelicato's son Anthony Bruno. For Rastelli, Sonny Black was the key to the struggle. The other captains respected and feared his growing strength, especially in light of his recent pact with Trafficante in Florida. From his cell in

Lewisburg, Rusty counted on Sonny to take the lead in his fight to retain family power, and Sonny intended to replace Cannone as consiglieri after Rastelli's release later that year.

Lefty called Joe on April 13. Lefty would be out of touch for a while, maybe a few weeks. He asked Joe to send his wife Louise $1,000 for bills in his absence. "I'm going to the mattress." This meant Lefty had a job to do, after which he was going to hole up somewhere. Joe was to stay available in case Lefty and others needed to contact him to hide out at The King's Court.

Joe called New York agent Jerry Loar and reported his conversation. A street team followed Lefty for three days, but nothing happened and the surveillance was dropped. Joe didn't hear from Lefty for a week. When Lefty called, he sounded elated. He said he was coming to Miami and told Joe to make the arrangements for his trip.

"We're going to be moving into Miami now in a big way," Lefty said. "I'm gonna introduce you and Tony to every fucking wise guy in town." Joe didn't ask questions. A connected guy is not curious. Lefty's upbeat mood told him something had turned out right for Sonny Black.

On April 23, Ed and Joe picked Lefty up in Miami and drove to the Deauville Hotel. At the piano bar, Lefty confided in them. "The case is closed. They lost. Nationwide. That's why it took me five fucking days to go out and do what I had to do." He, Sonny, Nicky Santora, and Joey Massino had done a "big job in New York for the Commission," Lefty said.

The Mafia Commission consisted of the head of each of the five families, and was the coordinating and ruling body for organized crime in New York. All hits on bosses, captains, or soldiers had to be approved by the Commission. In return for doing the "job," the Commission agreed that Rusty Rastelli would remain as Bonanno boss. Under Rusty, Sonny's power would soar.

Ed and Joe checked with their connections in and outside the FBI. No bodies turned up. What had the "job" been? Had it been done already, or was Lefty referring to a hit still in the planning stage?

Two weeks later, on May 6, the answer came. Information from two informants in New York led the FBI to believe there had been a major hit. Philly Lucky Giaccone, Big Trin Trinchera, and Sonny Red Indelicato, three of the renegade Bonanno captains, had reportedly been summoned by Sonny Black to a "peace meeting" at a catering shop in Brooklyn. There, the three were shotgunned. The fourth rival capo to oppose Rastelli's power, Caesar Bonventre, resided in the Nassau County jail on a weapons charge. Bonventre saw the light after the rest of the opposition was blown to bits, and was only too glad to come over to Rastelli's and Sonny's side. Indelicato's son, Anthony Bruno, a known coke freak, had also been beckoned to the meeting, but he missed it.

In subsequent conversations, Lefty revealed that the triggermen for the hit had been Lefty, Jimmy Legs Episcopia, Nicky Santora, and Bobby Capazzio. Boobie Cerasani and Joey Massino helped get rid of the bodies. Lefty told Joe he admired Boobie's strength, how Boobie had handled Big Trin Trinchera's fat, bloodied corpse all by himself. The bodies were cut up and put in plastic garbage bags for burial in remote parts of the city. The first body found was that of Sonny Red Indelicato. He was discovered two weeks after the hits in Queens. An article in the New York Post, under the headline MOB SNUFFS OUT AMBITIOUS BOSS, described two kids playing in a vacant lot who saw a cowboy boot sticking out of the ground. The body had been shot in the left side of the face, chest, and lower back. It was wrapped in a bed sheet and tied with clothesline. Sonny Black was furious at Joey Massino for the sloppy job of Indelicato's disposal, burying him whole in a shallow grave instead of deep and in scattered pieces.

* * *

Sonny Red's son, Anthony Bruno, was still on the street.

Sonny Black wanted Ed and Joe to search for him in Miami. If they found Bruno there, Sonny gave them the contract to whack him.

"Kill him, and leave his body in the street," he said.

In Miami, Ed and Joe looked for Bruno at an address given to Sonny by a "reliable source" who turned out to be Bruno's uncle, who also had a Bonanno contract on his head. Sonny had given him a pass in return for his help in whacking his nephew.

"You gotta give a little to get a little," Sonny said.

Ed and Joe made it appear they were looking for Bruno. They strutted around the bars and nightspots, making their presence known. If they had found him, they would have had him arrested to get him off the street and told Sonny the hit had taken place. But if Bruno knew he was going to be hit, if he'd gotten word that Tony Rossi and Donnie Brasco had the contract, he might take the initiative and try to hit them first. The scoop on Bruno was that he was a good guy until the coke turned him into a wild man. Then you had to be careful around him.

With Bruno's drug habit, they figured he couldn't stay underground for too long. For a week, Ed and Joe followed leads and tips. While they looked for Bruno in Miami, the mob searched for him elsewhere, as did the FBI, hoping to nab him for his own protection. Finally, Sonny called and said he didn't think Bruno was in Miami. He was probably back in New York. Go on home.

* * *

The war inside the Bonannos raised the danger to Ed and Joe astronomically. Sonny clearly believed he could rely on Ed and Joe enough to send them on a murder contract. This put the two agents at the heart of the battle, exposing them to preemptive strikes or retribution from the opposition. At the moment, Sonny was at the head of the Bonannos, but the pendulum could swing and there could be another flurry of hits from the other side. Joe could easily be hanging out with Sonny or Lefty in Brooklyn when the next round of shotguns blazed. Or Ed and Shannon could be wiped out at The King's Court, gutting Sonny's Florida power base.

A meeting was set up in late May at the Crystal City Marriott outside Washington, D.C., to discuss the plans for extricating the agents and shutting down Coldwater. Ed, Shannon, and Joe met with case agents and supervisors from Coldwater, as well as Headquarters officials and representatives from Fast Hit in Charleston, Operation Timber in Milwaukee, and several smaller undercover operations whose conclusions, for one reason or another, were tied to Coldwater's. A date was set: Everything would close up on July 26.

Weeks after the initial meeting, the key street and surveillance agents and supervisors met in New Jersey to resolve the final details of how to close Coldwater. They also decided to seek a Title III wiretap on Sonny Black's phone in Brooklyn and have it in place before revealing that Tony Rossi and Donnie Brasco were FBI undercover agents. This was called "tickling the wires." Sonny would surely emit a burst of phone calls once he found out that Tony and Donnie were "the G." The FBI would be listening.

Kinne led a discussion on how to approach Sonny Black. As soon as word hit the streets, Sonny, Lefty, Tony Mirra, and all the Bonannos who'd vouched for one or both of the agents with the family would be in dire peril. Kinne wanted to get Sonny to roll over, to turn informant. Lefty Ruggiero was never seriously considered for recruitment; he was unreliable, too unsavory and violent a character for any relationship with the FBI. Sonny was the one they would go for. He'd be the first to be told, privately, of the undercover operation. He would be offered a deal, not in words or writing but implicitly. The mob knows the Bureau wants informants, makes deals, and in return provides leniency and protection. If Sonny took a deal, he would be brought in off the street and protected in return for his testimony. The FBI would then be in possession of one of the most reliable, highly placed, and damaging witnesses against the American Mafia in history. If Sonny Black refused, he was a dead man.

Three agents were assigned to visit Sonny in Brooklyn—Jim Kinne and New York Agents Jerry Loar and Doug Fencl. Sonny would recognize Fencl, an agent who stopped by the Motion Lounge on occasion just to let the mob know the government was watching, and to give them a name and a friendly face in case any of them changed their minds and wanted to talk.

As proof of the sting, Kinne would have a photograph of Tony Rossi and Donnie Brasco standing arm in arm with the three FBI agents, taken at the New Jersey meeting on the Coldwater closure. The picture would identify Tony and Donnie as federal agents instead of mere stoolies in hopes that their official status would protect them from murderous retaliation. Kinne argued that Joe Pistone should be with them when they confronted Sonny, that such a shock might give them their best chance to persuade him to cooperate. But Joe didn't want to insult Sonny, and Kinne didn't insist.

*　*　*

During the final six weeks of the operation, Sonny showed signs of warming again to Ed and The King's Court. On a visit to Florida in the first week of July, Sonny gave Joe $4,000 in shylock money. He wanted $300 per month in return for the loan. In The King's Court office, Sonny rhapsodized anew about his plans for expanding the club and the costs involved. Ed admitted that his finances had been hurt badly by the bust; his operation had been set back six months. Sonny said not to worry. If everything goes right, there would be lots of money.

"That raid," Sonny said, "has made me a lot smarter and wiser." Sonny brought up the old pipe dream of running bingo games for Trafficante. "We need to buy our own land and build our own bingo hall. Five acres is what we need."

Ed agreed. "No one," he said, "is going to rent to us."

Sonny promised Ed and Joe he'd send them $5,000 a month to put on the street. By August, he wanted to have $100,000 shy-

locked out in Florida. Sonny planned to give $2,000 to The Old Man as a peace offering once the $10,000 taken during the raid was returned by the Pasco Sheriff's Office.

Two weeks later, on July 24, two days before the curtain would come down on Coldwater, Sonny was back in Florida with triggerman Nicky Santora. Sonny had Ed set up a meeting with Trafficante and Husick for the next afternoon in Holiday. Sonny's spirits were soaring. He'd consolidated his power in New York, and was the undisputed captain of captains in the Bonanno family. Lefty, of course, stewed about unfair treatment after all he'd done for Sonny, but Lefty couldn't draw a breath without bitching. Rusty Rastelli's release from jail would be in another few weeks, and Sonny wanted The King's Court operation humming. He needed to get back in Trafficante's good graces after the raid six months earlier. And he wanted to mend bridges with his chief earner in Florida, Tony Rossi.

Ed and Joe knew this was the last time they would see Sonny Black on the street, perhaps the last time alive. Joe had mixed feelings; he'd grown close to Sonny over the period of nearly six years, and had developed a "kinship" with the mob capo.

Ed harbored no sorrow or regret. Ed Robb, just like Sonny Black, had made his choices.

Ed and Joe decided to pump Sonny and Nicky Santora for all the information they could squeeze out about the New York murders, the shifts in Bonanno alignments and power, other crews, and mob families. It didn't matter now if they showed too much curiosity or stepped over their bounds as merely connected guys; the end of the game was at hand.

The evening started at Pappas'. Ed and Joe were merry, exhorting Sonny and Nicky to eat, drink, and loosen their tongues. From Pappas', the party moved to a hotel in Clearwater, then made a long, slow landing at The King's Court. By six in the morning, Sonny and Nicky were crashed in their rooms at the Tahitian. All they had done was party; no one talked business.

The next afternoon, Trafficante and Husick arrived at the

Tahitian. They stayed in Sonny's wired room for no more than a minute before heading for the coffee shop where they chatted amicably for forty minutes. After The Old Man and Husick left in Trafficante's car, Sonny called Ed and Joe into the diner.

He was thrilled with the meeting. He'd given Trafficante $2,000 and Husick $1,000 to split with the Miami guys who'd worked the Las Vegas Night. Trafficante had been very understanding. He'd called the bust "just one of those things." Everything was put back on track. Sonny and his crew were going to be sun kings in Florida again. Trafficante had spread before them a smorgasbord of crooked enterprises: gambling, sports book, the dog track, bingo, narcotics, numbers, shylocking, anything they wanted, just like before.

Ed and Joe tried to keep Sonny talking. Until dawn broke Sunday morning, Ed, Joe, Shannon, Sonny, and Nicky caroused with the bartenders and barmaids and regular customers of the club. But no matter how the agents turned the conversation, Sonny wouldn't talk business.

* * *

Late Sunday morning, after Sonny had taken one of the barmaids to his room and Joe had gone for breakfast with Nicky, Ed went into the lounge. He told all The King's Court employees to take two weeks off. The club was closed for remodeling. He gave them each two weeks' pay.

He picked up Sonny and Nicky and drove them, hung over and sleepy, to the airport. This was critical: If Sonny had spent another night in Holiday, as he'd mumbled he might do while in his cups the night before, the plan for closing Coldwater and the other operations would blow up in their faces. Besides, Ed had closed the club without telling Sonny. This would have looked suspicious, so Sonny simply had to leave on time.

* * *

At the Tampa airport, there were no big goodbyes, no emotion. Ed was just glad to see them go. Talk to you tomorrow. See you. Get busy, you two. OK, Sonny. Have a good flight.

That afternoon, The King's Court was shut up and locked. Agent Bill "Filefish" Garner took charge of the club. A team of agents emptied it out. Everything that could be moved was put in storage, including cartons of booze belonging to the members. The tables, chairs, glasses, and medieval decorations were sent to another undercover sting in Miami.

Ed went to his apartment and cleaned out his personal belongings. Under fictitious names, Shannon and Joe flew to Milwaukee to testify before the grand jury in the Frank Balistrieri investigation. Ed flew to Washington for a debriefing, then home.

CHAPTER SEVENTEEN
Curtains

When Sonny Black returned to Brooklyn from his last trip to Florida, Jim Kinne was watching. He sat on Sonny for two days, tailing him around the neighborhood, hoping to catch him alone where they could talk. The chance never came. Finally, at seven in the morning on Tuesday, July 28, Kinne, Fencl, and Loar knocked on the door of Sonny's apartment.

Sonny answered the door in his briefs. The agents identified themselves and Sonny let them in. He dressed while the G-men talked. When they reached the bad news about Tony and Donnie being federal undercover agents and showed him the photograph proving it, Sonny was putting on his socks. Kinne saw his hands jerk to a halt though his voice and face betrayed nothing.

Kinne left Sonny a card with a New York phone number, a direct line into the FBI Offices. All Sonny had to do was call, any time of day or night. An agent would bring him in.

"You know I can't do that," Sonny said.

Just as they had anticipated, Sonny flew into action after the agents left his apartment. He met immediately with his trusted soldiers at the Motion Lounge, where the installed microphones recorded him saying: "I can't believe Tony and Donnie are FBI agents." But he gave orders to Lefty, Boobie, and Nicky to find Tony Rossi and Donnie Brasco and hit them hard. The crew called everyone remotely connected to The King's Court and scoured the familiar places in Florida: Holiday, Tarpon Springs, St. Petersburg, Tampa. Lefty flew to Miami where he and Steve Marucca found a cold trail. Sonny called Trafficante, then alerted

Rusty Rastelli in prison. Then he disappeared.

The Commission met in emergency session. Two nationwide contracts were put out, a $500,000 bounty each on Tony Rossi and Donnie Brasco. The contracts were open; anyone could make the hits and claim the reward.

The New York Office acted quickly to quash the mob initiative to murder two of its undercover agents. Delegations of three agents were sent to each of the mob bosses, including Trafficante, and told them that the FBI was aware of the contracts, leaving the clear implication that the FBI was watching and would know where and when a hit was planned. They told the mob bosses that if either Rossi or Brasco were harmed, the U.S. government would declare war and bring to bear its full resources and every legal means to destroy their families and operations. It was implicit in the message that the pursuit of justice would be conducted with such vigor that there could be accidents resulting in collateral damage.

Furthermore, the bosses were told, the FBI beat you. These weren't snitches and they weren't your boys, never were. They were ours, just doing their job. Lay off or else. Rusty Rastelli received this message while still in jail, and went into a rage, screaming for revenge, but later apologized and conceded that the FBI had indeed just been doing its job.

Informants told the Bureau of a sitdown the Commission held on August 14 in New Jersey, called by the bosses to assess damage from the revelations. Sonny was called in. Before heading over the Hudson, Sonny left his jewelry and apartment keys with the bartender at the Motion Lounge. He asked the man to make sure that Judy Brown, his girlfriend, got them. Sonny knew he wasn't coming back.

On a Sunday morning two weeks later, agents picked up Lefty Ruggiero outside his Brooklyn apartment building. Word of a contract on his head had spread all over town, and he must have known. Typically defiant, Lefty strolled around Mulberry Street as if he owned it. Anthony Mirra, who had originally introduced Joe Pistone into the New York underworld six years earlier, was shot four times in the head in March of 1982. His body was found in a car in a parking lot beside the building where Bonanno consiglieri Steve Cannone lived. Mirra had $6,700 on him.

Joey Massino disappeared soon afterward, presumed murdered.

* * *

The first sting to bring its targets before justice was Operation Fast Hit in Charleston. On September 3, 1981, former Berkeley County Sheriff Jimmy Rogers and his Goose Creek go-between Ray Scarboro were indicted on federal racketeering and conspiracy charges. The evidence against both included more than 50 wiretap recordings and 100-plus Nagra tapes, resulting in more than 9,000 incriminating transcript pages.

On January 15, 1982, U.S. District Judge Falcon B. Hawkins accepted a plea bargain recommendation, dropped the racketeering charges against defendants Rogers and Scarboro, and sentenced them only on the conspiracy counts. Rogers received a sentence of fifteen years out of a possible twenty. Judge Hawkins displayed slightly more sympathy for Scarboro, whose defense attorney stated that his client had wanted only to sell the Goose Creek property and "go live with his seventy-seven-year-old mother in Georgia." Scarboro's lawyers claimed that their client had been sought out by undercover agents posing as "high rollers who took him to Florida where they wined and dined him and led him to believe they only wanted to open a small gambling casino for a select few." The Judge, unconvinced, replied that Scarboro would have "allowed organized crime figures from another state to operate in Berkeley County. Scarboro did procure money from them and passed it to the Sheriff." Scarboro was given seven years.

No charges were brought against Nick Tsachilis. His Charleston champagne room for sailors did not fall under federal jurisdiction.

*   *   *

Another tug-of-war got under way between U.S. Attorney Offices. The murders of Bonanno captains Indelicato, Trinchera, and Giaccone in New York City brought the Southern District (Manhattan) and the Eastern District (Brooklyn) of New York into the prosecution sweepstakes late in the game. For two years, the cases arising out of Coldwater had been the sole prerogative of the Middle District of Florida, but with the discovery of Indelicato's body in Manhattan, murder became the lead case and the widespread racketeering charges stemming from The King's Court were moved to second chair.

The Southern District's claim of jurisdiction was based on Joe's testimony of statements made to him by the defendants and the location of Indelicato's corpse, all indicating the murders took place in Manhattan. The Eastern District U.S. Attorneys held that most of the conspiracy elements originated in Brooklyn, in the Motion Lounge, The Italian-American War Veterans Club, and the defendants' dwellings. The Manhattan federal attorneys won. The trials opened to New York media fanfare in late July 1982, exactly one year after the FBI closed the doors of The King's Court.

*   *   *

The New York federal court case was U.S. v. Dominick Napolitano et al. Accused of various racketeering charges, including the murders of the three rival Bonanno captains, were Sonny Black in absentia, Benjamin "Lefty" Ruggiero, and Nicky Santora. John "Boobie" Cerasani was charged with truck theft, armed robbery, and the attempted robbery of Princess Ashraf Pahlevi's apartment.

Before the trials began, U.S. District Court Judge Robert Sweet denied a government request to keep the two central undercover agents' true names a secret during the hearings. An FBI affidavit claimed that the mob had threatened both men's lives; Lefty had told an informant in prison the year before that he was going to find and kill Rossi and Brasco if it was the last thing he did. Nonetheless, Judge Sweet insisted that both Tony and Donnie face the accused as agents Ed Robb and Joe Pistone. On August 2, Joe took the stand for the first time, with Lefty, Nicky, Boobie, and the rest staring bullets at him. He testified for two weeks, under direct questioning from Assistant U.S. Attorney Barbara Sue Jones. While Joe sat in the witness chair in Manhattan, heavy rains washed ashore a laden body bag in a swollen Staten Island creek. The badly decomposed corpse inside had been shot in the head. The hands had been cut off in the gruesome trademark of Mafia revenge taken on one who had violated mob security. The mutilated body wasn't identified until November 10 when dental records and a panther tattoo on the shoulder revealed it to be Dominick "Sonny Black" Napolitano.

Ed testified in New York for two days, questioned by then Assistant U.S. Attorney Louis Freeh. Ed detailed his knowledge of the defendants as a Mafia clan in order to help establish the racketeering conspiracy charges against them.

During the five weeks of hearings, a series of articles in the local papers reported the killings of up to thirty known under-world figures. Informants indicated that these hits were the work of Mafia "death squads" authorized by the heads of the five crime families. The Commission had allegedly selected twenty-five trusted members—five per family—to conduct a purge of suspected informers, malcontents, weaklings, and unreliable characters from their ranks. The bosses were described in the articles as "vulnerable and insecure now" as a result of the FBI's demonstration of its ability to penetrate to their core. Also, some big organized crime players, including Jimmy "The Weasel" Fratianno, a former mob boss and executioner, had been key federal witnesses in Mafia cases. The aura of invulnerability and impenetrability that had surrounded La Cosa Nostra for decades now flickered about them like cheap incandescent lamplight. Internal security in gangland lay in chaos, resulting in a spasm of bloody house-cleaning.

The five New York crime families later met and banned the Bonannos from the Commission for a decade. The Bonannos were punished for their vulnerability to government infiltration and their involvement in narcotics. Suddenly finding themselves the weakest of the New York families, the Bonannos tried to rejuvenate themselves by opening up the books and recruiting immigrant Sicilians. The Sicilians were considered more tradition-bound and less likely to become turncoats than their American counterparts.

* * *

At the conclusion of the New York trial, Sonny Black (in absentia,) Lefty Ruggiero, and Nicky Santora were sentenced to fifteen years in federal prison on racketeering charges, including murder. Boobie Cerasani was acquitted on all charges. Lefty and Boobie still had to face racketeering and conspiracy charges in Florida.

* * *

In early March of 1983, Ed rented a safe house condo in Indian Rocks Beach where he and the other Coldwater agents, under fictitious names, could prepare their testimonies for the Florida trials in safety and privacy. Five miles away in Clearwater, another safe house was set up with audio and video equipment. There, the agents and federal attorneys held strategy sessions, reviewed some 500 audiotapes plus 97 videotapes and compared them with transcripts. They looked at thousands of photographs and catalogued and classified innumerable bits of evidence and personal recollection.

During the grand jury hearings, the FBI chased down witnesses to serve them with subpoenas. The witness stand in the grand jury room in Tampa was where most of them learned that Tony Rossi was an FBI undercover agent and The King's Court had been a government sting.

Jim Kinne pursued Jimmy Acquafredda to serve his subpoena. Acquafredda ducked him for a week. Finally, Kinne caught up with two of the mobster's kids driving a garbage truck. He told them their father would be wise to contact the FBI soon or answer additional charges. The kids passed the message on, and Jimmy called Kinne's office.

Joe Pete Pullicino got furious at Kinne when he was handed the subpoena. He tried to pump Kinne for information about the case against him. The Shark merely advised Pullicino to cooperate for his own good. Similar scenes were played out with the eleven members of the garbage association. In each instance, Kinne tried to get them to roll over and testify, to see if one would rat out another or give up names unknown to the FBI. Not one of the garbage guys made a deal.

Joseph Donahue accepted his subpoena quietly at home. On the stand before the grand jury, Donahue was asked if he knew a Mr. Anthony Rossi. He replied that he did. Had the captain ever accepted money from Mr. Rossi? No, he had not. Outside the hearing room, Kinne circled, waiting for Donahue to finish his testimony. When the cop appeared, Kinne drew him across the street to the FBI Office where they showed him videotapes of him taking money from Ed.

Donahue confessed. Did he want to cooperate? Donahue said he'd have to think about it. If Kinne could get Donahue to testify for the government, who else might the captain implicate? If Pasco Sheriff John Short was corrupt, as many in the FBI suspected, Joe Donahue might give him up to save his own skin. Kinne targeted Donahue.

The following week, while the grand jury continued to deliberate, Kinne devised a good-cop, bad-cop tactic to use on the captain. Kinne and Jack Case set up a meeting with Donahue in the parking lot of a pancake house. Donahue sat next to Kinne in the front seat of the government car. Kinne chewed on him with an Irish frenzy. Donahue tried to speak.

"Keep your fucking mouth shut!" Kinne bellowed. "I don't

want to hear your fucking voice! If you got anything to say, you call Jack Case. If you want to save your ass at all, because you're gonna be indicted and you're gonna go to jail for the rest of your miserable life, you call him, you piece of shit!"

All Donahue uttered was, "Yes sir."

"Now," Kinne turned away in disgust, "get out."

Donahue opened the car door and slid out. When he stood, Kinne saw the damp darkness on the back of the cop's pants. The car seat was soaked.

* * *

Joseph Donahue faced a maximum forty-year term in a federal penitentiary on corruption charges. Following his arraignment on April 1, Donahue's lawyer contacted prosecutors and began negotiations for him to testify against others in the criminal proceedings. Donahue's interview with federal prosecutors was scheduled for April 19.

On the morning of April 19, an article appeared in the St. Petersburg Times, written by investigative reporter Lucy Morgan. Morgan had checked up on Donahue's exemplary background in New York and discovered most of it to be falsified. Donahue's resume on file with the Pasco County Sheriff's Office claimed that he'd attended St. John's College and served in the U.S. Navy in the 1940s. Neither institution had any record of Joe Donahue. His Pasco job application neglected to mention two previous divorces. The most important item in his personnel file was his assertion that he'd been an officer with the New York City police department for twenty years. Despite the detailed stories he told of big city police work as a New York "flatfoot," despite even the prized paperweight—sitting for years on Donahue's desk—made from a gold shield given only to those who achieve the rank of detective, reporter Morgan discovered that Donahue had spent the years before he came to Florida in 1957 as a plumber in Queens. In Pasco County, his credentials had never been checked.

At 10:30 on the same day, his father-in-law and neighbor, Leslie Stocking, brought the mail inside Donahue's house. Stocking found Donahue's body, face up on the bathroom floor. Beside the body lay a .38 Smith & Wesson later determined to be the death weapon. The revolver's barrel bore a small silver plaque, reading "Chief of Police." The pistol was not of police issue.

No suicide note was found. That morning's St. Petersburg Times, with Lucy Morgan's exposé published large on page 1B, was folded carefully on the bed. A bath towel was arranged neatly on the tile floor beneath the body, leaving the impression that Joe Donahue, in his final moments, had figured he'd caused everyone enough trouble and didn't want to cause more. Despite the appearance of suicide, Sheriff John Short declared immediately that his former captain's death was to be investigated as a homicide. After all, Donahue had recently agreed to become a government witness against several powerful members of New York crime families, perhaps even against Santo Trafficante.

Local people were not persuaded that Donahue had taken his own life, even though he had ample worries to depress his outlook. Donahue faced certain conviction and it was well known that ex-cops and government stoolies fared poorly in prison. Nonetheless, conspiracy theories abounded: Speculation ran rampant as to whom Donahue might have sullied if he'd lived to testify.

The St. Petersburg Times ran the following quotes:

Donahue's third wife, Nita Keebler, from whom he'd been divorced since 1971, doubted his suicide. "I never would have thought he could have killed himself, and I don't think he did," she said. "He probably knew enough to write forty books."

"The Joe Donahue I knew was more the type to just move on down the road," said a courthouse employee who'd worked with him. "If Napolitano had been found dead in Pasco County, they'd have ruled that a suicide too."

"He was playing with some bad guys," a local cop mused. "Maybe they called and said, you do it or we do it."

The case was eventually closed by the Pasco County Medical Examiner. Joseph Donahue's death was officially ruled a suicide.

More arrests followed in Florida, including Jimmy Acquafredda, JoJo Fitapelli, and Bernie Agostino. Eleven members of the garbage association were indicted on charges of extortion and price fixing to control the Florida west coast refuse collection business. Theo Nicholis, Rick Renner, and Bill Sakelson were brought up on narcotics charges. Professional gamblers Billy Jones, Barry "Winter" Bienstock, and bodyguard George Petry were charged with operating an illegal gambling establishment.

Special Agent Edgar S. Robb testified in state and federal courts in Florida and South Carolina for three and a half years, until the last convictions or guilty pleas arising out of Fast Hit and Coldwater were entered.

Santo Trafficante won a reprieve from U.S. District Judge William Castagna, who separated The Old Man's case from those of a dozen co-defendants in the Coldwater trials. Trafficante, seventy, was temporarily released from having to stand trial on racketeering charges because of his poor health. Doctors called to the stand by defense lawyer Henry Gonzalez testified that Santo was suffering from several ailments, including hardening of the arteries to the brain, which caused "periods of confusion during which he has trouble thinking, putting things together." Trafficante's kidneys had failed, causing him to undergo dialysis three days a week, four hours a day. He had severe angina, prompting his heart doctors to conclude that standing trial would be "extremely risky and life threatening." Trafficante, the doctors said, "could easily have a heart attack watching the fights on TV tomorrow."

Strike Force prosecutor Kevin March protested, claiming the government wanted Trafficante to stand trial so badly that "the United States would even try Trafficante by closed-circuit television in a hospital room paid for by the government."

In October, Santo Trafficante underwent successful heart

bypass surgery in Houston. He was released ten days later to recuperate at home in Florida. In July 1986, Trafficante won another round in court. Halfway into the government's presentation, U.S. District Judge Castagna dismissed the case, ruling that the prosecution had failed as a matter of law to produce sufficient evidence of Trafficante's membership in a conspiratorial enterprise to allow the trial to continue to its conclusion.

The government appealed Judge Castagna's decision to the 11th Circuit Court of Appeals. Before the verdict could be handed down, The Old Man died on March 17, 1987, at age seventy-four, without ever serving a day in a U.S. prison.

* * *

With the final settlement of Richard Milbauer's estate in the spring of 1987, The King's Court was torn down. Jim Kinne, who lived nearby, drove past the site every day and watched the stages of demolition. The location on Rte. 19 was soon occupied by a medical center for the quiet retirement community of Holiday. After the club was gone, Kinne heard that the building's roof, which had kept the Florida weather off of so many dark conspiracies, had been taken away and nestled atop a new church.

CHAPTER EIGHTEEN
Re-Entry

Special Agent Edgar S. Robb did not exist.

Callers to the Charlottesville or Richmond FBI Offices were informed there was no record of an Ed Robb anywhere in the Bureau. No one with that name had ever been an FBI agent. The thick, dark man in the new "Bu" suit, who traveled to FBI Headquarters, Quantico, and across the country to give lectures on criminal undercover work or consulting on other undercover operations, was named Stanley I. Nesbit. He answered to "Stan" or "328," his FBI vehicle number.

"Stanley I. Nesbit" was the brainstorm of the Richmond Special Agent in Charge, Al McCright, for the fun of the initials: S.I.N.

Ed never took to heart the name Stanley Nesbit. It lacked the hard edge of "Tony Rossi" or the alert clarity of "Edgar S. Robb." Stan Nesbit sounded like a nice guy but perhaps too quiet or studious to be the lead agent in one of the Bureau's longest, most complex, and successful undercover operations. On his travels for the Bureau, Ed heard accolades in another's name: "Great job, Stan," and "We're looking forward to working with you, Mr. Nesbit." Ed felt sometimes that this Nesbit fellow was an imposter. Ed Robb had done all the work.

The precaution of a new identity was necessary, and Ed let it play out. It was true that the mob had put a half-million-dollar bounty each on him and Joe Pistone. The government installed a sophisticated alarm and motion detector system at his secluded house in the hills outside Charlottesville. He drove a high-powered, police-package Ford with a remote-control ignition and kept his Glock 9-mm automatic close at hand, though he insisted the official protection stop there. He did not allow surveillance of himself or his family, considering it intrusive and unwarranted. He believed his home was secure enough: He had the alarm system, two robust and loyal Rottweilers, and his Glock.

But the threat to Ed's life was real. Coldwater had left a deep scar on the Mafia. Power, fortunes, and lives had been forfeited as a result of the evidence he and the other agents had uncovered in Florida and New York. Nonetheless, Ed remained unconvinced that the mob was coming after him full bore, in light of the FBI's direct warning to the Commission bosses of the consequences if they harmed Bureau agents. The mob, like any other business, is reluctant to make a play it can't win, and all-out war with the FBI and the Department of Justice was likely to be judged an unprofitable trade for the lives of two clever undercover agents. Besides, if the mob were actually to make a concerted effort to get him, Ed knew he couldn't escape, despite all reasonable precautions. Instead of jumping at shadows and alarming his family, he threw himself back into his old job as a Special Agent and answered to Stanley Nesbit.

Never before had an FBI agent surfaced from such a lengthy covert operation as Coldwater. For Ed Robb and Joe Pistone, a difficult psychological transition lay ahead, from the unstructured environment of undercover life to the four walls and ringing phones of a government office. Ed was lucky to have the support and cooperation of his supervisors in the Richmond and Charlottesville Offices. They allowed him ample time out of the office for his schedule of lecturing and consulting on new undercover operations. His bosses understood and appreciated the challenges he faced in acclimating to the procedural and technical changes that had taken place in the Bureau during the years when he was undercover. They stood by him during his long, tense period of testifying, where he was forced in federal court to re-enter the role of Tony Rossi and confront many an old associate, point fingers, name names, and relive sordid and dangerous events.

Tony Rossi was slow to relinquish his hold on Ed's psyche. Ed bought a 1978 Cadillac two-door Coupe de Ville, a bright green gangster-mobile with a white Landau top. He didn't throw away his mob clothes but hung them in the back of his closet. He continued to accessorize his Bureau suits with gold bracelets and wore his hair longer than the office fashion. Under his starched white shirt and Bureau blue tie swung Tony's gold chains, and Ed wore a pinky ring for years after Coldwater ended. In shopping malls with Gretchen, he paused at shoe store windows to ogle the shiny, high-heeled Italian models, to the point where Gretchen had to tug him away. Ed strolled with Tony's arrogance. His speech was marred by the rhythms and foulness of the Italian Mafioso's tongue. The suddenness of Tony's temper, his surly mien, drinking and smoking habits, and his peacock strut that had worked so well with JoJo and Acquafredda did not go down well with Ed's wife, co-workers, and friends. Ed had Tony's nightmares.

He was considered a star by many of his fellow agents, a prima donna by others. The occasional aloofness he encountered was inevitable, a sort of "Where have you been while we've been in the trenches?" retort to his gaining notoriety. After all, he'd been gone for three years. A lot of new faces had come into the office, men and women who'd been busily carving out their own careers. Here was a new guy coming in out of the blue, acting, dressing, and talking like the king of the mountain. Ed reacted as he always had, by working harder to show how he had climbed to the top of the game in the first place. Along with his other credentials, he became the narcotics expert for the Richmond Office.

At home, he couldn't relax and be Ed Robb. The phone was in the name of Gretchen Brown. Gretchen was offended by her husband's gaudy Cadillac, hair, and jewelry. She advised him to drop the swagger and the colorful language around the house. She wanted Ed Robb back, the man she'd loved and married. Tony Rossi was not welcome in her home.

Ed applied for a bank loan under his real name. He was turned down because no history existed of his employment with the FBI. All the records, deeds, and licenses of his life were in the name of Edgar Robb but his birthright hit a dead end when it reached the Bureau. It seemed like an episode out of the Twilight Zone.

He walked around in Ed Robb's body, slept in his bed, thought his thoughts, but Ed Robb no longer existed, couldn't take a phone call, couldn't get a damned loan. Stanley Nesbit couldn't get a loan either. He wasn't complete enough—the way Tony Rossi had been—for a full credit check. Ed never took the Nesbit role seriously enough to fully develop the identity, feeling even a bit foolish while explaining to his old friends that they had to call him "Stan" in public. Rossi had been the whole package. He'd had everything, a driver's license, a Social Security number, a detailed background. Nesbit was stunad, period. He had funny initials.

* * *

The obstacles Ed and Joe faced during re-entry were unprecedented in the Bureau. No guidelines or experience were in place to deal with their situations.

A thousand miles away in the Dallas FBI Office, Joe Pistone was also encountering the reluctance of his undercover alter ego to let him go. The same fierce individualism that had drawn both Ed and Joe into undercover work in the first place, and which had served them so well in their undercover roles, now asserted itself in their return to office and family. Agents who knew the two men well and who watched them during Coldwater and now in their re-entry period saw them chafing under the sudden return to the strictures of regulated work, after years of freewheeling action on the street. Ed and Joe had lived lives of constant danger, where their bosses were psychopaths, their associates were killers and con-men, and now they were both at desks, with bosses who demanded paperwork and office hours, and co-workers they'd never met before. Whenever Ed encountered Joe before testifying or spoke to him on the phone, he recognized in his partner's voice the same strains of his own problems trying to deal with the real worlds of office, friends, and family. Ed Robb knew Joe Pistone intimately after their long adventure together, and suspected what Joe was going through. But Ed felt that the two partners could not reach across the chasms of distance, time, even pride, to help the other.

The two also had available to them staff psychologists, but because of a legal catch-22 they knew they couldn't go anywhere near them. A defense attorney might later ask an undercover agent on the stand if he had ever sought psychological or psychiatric help. A "Yes" answer could be used to discredit him. So, for reasons beyond their control and perhaps understanding, both men charted their own courses back into the real world.

Their return to the fold was made even more difficult by many of the old hands at the Bureau, most of them Hoover-era agents who could not appreciate the critical nature of the undercover agent's re-entry period. They were reluctant to admit that Ed or Joe could be emotionally taxed, disoriented, or even psychologically altered after such a feat as Operation Coldwater. These older agents, most of them supervisors, viewed the recognition of "re-entry problems" as mollycoddling. To them, it was weakness in an organization built on strength.

In September of 1986, Joe resigned from the Bureau to write a book about his time spent in Coldwater, Donnie Brasco. The book became a popular success and was turned into a movie of the same name. During publicity for the book and subsequent movie, he took to obscuring his face and voice to protect his identity. In 1992, Joe rejoined the FBI and finished out his career to retirement. Ed remained in the FBI until his own retirement in 1990, taking part as the lead undercover agent in another, even bigger, international undercover operation targeting the Sicilian Mafia.

The re-entry of Ed Robb and Joe Pistone from their lengthy undercover roles was not simple or seamless. But both men retained their balance and sanity, productivity and, most importantly, their commitment to the FBI. These were not easy accomplishments, especially in light of the fact that a handful of other agents before them had gone undercover for shorter durations and never "come back." There was work to be done to select men and women with the best attributes for this wearing and dangerous kind of work. Ed, who embodied these traits, teamed with Howard Teten, head of the FBI's Behavioral Science Unit at the Academy in Quantico, to develop selection criteria for undercover work, still in use in the FBI today.

Again, Ed Robb and Joe Pistone found themselves in the roles of pioneers. And again, the ground they broke was difficult and rewarding for them both.

CHAPTER NINETEEN
Councilman Chuck

In 1981, Congress gave the FBI joint jurisdiction with the DEA over Title 21 U.S. Code violations of the federal narcotics laws. News reports teemed with references to illegal drugs.

President Reagan made the war on drugs one of his administration's priorities. His "Just Say No" campaign was the softer side of an official reaction to the rising tide of narcotics in America. The FBI was told to get involved.

This was music to Ed Robb's ears.

In 1982, a year before his Coldwater testimony began, Ed volunteered for a three-week intensive course at the Federal Law Enforcement Training Academy in Glynco, Georgia. This was a first-class facility where agents from all federal law enforcement branches except the FBI were trained. Ed joined agents from Immigration, Border Patrol, DEA, and Customs in an in-depth study of narcotics and the specific nature of undercover investigations inside the drug trade. When he returned to Virginia, Ed searched for a chance to apply his new expertise. He worked with the Justice Department to sift through opportunities to involve the FBI's Narcotics Task Force. He started drug investigations in Harrisonburg and Charlottesville.

It wasn't until Ed was assigned to work with an informant in Richmond that he next went undercover. The Richmond FBI Office had developed reliable information that a city councilman, Chuck Richardson, was a small-time heroin user probably dealing at least enough junk to support his own habit. Richardson's involvement with narcotics alone wouldn't have been enough to

involve the Bureau, but he was an elected official, so his situation raised the likelihood of corruption.

Ed pushed aside the blue serge suits and starched white
shirts in his closet and reached in for his old sharkskins and
silks. He buckled on some gold and ran a chamois across his
Florsheims to bring out the sheen. He arranged a Pittsburgh
phone number to ring on his special line at home in
Charlottesville. At the Richmond airport, he rented a Cadillac
under the name Edward Rizzi. He slapped on out-of-state tags
licensed to Rizzi in Pittsburgh and hit the streets.

Ed was aware of the risk he ran by re-entering the underworld.
Though Chuck Richardson was just a punk by organized crime
standards, he was nonetheless, because of his habit, a denizen of
the criminal world. The underworld network was strong and, as
Ed had seen, information in it often flowed as fast or faster than
within the law enforcement community. Who knew who Ed
might be exposed to in his pursuit of Richardson, and which one
might recognize Rizzi as Rossi, now known to be undercover
agent Robb? But Ed's eagerness to return to undercover work
and his promises to his supervisors and Gretchen to be circum-
spect overrode their concerns for his safety.

Ed and the informant hung out for several evenings in a row
at Richardson's favorite watering holes, leaving the old tried and
true impression. The city of Richmond, a belle of the South and
capitol of the Confederate States, had always been a provincial
town, more village than city, despite its size and history. As in
any other village, word traveled fast in Richmond. The underworld image Ed cut was remarkable in the way it stood out from
the yuppies and college dinks drinking at the tables around him.
No one could mistake what he was. He was a bad man.

Finally, City Councilman Chuck Richardson came into the
Stonewall Café, an old elementary school turned fern bar. The
councilman was a handsome African-American, with long,
straight hair and a full mustache. He glided among the tables,
squeezing flesh, working the politician's affable craft.

The informant, an old pal of Chuck's, called the councilman

to the table and introduced Ed as Eddie "Ritz" Rizzi from Pittsburgh. Chuck said hello, made small talk, then kept moving and shaking.

Soon afterwards, Ed encountered Chuck again in the Stonewall Café. This time, Chuck had a drink at Eddie Ritz's invitation and the two spent more time chatting. Chuck elaborated on his political aspirations, claiming he was going to be elected the next mayor. Ed sat intent, working the undercover magic he'd perfected over a decade of listening and agreeing, drawing secrets out like a poultice. Before letting Chuck go to work his way to another table of well-wishers, Ed handed him $500 cash. He said he wanted to support Chuck's bid for the mayor's office.

"But," Ed said, dark and conspiratorial, "I might want something in return." Chuck left his phone number with Eddie Ritz.

* * *

A week later, Ed met Richardson at the Hyatt for dinner. As a sort of avatar of his power, Chuck brought along an attractive young woman, bragging to Ed how he'd used his influence to get her a job with the city.

After a meal of steaks and fine wine, Ed laid his first set of cards on the table. He told Chuck he was with "one of the Italian families in Pittsburgh, you know what I mean?" Chuck assured Eddie Ritz he did know what that meant. He put his lady friend in a taxi.

With the Nagra recorder working, Ed made his position clear.

"I want to get a toehold in Richmond. I don't want to screw around. So here's the facts. I'm in the narcotics business. You got a problem with that, get up and walk away right now."

Chuck stayed put. Ed had made an important opening move for prosecution purposes; he had given the target a way out. With this offer recorded on the Nagra, Chuck couldn't later claim entrapment as an effective defense.

Eddie Ritz wanted to set up some legitimate businesses to cover his drug operations in Richmond. He'd need some zoning assistance. Could Chuck grease the skids with zoning? And no hassle with the cops. Could Chuck help out with that? What about the judicial side of things if a bust went down? Was Chuck connected there?

Richardson was expansive. He said he could do more than help out, repeating his assertion that he was soon to be elected Richmond's mayor. Chuck claimed to control Richmond's political world; he had all the hooks Eddie Ritz would need. He also sat on the Richmond Port Authority. He and Eddie could utilize that avenue to move the drugs into the city. It also put him in a position to trade favors so Eddie's people could operate easier.

Chuck wanted to do business. Ed got clearance from his FBI bosses to take the councilman to the next level.

Ed and Chuck stayed in regular phone contact. Ed made plans to bring Chuck up to Pittsburgh, to wine and dine him there, and display what a big hitter Eddie Rizzi was. But these trips never became a necessity; Chuck Richardson was already sold. He wanted to get down to work as Ritz's partner in the narcotics trade.

Ed set up a meeting in a room at a Howard Johnson's several blocks from the city's baseball stadium. He rented adjoining rooms and installed FBI sound man Bob McCluan in the second room. The meeting was wired with bugs and video. No Title III approval was needed because the agent would be a party to the meeting. Beside Ed was an experienced DEA agent, John Lee. Lee was slated to take over the investigation; Ed planned to tell Chuck that, from now on, Lee, also an African American, was his connection. Eddie Ritz would still be running the show but from behind the scenes.

Richardson was late to the meeting; Ed called him and ate him out for it. When the councilman arrived, Ed introduced John as the man who had been running his family's operations in Maryland and Northern Virginia and would be the local boss in Richmond. Chuck was leery, slow to accept the notion of Ed's naming a replacement for their arrangement. With John in the room, Chuck would only refer to "statues" or "artifacts," though they were plainly discussing the buying, selling, and transportation of heroin and cocaine. Ed said that he counted on Chuck to introduce John around to the right people. He placed responsibility for the success of their narcotics business squarely on Chuck's shoulders.

Over the next several months, Ed, John, and other DEA and FBI agents contacted Chuck to bring the investigation to a head. Finally, a meeting was set up for Chuck to take delivery of a sample of coke from John. The FBI rented two adjacent motel rooms on the outskirts of town, installed an audio/video bag of tricks in the room, and then the agents settled in to await the target.

Chuck never showed up.

The next day, a local criminal defense attorney, Michael "Magic Mike" Morchower, called the Richmond Office. He represented Councilman Chuck Richardson. His client wanted a sit-down. At that meeting, Richardson told the FBI that he had been contacted by a black guy named John, who wanted to do a drug deal. Chuck was being a good citizen and turned John in. He never mentioned anything about Eddie Rizzi from Pittsburgh, or Eddie's $500 campaign contribution.

Ed Robb wanted to know what had gone wrong. His best guess was that Chuck smelled a rat. Indeed, the motel clerk later reported that Chuck had come into the office and asked for John. The clerk had replied, "What room do you want? He rented two of them side-by-side." Chuck probably put two plus two together and ran for Magic Mike.

His tale that he was doing his own undercover job on John was a classic defense from a public official on the verge of being caught. Though implausible, it was nonetheless effective. All the evidence against Chuck up to that point was consistent with an investigation of his own; no overt actions had been taken.

Ed went to FBI Headquarters and argued for prosecuting Richardson, convinced that the taint of corruption among Richmond's public officials went higher than Chuck. The

Bureau refused to prosecute. Though they badly wanted to land Councilman Richardson and squeeze him for his connections in and outside of government, the only way to secure a federal conviction would be to put Special Agent Edgar Robb on the stand to testify. This, they were not prepared to do. The drug trial of an allegedly corrupt city official, and those others he might lead the FBI to, would be a very public affair. Mafiosi read the papers. Ed would be blown for sure, and the lingering threat to his life re-kindled. Frustrated but resigned, Ed backed off.

Richardson walked out, but he didn't walk far enough; his problems with narcotics followed him. In October of 1987, he was arrested in a car with a local man, Charles Alexander. At the instant the police moved in, Alexander had in his hands cocaine and drug paraphernalia. A search of Richardson's briefcase revealed more drug paraphernalia, containing residues of cocaine and heroin. Richmond City police charged both men with felony possession of cocaine. In February of 1988, a plea bargain by Richardson's lawyers reduced his charges from felonies to two misdemeanor counts of possession in return for $200 in fines and a promise to seek drug counseling and treatment. The misdemeanor counts drew a firestorm of criticism to the city's commonwealth attorney, Aubrey Davis. The allegations of cronyism contributed to Davis's failure to be re-elected. The reduced charges allowed Richardson to run for re-election to his council seat, which he won despite additional brushes with the law, including a contempt charge for missing probation meetings and drug counseling sessions. In 1994, his problems with narcotics returned and he re-entered drug rehab. Richardson stepped down from his council seat late in 1995. He was never elected mayor.

CHAPTER TWENTY
Pizza and the Wolf

Another good man has bit the dust, thought Ed Robb when Eddie McLaughlin phoned.

McLaughlin, the undercover bookie "Eddie Shannon" from the Coldwater days in Florida, had been a first-rate undercover agent, but he'd taken a fork in the career road and turned to administration. In September 1986, McLaughlin was the supervisor of the Narcotics Squad in the Washington D.C. Field Office.

"Hey, Tone," McLaughlin greeted his old undercover mate, "I've got a Group 1 undercover operation in D.C. It's drugs. You interested?"

During the five years since emerging from Coldwater, Ed had kept a full schedule: testifying in federal and state courts, traveling as a consultant and lecturer inside the FBI on undercover issues and operations, helping to promulgate guidelines for covert operatives, developing new undercover techniques and expertise, and carrying most of the routine case load of a street agent. He'd been Stanley Nesbit for those five years except for his brief stint as "Eddie Ritz" in the Richardson case. He had finally been able to be with Gretchen and his children regularly to make up for lost time as husband and father. His standing within the Bureau as one of its first and most accomplished undercover agents was unchallenged. He was forty-nine years old, three years away from his twenty-year retirement.

"Sure, Eddie. I'll take a look at it."

Organized narcotics trafficking had become the new investigative frontier for the FBI. The Bureau's first big strike came with an operation code-named the Pizza Connection. The case got its name from a network of pizza parlors in four eastern states that were used as distribution points for a huge Sicilian-based heroin ring.

The Pizza Connection traced its roots back to the days of Coldwater. It began immediately after The King's Court was shut down in the summer of 1981. The war between rival factions of the Bonanno family—resulting in the murders of three captains by Sonny Black's crew—gave rise to thirteen Title III wiretaps in New York City. These wiretaps led the FBI to a ring of American and Italian drug dealers who, in five years, had smuggled into the United States an estimated 1,650 pounds of heroin, with a street value of $1.6 billion.

The Pizza Connection investigation lasted for three years, and the trial, United States v. Badalamenti et al., was one of the longest and most expensive in federal prosecutorial history, going on for seventeen months. The evidence consisted of recorded telephone conversations, surveillance, informant testimony, and cooperative statements by some of the defendants. No undercover agents from the FBI or DEA had been involved in the case.

At the center of the prosecution was Assistant U.S. Attorney Louis Freeh, the federal lawyer who had prepared Ed and questioned him during his testimony at the Coldwater trials in New York. The Pizza Connection resulted in convictions on federal drug charges for twenty-one out of the twenty-two persons indicted, including a boss of the Sicilian Mafia. Sentences of twenty to forty-five years were meted out, along with millions of dollars in fines.

After the Pizza Connection drug circle was swept up, the Bureau was left with a thick file of contacts, suspects, and informants still on the streets of Los Angeles, Houston, New York, Boston, Miami, Washington, and Charlotte. Though an important group of dealers was now behind bars, Pizza had failed to disrupt other major drug gangs from filling in the gap and importing more heroin into the United States. The Sicilian zips were regrouping, and with alarming speed they again became the biggest players in the domestic heroin trade.

A summit meeting was called in Boston in 1985, attended by seventy-five key FBI agents and supervisors from around the country. They agreed that the number one narcotics problem in the United States was cocaine. Because of the glut of Colombian coke in this country, it sold on the streets of New York for only $20,000 a kilogram, whereas the same kilo in Europe sold for $55,000. The Italians and Sicilians, with limited supplies of cocaine but flush with their own mountains of Middle Eastern heroin, were beginning to barter heroin on a one-for-two basis with American coke dealers. Heroin cascaded into the United States, cocaine flowed out, and millions of dollars changed hands routinely. The Bureau wanted to mount another strike against the Sicilian heroin dealers.

The assembly of agents in Boston decided to build on the foundation of the Pizza Connection, but this time, Title III wiretaps, the backbone of Pizza, wouldn't be enough. For the first time, the FBI would attempt to insert undercover agents into a major international narcotics cartel.

The original Pizza Connection case became known as Pizza I. The new investigation, a broad-based, fully financed Group 1 covert operation, was code-named Pizza II.

Ed knew all about the Pizza Connection case. It was the biggest bust in terms of suspects and money the FBI had ever pulled off. Pizza II would top it, and McLaughlin wanted to put Ed right in the middle of it.

In Washington, Ed met with McLaughlin and Case Agent Glenn Tuttle. He gave Tuttle the same line he'd given Jimmy Kinne seven years before in Florida: If you want this job done right, I'll do it for you. If you don't like something, my behavior, my decisions, whatever, you come straight to me about it and not behind my back. We'll work it out. Tuttle and McLaughlin made the easy decision to bring Ed on board Pizza II, as the lead undercover agent.

*   *   *

Heroin was imported into the United States from the Middle East via Italy in a variety of ways. It was muled in body packs or stashed inside crates of Italian tile, furniture, leather goods, and pizza fixings such as tomato paste and cheese. Once inside the country, the narcotics were distributed through a string of Italian restaurants and pizzerias. The workers in these restaurants were often Italian or Sicilian men and women who'd taken jobs on cruise liners as wait staff or kitchen help, then jumped ship in New York or Miami. Since they spoke little or no English, they relied heavily on their jobs and the network of other immigrant workers. Many of them were easily lured by the quick money of the drug dealers or their Sicilian brethren who'd come to America before them and formed their own crime families.

The Sicilian Mafia existed side by side with the American mob. Cooperation between the two underworld networks was rare, unless there was a very profitable purpose, and the drug trade in the United States became one of those occasions.

The zips were far more loosely organized than their American counterparts. They were wilder and more unpredictable; they surpassed the American Mafia in brutality. These immigrants had neither homes nor families in America; they were cut loose, free from all rules and restraints. These were men who had not grown up with Miranda rights or the civil protections of the U.S. Constitution. In their homeland, the police often surpassed the criminals for cruelty and corruption. The Sicilian crime families, such as the N'Drangheta in Calabria and the Cammora near Naples, ruled through ruthless force. They did not hesitate to murder a judge, prosecutor, or policeman closing in on them. Bloodbaths between rival gangs were common. Entire towns were often the turf of one family or another. The Sicilians had a joke about their lawlessness. The gag ran that, every morning, whoever woke up first in the village grabbed the shotgun. He was the mayor for the day.

Those Sicilian immigrants who drifted into the underworld had come to carve off a piece of the American Dream but wound up instead at war with their new country. As illegal aliens, they began skirting the law the moment they touched American soil. They were wary of all official authority, forming clans for survival. They found work in the Italian restaurants, safe from Immigration, where their lack of English was no drawback, but they could not negotiate the streets and stores outside their close neighborhoods, trapping them in their small corner of the city. They might earn their way up the drug gang ladder, first unpacking the crates of heroin in the pizzerias, then muling the narcotics around the neighborhood. Then, perhaps, they would deliver the drugs to other cities and states, often exchanging the heroin for U.S. cocaine, then obtain a passport and body-pack the coke back to Sicily. These lucky few would arrive home with pockets full of cash, returning as conquering heroes with tales of the possibilities in America. For many who had been uneducated and powerless in Sicily, drugs provided the way to status and power in America, and a way of belonging to a family to replace the one they'd left far behind.

The springboard for the several Pizza II investigations was to be Eddie McLaughlin's undercover operation in Washington, code-named "Infamita," the Sicilian word for family. Infamita would work in tandem with three other investigations: "Chokehold" in Boston, "Crimson Sky" in Charlotte, and with another undercover agent from Los Angeles. Infamita would be the first of the Pizza II operations to insert an undercover agent into the midst of the zips.

The goal of Pizza II was to bypass the street corner heroin dealer and reach up the ladder to the organizations, domestic and offshore, actually importing and distributing the heroin. McLaughlin's Narcotics Squad had developed information about illegal Sicilian immigrants running a heroin operation in Washington similar to the one the Bureau had mopped up in New York in Pizza I. McLaughlin wanted to plumb the depths of this new ring to see how much of Pizza I was left alive and doing business in his city. Ed was to be introduced by an informant. The strategy was simple: Ed would buy his way up the drug ladder as far as he could go, then look around at the top when he got there.

His new identity was Kurt Wolfe, German-Jewish business-man and international drug dealer. Kurt was nothing like the mob-businessman Tony Rossi, or the oily, unctuous Eddie Ritz, or Operation Talon's tough guy Eddie Rossi, much less the lik-able, front porch bumpkin of Special Agent Ed Robb in Tennessee. Kurt Wolfe was a bastard, a money-grubbing, immoral, paranoid SOB with world-wide narcotics ambitions. Kurt was an aloof, independent operator; he would not be one of the guys, he would not hang out. Kurt disappeared once in a while and no one dared ask him where he went. Kurt didn't care if you liked him; he didn't like you and wanted you to know it. Kurt was concerned only that you did your job, showed up on time, made him a profit, pocketed only your share, and kept your mouth shut.

Ed and the Washington Field Office set about establishing Kurt Wolfe's identity. This meant the usual credit cards, driver's license, passport, former addresses, family history, employment and banking records, Social Security number, title and insurance on his automobile, plus authentic memories and stories of his full life. Kurt rented an apartment in a complex in Georgetown, on the corner of 22nd and L. The FBI filled it with bugs and pin-hole cameras, then rented another apartment three floors up. This was the safe house where the monitors and recorders were set up and could be staffed twenty-four hours a day.

Unlike Coldwater and Fast Hit, Infamita and Pizza II fea-tured a large, inter-departmental federal team. There were agents from the Internal Revenue Service, Immigration and Naturalization (INS), and the DEA working on the case. Also, the communications technologies that had emerged in the mid-1980s (such as cellular phones, beepers, and fax machines) were now used by the mob, which meant more manpower was needed for surveillance. No longer could the FBI rely on a simple wiretap on home and office phones. The extra personnel in and around Infamita increased the risk of leaks and mistakes.

* * *

When the identity had been established, and the backup was in place, it was time to meet the snitch, Gino.

Ed picked Gino up in Kurt Wolfe's flashy red Cadillac convertible, which the FBI had confiscated from a drug dealer in Baltimore named Big John. Before meeting the informant, Ed had to remove a brass plate from the glove compartment door that read "Custom Built for Big John."

Ed and Gino drove around D.C. to get acquainted. Ed schooled the informant in Kurt Wolfe's cover story: He'd been in the legitimate construction business in Pennsylvania for years. Wolfe's company had been a success but he'd grown tired of his life, his family, and of working. He'd liquidated the business for a million bucks and split, leaving everything behind. Wolfe was now a narcotics trafficker on a global level. Gino, the story went, had done some jobs for Kurt and knew him to be a reliable professional and an up-and-comer.

Gino was a naturalized Italian immigrant. Sleek and trim, with Neopolitan good looks and an urbane style, he was the embodiment of Euro-suave. He was a smooth talker and a slick dresser who wore his coats like capes without putting his arms inside the sleeves. Gino considered himself a playboy and, though he was a bit smarmy, he was well connected socially. He knew people in very high and very low orbits around the D.C. scene.

Gino was a full-time professional information peddler. He was the highest-quality informant Ed had encountered in his seventeen years in the FBI. Gino provided McLaughlin's Narcotics Squad with regular and excellent intelligence, and his rewards were an annual income of almost a hundred thousand dollars, a furnished Georgetown apartment, a tailored wardrobe, and a snazzy Italian car. It was very expensive to maintain

Gino's image in the underworld as a key figure in the international drug game.

In the Cadillac, idling around Georgetown, Ed gave Gino his standard agent/informant lecture. Don't expect to be involved in this case long, Gino. Just get me in the front door with the zips and you go out the back door. No matter how good a snitch you might be, you are still dangerous and unreliable. Gino, his pride only slightly bruised, kept his spirits up and his manner gentle. He looked at the stocky man opposite him driving the car, dressed like an FBI agent rather than a well-to-do narcotics entrepreneur, and gave Ed tips on his ensemble.

"Kurt, really, after five in the evening, you must wear a dark jacket."

"The kerchief should match the tie."

"Try a less pungent toilet water, Kurt."

Ed and Gino were slated to be partners in a wine importing business. Ed obtained a letter of credit and an introduction from First American Bank to establish Ital Wine Import. He had stationery and business cards printed. Gino was told to search for a storefront where they could set up shop.

Gino was charming, but it was the charm of a snake. On one occasion, he suggested to Ed that they recruit a friend of his as an additional informant for Pizza II. Gino volunteered to plant a packet of heroin on his friend and get him busted to compromise him and make him vulnerable to the FBI's influence. Ed refused angrily. Play by the rules, he told Gino, or don't play. The rules are what make us different from the mob.

Gino used drugs and supported his medium-sized cocaine habit with FBI money. He was also at times, for an informant in a highly dangerous world, hazardously indiscreet. Obviously, Gino was to tell no one that Kurt Wolfe was an undercover operative or that he himself was an informant. Several weeks into the investigation, Ed answered his phone as Kurt Wolfe in his Georgetown apartment. It was Gino's brother looking for Gino. "Yeah, Kurt. How's Glenn doing?" This referred to Glenn Tuttle, Infamita's case agent. Ed grew livid at the breach in security. If

Gino had crowed to his brother about the important FBI under-cover case he was working on, who else, and what else, was he telling? Ed found himself again in the unavoidable and nerve-wracking position of having his safety linked to a man he couldn't trust out of his sight, and whose profession he detested. A careless comment from Gino could result in bullets for both of them, continuing their linkage into death. Ed knew from experience that he would only sleep well after the lethal little toady Gino was gone from Pizza II.

*   *   *

On September 30, 1986, at 10:30 p.m., Gino, wearing a wire, held a conversation with a narcotics connection he'd been courting for weeks. Luigi Visciano was a waiter at Il Giardino, a chic Italian restaurant in Georgetown. Gino told Visciano about a major dealer he was hooked into, for whom he scouted coke and heroin contacts. Luigi was thrilled; he told Gino they could get heroin from New York City from two sources, or cocaine in Miami from several connections. He wanted to meet Gino's guy and maybe get a piece of him for himself.

The next afternoon, Luigi called Gino again. He said he would call his cousin, Tony Cascone, in Miami to get the price for coke delivered to Washington, D.C. Over the course of the next two weeks, Gino and Luigi spoke several times about the availability of heroin from New York and cocaine from Miami. Gino primed Luigi for an upcoming meeting with his new drug boss and got everything on tape.

On October 15, Gino introduced Luigi Visciano to Kurt Wolfe. Ed was relieved that his new undercover persona, Kurt Wolfe, would not be spending a lot of social time with the characters surfacing in Infamita if Luigi was a representative specimen. Luigi was tall and stooped, with thin shoulders and a pear shaped middle. His hair was slicked back to reveal mounds of baby fat on his cheeks and neck. He stank of oil and garlic and his delicate hands reminded Ed of limp fish. Like Gino, Luigi

Visciano had an ingratiating manner, greasy and continental. He was an excellent waiter but he might steal your watch if he shook your hand.

Luigi was enthusiastic about working with Kurt. He described his numerous contacts in New York and Florida and claimed he could obtain all the drugs Kurt could want. He volunteered to act as the broker for purchases from his contacts and to help Kurt find more narcotics sources. Ed told Luigi he would make him a lieutenant in his drug operation. Ed had the buyers; Luigi's job was to find the sources. But he was interested only in heroin unless a big buy of hash, coke, or grass made itself available. Kurt didn't like dealing with Colombians, they were too unreliable and expensive. He wanted to work only with Italians and Sicilians.

Ed's strategy was to use the waiter Luigi's connections to locate and purchase increasing amounts of drugs. Once an airtight case was made against Luigi, and Ed had made direct contact with his suppliers, he would discard Luigi and forge newer, more powerful associations at the next level up. He would, in turn, move beyond these contacts at the right time, until he had climbed as far into the narcotics organization as he could.

Every penny of Bureau money Kurt Wolfe laid out had to be justified: How did the expenditure further the investigation? Unlike Coldwater, where the agents spent money in dribbles of a couple hundred here and a few thousand there, one major narcotics buy in Infamita might consume several hundred thousand dollars.

Once Infamita got under way, Ed embellished his characterization of the aspiring drug czar Kurt Wolfe. Luigi, Gino, and their widening circle of drug connections were treated to a vintage Ed Robb undercover performance, featuring a veritable sideshow of quirks and idiosyncrasies calculated to throw the zips off the scent. Kurt demanded punctuality, not just to the minute but the second. He refused, sometimes wide-eyed and terrified, to ride in an elevator or the back of a car. Kurt was suspicious to a fault. He never entered a doorway first, always making sure that everyone else had walked through before him. He had his hair cut only by hairstylist Sal Cattano at the Watergate, who knew a lot of the people Ed was secretly investigating. Often, Luigi or another target of the case would accompany him for a haircut, and Ed pitched a fit if they spoke Italian in his presence. He reminded them loudly, publicly, that he was the boss and the boss spoke "fuckin' American."

Ed never answered his telephone, but always allowed the answering machine to pick up before he took the receiver. He lectured his circle of associates constantly about being careful with the telephone, telling them the phone was the biggest rat in the world. He designed a heroin testing kit. A drop of hydrochloric acid revealed by a change in tint the purity of the heroin. The deeper the shade of purple, the better the sample. In another tube, he tested the heroin with ammonia. This separated the "cut," or impurities. The cut would drop to the bottom of the tube while the pure narcotic floated. The zips considered Ed very sophisticated; they tested their own samples by using a "pig" or, if they were users, snorting, eating, or injecting the drugs themselves.

In a crowning, inspired display of caprice, Ed purchased a complete Catholic priest's outfit, the full black suit and white collar, and often walked around Georgetown in it to blend in with the many clerics who taught at the Jesuit Georgetown University. He hung out in the bars in this garb, drinking and smoking alone in his surly mien, leaving a whirring rumor mill. His criminal associates thought this an incredibly clever disguise; it was also irreverent and wacko, far beyond the pale of what a cop might do, and that was the point.

Ed was concerned about the new counter-espionage technologies any citizen could purchase to uncover electronic surveillance. Radio Shack and Sharper Image sold electronic gadgets to detect radio transmitters; other devices revealed the presence of a tap on your telephone by measuring a drop in voltage on the line. Another monitor told you if someone in your building had picked up an extension phone to listen in on your conversation. Also available were hand-held metal detectors. Ed figured that a good defense was a good offense so he purchased every one of the devices he could find and made them proof of Kurt Wolfe's uncontrollable paranoia. He assembled them all into a kit in a suitcase and pulled them out whenever someone new visited his apartment. The fact that Kurt had all these beeping, buzzing, needle-waggling toys gave the Sicilians a sense of security when dealing with him. They felt they could talk more freely on the phone with Kurt—despite his admonitions to the contrary— knowing that he was always on guard against electronic interloping from the cops; they believed that Kurt was even more mistrustful than they were. His gizmo collection also prevented them from bringing their own anti-surveillance equipment around. If by chance one of them owned the same or a similar unit and had it on him, he would inevitably, stupidly, pull it out and say "Hey, Kurt, I got the same fuckin' thing. Let's see yours," and they'd compare machinery.

Most of the Sicilians were very impressed with Kurt's almost comic concentration on counter-surveillance. Still, Ed underestimated the superstitious naivete of a few of the immigrants, men who'd remained essentially strangers to American and Japanese technology. These men were accustomed to the traditional pat-down by hand, not a beeping space-age contraption waved over their body crevices.

One of the early suspects of Infamita, a drug connection Luigi brought to Ed, was a three-hundred-pound Sicilian named Alfreddo, owner of a pizza place on Pennsylvania Avenue a few blocks from the White House. Alfreddo allegedly ran heroin out of his kitchen, and he was invited to appear before the cameras and mikes in Ed's apartment to discuss a deal.

Moments after Alfreddo crossed the threshold, Ed dragged out his Sharper Image suitcase and started trailing a transmitter detector over his guest's large, jiggling frame.

"What the fuck are you doing? What the fuck is that?" Alfreddo turned the color of pizza sauce.

"Shut up. I gotta make sure you're not wearin' a wire."

In seconds, Alfreddo, his hands in the air, his massive legs spread, got spooked. This was too weird. "I'm outta here." He hit the door and never came back. Ed realized he would have to phase in slowly this part of Kurt Wolfe's funky personality. This time, with Alfreddo, he'd outsmarted himself.

To round off Kurt's remarkable facade and to drive home a very powerful spike of credibility, Ed had a million dollars in hundred-dollar bills nested in a safety deposit box in a bank at 21st and L Streets. Ed showed Luigi the money to cement the Sicilian's loyalty. Luigi became euphoric. He dug into the stacks of cash and held a pile of it to his chest, hypnotized by the heft of real wealth in his hands. Ed gazed down into the green bowels of the box and knew that he could at any time pack up the money and disappear for good. With the several fake ID's he carried in his wallet for Kurt Wolfe, with what he knew about local, state, and federal law enforcement and the tracing of fugitive suspects, with his experience at establishing new identities and blending into his surroundings without making a ripple, Ed Robb could make a clean getaway with the fortune and disappear. It crossed his mind once and not again.

* * *

During the last week of October 1986, Gino and Luigi Visciano got serious about finding heroin for Kurt Wolfe. The afternoon of the 26th, Luigi made a phone call from Gino's apartment to a connection in New York City. Giuseppe "Peppe" Vitiello was a waiter at the restaurant Casa di Pizza on Mulberry Street, Lefty Ruggiero's old neighborhood. Peppe told Luigi he had heroin for sale at $200,000 per kilo, with a 20 percent discount for purchases over a kilo. The drugs were available in one to eight-kilo buys. Gino told Luigi to go to New York and bring back a sample. Gino would talk to Kurt, whom he claimed grandly might buy a full eight kilos.

On November 4, a New York FBI surveillance team was in place as Luigi Visciano entered Casa di Pizza at one o'clock in the afternoon. Luigi was met by a short man with curly grey hair, later identified as Luigi Silvestri. Silvestri went to a shelf and took down a can of Italian tomatoes. The two walked to the rear of the pizzeria and disappeared. An hour later, Luigi Visciano called Gino and told him he'd completed his business in New York and was returning to Washington. That night, Luigi delivered the sample of heroin to Kurt Wolfe's apartment. The taste, worth $100, was the first narcotics buy of Pizza II.

Ed delivered the packet to Glenn Tuttle, who had it tested at the DEA's Mid-Atlantic Regional Laboratory. The white powder was found to be only 17 percent heroin hydrochloride, with a net weight under a quarter of a gram. This initial sample of heroin from the New York zips was of ridiculously low quality.

Luigi and Gino were eager to make something happen. Without checking with Ed, they called Peppe in New York and told him they liked the sample. Three days later, Ed phoned Luigi and jumped down his throat about the quality of the heroin. Luigi calmed him down, assuring him that Peppe and Silvestri would come up with better stuff next time and plenty of it. Ed said, OK, they could still do business with Peppe and Silvestri but no more bullshit quality goods. He told Luigi to set up a buy.

Luigi went back to New York and found another supplier who would sell Kurt a kilo of heroin for $200,000. In a phone call to Gino, Luigi said the supplier was "Mario," later identified as Mario Digrazia, a former waiter, and the man behind the poor sample of heroin Luigi had delivered to Ed.

Gino and Luigi met with Mario at Ecco Restaurant in New York. Gino told Mario about the bad sample. Mario agreed that the taste was shit and explained that it was "street quality" heroin because he wasn't sure Luigi, Gino, and their master Wolfe were serious about doing a large deal. Mario claimed that he and his associates handled only kilo quantities of heroin. Their packages arrived sealed from the refinery in Palermo, Sicily. Now that Kurt had shown himself to be a player dealing in significant amounts, Mario was ready to move ahead with a one-kilo buy, to go down in New York. Gino called Ed with the news. Ed told him to schedule the deal for December 3. This would give the New York FBI time to set up surveillance and allow Ed to get the money approved by FBI Headquarters.

The morning of the 3rd, Ed flew to La Guardia with $200,000 stacked tightly in a briefcase. He picked up a rental car and drove to a motel in Brooklyn where he waited for a call to tell him the deal was on. After lunch, Luigi called to give him the address. Ed drove through Brooklyn, followed by an unmarked FBI van carrying three armed agents. He parked next to an empty schoolyard; the support van watched from the next block.

Across the street, Gino and Luigi sat inside Mario's apartment. The cash-laden briefcase on the seat beside Ed seemed to scream like a police siren in this run-down neighborhood. It made him feel vulnerable; the Walther PPk clutched in his hand under his coat kept him from sweating.

Mario didn't want to meet Kurt Wolfe. The plan on this day called for Mario to hand the kilo of heroin to either Gino or Luigi, who would call Ed on his cell phone to alert him they were coming down. Not meeting Mario face to face didn't concern Ed; he knew if this first buy went well, Mario himself would soon suggest to Kurt that they cut out Gino, Luigi, and their commission and deal directly with one another. At that point, Ed would insist that Mario deliver the heroin straight to him in Washington, thus making the case under the jurisdiction of Eddie McLaughlin instead of the New York Office. Mario might prove to be the next rung up the narcotics ladder. Ed would then try to buy above him, and so on.

His car phone rang at 6:30 p.m. Gino said Mario was having trouble getting the heroin from his source. Ed was angry but Gino talked him into waiting for one hour. At 7:00, Mario's source had still not shown. Ed called the apartment and cursed up a storm that fogged his windshield. He told Luigi he had fifteen more minutes. After that, he was gone. The three agents in the van who'd been monitoring the calls to and from Ed's cell phone called him to argue that he shouldn't abort the buy. Stay there, they said, we've got a chance to make this deal.

"No fucking way," Ed shot back. "If I don't stick to my word, I'll look like a schmuck. I've got to do what I say with these guys. Kurt Wolfe don't wait like this."

At 7:15, Gino phoned Ed to tell him that Mario might come up with half a kilo later that night. The price was $105,000. Mario would send the other half of the buy to D.C. tomorrow.

"Tell him," Ed said, "to get fucked. I want a kilo of H, I want it tonight, and I wanted it a fucking hour ago."

Mario took the phone himself to ask Ed to go ahead with the deal.

"Listen, you cock smoker," Ed rammed his anger into the phone, "the next time you do a deal with me, you keep your end of the bargain. You deliver what I ask you for on fucking time, or don't bother me!" Ed drove away, the dismayed agents in the van chasing close behind. When Gino and Luigi left, Mario promised them that the next time they came to New York they wouldn't leave empty handed. Luigi got so upset at the score falling through his fingers that he broke into tears on Gino's shoulder.

Ed led the support agents' van to the New York Office. There, opinion was divided over how Ed had managed the episode. Half the agents applauded his gumption and discipline in squelching the buy; a cop would have sat there all night, they agreed, anxious to make a case. Perhaps Mario was testing this new player Kurt Wolfe, to see how long he'd twist in the wind. The other half of the agents thought Ed had been showboating and too quick on the trigger. Ed was sure he'd made the right move. Mario wasn't bringing the heroin down to Ed's car personally so no case would have been made against him. Ed would have spent the FBI's $200,000 just to establish Kurt Wolfe's authenticity with Mario. Perhaps, by leaving as he did in a huff, Ed had done this for free. Mario would be back, more eager than ever, and Kurt would be waiting. In time, Ed was proved to have been right.

* * *

Ed and Mario talked several times over the next few weeks, trying to set up another buy. Ed realized quickly that New York City would play a pivotal role in Infamita and Pizza II. The city remained the main arrival and distribution point for the Sicilians' narcotics.

Because of his exposure during The King's Court days in these very same Brooklyn neighborhoods hanging out with Sonny Black, Lefty, and the Bonannos, Ed couldn't travel here safely. Even though he hadn't been seen on Mulberry or Madison Streets in six years, the Mafia has a terribly long memory. Their recollection is tribal, kept alive in oral tradition. Ed Robb was not forgotten. Tony Daniels, the original Tampa supervisor of Coldwater, now the FBI's assistant director in charge of the Criminal Division, put a limit on Ed of two trips to New York during Infamita. This limit wouldn't hold up over the course of the case, but it did mean that, for now, Ed needed a connection in the Big Apple, someone who would do Kurt's work so he wouldn't need to go there. Ed told Luigi to invite Peppe Vitiello down to D.C. for a recruitment trip.

When Peppe arrived in Washington, Ed saw that he was cut from the same thin Mediterranean cloth as Luigi. Guiseppe "Peppe" Vitiello was another illegal immigrant from Naples, cunning, obsequious, slimy. Ed escorted Peppe around Georgetown and made a pitch for him to spearhead Kurt Wolfe's business in New York.

Luigi and Peppe now provided Ed's team with branches in Washington and New York. Ed instructed Peppe to phone every day at 5:00 p.m. Routinely, Peppe forgot and Ed had to make the call. Peppe lived in a small walk-up apartment with his immigrant mother and sister, neither of whom spoke a word of English but had no qualms about answering the telephone. On more than one occasion, Kurt Wolfe lost his already shaky reserve with them, though he knew they didn't have a clue what he was yelling about.

＊ ＊ ＊

Luigi, Peppe, Silvestri, and Mario all believed they were forging the nucleus of a new dope smuggling ring. However, by New Year's Day, 1987, Ed hadn't managed a single major drug buy. He'd scared Alfreddo out of his apartment with his suitcase of space-age, counter-espionage toys, he'd nixed the deal in Brooklyn because Mario had been late, and Luigi and his contacts had spun a lot of wheels setting up dead-end deals. Though he'd developed excellent intelligence, gathering names and connections in both New York and Washington, Ed was concerned that Luigi and his contacts might begin to lose faith in Kurt Wolfe. To give the impression of illegal activity—without committing any FBI money—Ed and Glenn Tuttle set up a scam buy with Luigi as participant and sole audience member.

A one-kilo football of sham "coke" had been placed inside a locker at the Washington bus terminal. Ed instructed Luigi to take a cab to the terminal and retrieve a package from a locker there, to be opened with a combination Ed provided. Luigi was to take the package to a Metro subway station in Alexandria, then sit on a particular bench and wait with the package. An Air Force colonel would sit next to him. Luigi was not to speak, just give the man the package. All of this had to be done at precise times. The colonel, Ed confided to Luigi, was a powerful connection to some very big people in the Pentagon and the government for whom he supplied narcotics. This was an important and secret assignment, so Luigi shouldn't fuck it up.

The colonel was, of course, an FBI agent who served in the Air Force Reserve, and the football was talcum powder.

Luigi was under surveillance from the moment he left Georgetown. At the bus terminal, combination in hand, he tried several times to open the locker door. He couldn't make it work. Frustrated, Luigi kicked the row of lockers and cursed in mad Italian. He dialed Ed's beeper and asked to have the combination repeated. Ed gave him the numbers and told him to calm down, just take care of business.

Again, the locker thwarted Luigi. He shook the door handle and kicked again to punctuate his rising dismay. The surveillance team stood by, watching Luigi bungle this simplest of tasks. One agent, looking over his newspaper, noticed that Luigi's banging fit was attracting the attention of the cops and security guards who are always in ample supply in big city bus terminals. A police officer walked toward Luigi. The FBI agent, afraid that the zip would get himself busted, stepped up fast and asked Luigi if he could help him out. Luigi sighed, "Yes," and the agent took the combination and opened the locker door. The cop kept walking as Luigi took the parcel, thanked the good Samaritan, and hurried to stay on schedule.

The surveillance agents tailed him to Alexandria where he made the handoff to the colonel. Later, the Washington Office weighed the talcum powder football to see if Luigi might have secretly carved off a taste for himself. He had not. Luigi Visciano, for all his criminal bent and loathsome ways, was stand-up. If he'd been busted, Ed knew he would never have ratted out Kurt Wolfe.

A week later, Ed again sent Luigi with a briefcase, this time to Union Station. At exactly 11 a.m., Luigi stood by the men's room. He recognized the Air Force colonel, and followed him in. Inside and alone, the two exchanged passwords. Luigi set down his briefcase. The colonel placed an identical one beside it; they made a swap and left the men's room separately. All was very cloak-and-dagger, all just for Luigi's eyes.

Luigi's enthusiasm for playing on Kurt Wolfe's narcotics team skyrocketed. He wanted to learn everything Kurt could teach him about smuggling. Kurt seemed very advanced in the ways he did his business.

"Never," Ed lectured, "let the drugs and the money be in the same place. You'll get ripped off, you'll lose the money and the junk. You could even get killed. Put the money in a car, give the guy the keys to the trunk, and walk away. Put the dope in a locker at the bus station, or in a trashcan a couple blocks away, and take the buyer a briefcase with the address in it. And never bring me the junk. I don't touch the shit, I only touch money." Behind Ed's back, Luigi began calling him "El Presidente" or "Lupo," Italian for wolf.

Every once in a while, Kurt Wolfe screwed Luigi, Peppe, or Silvestri out of money, just to maintain the pecking order. Lupo was a bad guy, a distrustful, mean bastard, and his crew wasn't allowed to forget it.

"Luigi," Ed told him, "you think sometimes you're smarter than me. You think you're a fox. Well you might be. But never forget. The wolf will kill the fox every time."

CHAPTER TWENTY-ONE
The Ladder

Luigi soon added one more connection to the cadre of brokers sniffing out heroin deals for Kurt Wolfe. Silvio Falleroni was another illegal Sicilian immigrant in New York who saw his path out of the pizza kitchens paved with narcotics and American money.

Silvio's voice joined the swirl of phone calls recorded by the FBI between Ed, Gino (both of whose phones were tapped voluntarily), and Luigi (who had a Title III wiretap on his phone) to and from their zip connections in New York—Peppe, Mario, Silvestri, and Falleroni. During these conversations, in a poor attempt at security, heroin and cocaine were given a hodgepodge of code names including red and white wine, red and white shoes, little shoes (samples), fifths, shirts (the quality of the "cotton" in the shirts referred to the purity of the narcotics), mozzarella, and farina (the Italian word for flour).

The Sicilians spoke almost daily among themselves, chatting like anxious housewives on the gossip wire, until three or four in the morning after getting off work in the restaurants. Each conversation featured a claim to know "this guy" with "the things" who could sell "all the shirts you can wear," but with no tangible results.

Luigi finally set up a six-kilo buy of cocaine with Silvio, but the price for the "white shoes" was too high for Ed. He nixed the deal, because the Bureau wanted only heroin, not coke. If the coke cost too much, Silvio told Luigi, then Kurt "should go somewhere else." Another dead end.

The next morning, Peppe and Luigi had a talk that would prove to be pivotal to Pizza II's progress up the supply ladder. Peppe said that "Michele" had called him to inquire what had happened to the six-kilo cocaine deal. The FBI, monitoring the call, was anxious to know who Michele was. Was he the source behind Peppe, Silvio, and Mario?

Ed still refused to buy cocaine at high prices. Luigi phoned Peppe several times and begged him to get in touch with "Michele," to ask him to get involved personally and set up a score for Kurt.

On January 29, Michele Bernardo phoned Luigi to tell him he was ready to supply heroin to Kurt Wolfe, deliverable in New York. When Ed heard the news, he knew he had to make a buy. This was Infamita's chance to take a step up the ladder, to the rung where Michele Bernardo stood. Ed agreed to purchase "one-fourth of a bottle" (a quarter kilo, slightly over a half-pound) from Bernardo in Brooklyn for $40,000.

High-quality, uncut heroin sold in New York for up to $250,000 per kilo. For a drug dealer, this figure represented simply the cost of doing business; he would probably triple his investment after shaving the kilo and selling it on the street. For a federal law enforcement agency that had to count and report every dollar, a quarter million dollars for a drug buy was a great act of faith in its undercover operations and its agent. The Bureau reasoned that a mere $250 sample, a taste, would secure a conviction of the seller, so why make the big deals? Pressure fell on the undercover agents to make smaller buys.

At the broker level on the narcotics totem pole—occupied by mopes like Luigi and Peppe—a taste was easy to get. Often, it was all the suppliers would entrust to them. But a New York dealer, a Michele Bernardo, was bound to grow leery of anyone claiming to be a major dope smuggler who only wanted to buy samples. Bernardo would want to make all his transactions expensive as a weeding-out process, knowing that most undercover cops couldn't last in too expensive a game. Insist too often or too stubbornly on a taste and you're a cop.

Ed later learned that it had been Bernardo who'd instructed Mario two months earlier to leave the newcomer Kurt Wolfe lingering in his car beside the Brooklyn schoolyard waiting for the kilo of heroin. It had been, as Ed suspected, a test, which he'd passed. Now Bernardo was willing to deal with Kurt Wolfe directly even if, at first, the buy was only for a "quarter bottle."

* * *

The morning of January 31, Ed, Luigi, and Peppe checked into the Sheraton Hotel near La Guardia Airport. Luigi had made arrangements with Bernardo to bring the heroin to their hotel where he could meet Kurt Wolfe. The drugs would be taken up to Ed's room, tested and, if satisfactory, paid for with $40,000 in a briefcase.

Ed and his Italian cohorts waited for four hours in the hotel lounge. This time, Kurt wasn't so antsy about the delay. Waiting in a warm bar beside loyal henchmen was not as tense as sitting alone next to $200,000 in a cold, strange neighborhood, your finger tapping on a trigger. The morning wore into afternoon. Luigi burned a path back and forth to the lounge pay phone.

"When are you coming?" Ed overheard Luigi's anxious pleas. "Alright. Alright. Yes, we're waiting."

After lunch, Ed sent Luigi in a taxi to fetch Bernardo. Finally, just after 2:00 p.m., Peppe perked up and jumped from his seat.

"They're here," he said. Ed remained seated.

Luigi entered the lounge, happy and excited, followed by Michele Bernardo who carried a briefcase. Michele exchanged pecks on the cheek with Peppe. Ed stood to shake the man's manicured hand. Bernardo's bearing, juxtaposed between Luigi and Peppe, was a total contrast to them. Like Gino, Michele reeked of class, but unlike Gino, it was real class. His clothes and overcoat were expensive, European in fit and flair. Michele spoke perfect Italian though he'd been born in New York. His air was that of Mediterranean royalty, looking down his long nose when he spoke, turning his head slightly as if to always give his best profile. Where Luigi and Peppe were street mongrels who scrambled for a living, Michele was a merchant prince, buying and selling anything in New York. He was the quintessential big businessman, borne and raised to cut million-dollar deals. Today, his deal was narcotics.

Michele's eyes swept away from Ed as they dropped hands. The drug dealer's gaze took in the Sheraton lounge and the lobby, calculating some risk: Something was wrong.

"I don't like the smell of this. I don't like this at all. Too many cops." Returning his eyes to Ed, he apologized. "Mr. Wolfe, no offense, but this is a favorite hotel for the police to do their drug deals. It's near the airport. Very convenient for them. Sorry."

As he turned for the door, Michele threw a quick glance at Luigi. "Call me, Luigi. Guiseppe, come."

Bernardo spun on his heel. Peppe gave Ed a shrug and fell into the man's sleek wake. The two got into a champagne-colored Cadillac and drove away. In fact, Bernardo had been right. There were too many cops in the hotel. By an unfortunate coincidence, another FBI undercover drug buy took place in the Sheraton that same afternoon, and there was other surveillance in place in the lobby, alongside Ed's team.

As Bernardo's car disappeared from the Sheraton lot, Ed's glare sent Luigi scurrying for the pay phone. Luigi reached Bernardo on his car cellular phone. The transaction was set for an hour and a half later at El Torrito, a restaurant behind the Yonkers Raceway. Luigi hailed a taxi. Ed sent him ahead to El Torrito, to make certain that Bernardo was there and that everything was in order.

"You coming with me, Kurt?" Luigi asked.

"No. I'll rent a car and meet you and Peppe there. I need my own wheels. I don't trust this guy yet."

What Ed needed was a car wired for sound. He couldn't safely wear a wire during his first meeting with a dealer as cagey and observant as Bernardo. Ed had no idea what he'd be walking into at El Torrito. Clearly, it was home turf for Bernardo. He might have Ed body-searched before approaching. A recorder or transmitter in a car would be the safest bet for this opening trip to Yonkers. And, he wondered, where the hell was Yonkers?

Ed rented a Grand Am Pontiac at the hotel desk. He drove it around the block, then stopped for the surveillance agents, who slapped a transmitter under the carpeting in the trunk and wired up two hidden mikes. The bugging job was fast and invisible.

"Can I follow you guys to fucking Yonkers?" Ed asked. The agents led him to the Yonkers Raceway. Had Ed lost them in the Gotham maze of stoplights and side streets, he knew he'd be irretrievably lost.

On the way, the agents detoured into a Howard Johnson's parking lot. Ed pulled in behind them and a supervisor drove up beside him. They conferred through open windows for five minutes. Two distress signals were arranged: If, during the transaction at El Torrito, Ed dropped his hat, this would be a sign to the armed surveillance team that he was in trouble. If he uttered the phrase, "Everything has turned to shit," the team would turn cavalry and rush with guns drawn to his rescue.

Ed tailed the van to Yonkers while another surveillance team picked up Bernardo's Cadillac and followed him to El Torrito. There, Bernardo was seen with a man who passed him a package.

When Ed arrived at El Torrito, the first thing he saw was Luigi and Peppe patrolling the property like guard dogs, peering around corners. Luigi gave a serious thumbs-up sign as Ed parked the rental car and flipped the transmitter and recorder switch to "on." Michele Bernardo came out of the restaurant. Ed checked the 9-mm Walther under his seat. Bernardo got in the passenger side. Peppe and Luigi climbed in the back.

Bernardo shook Ed's hand again.

"Now we can do things the right way," Michele said. "The heroin is good. It's the same quality as the sample Peppe brought you two weeks ago."

"Good. That was good shit." Indeed, Peppe's last score had passed the FBI test.

"You have the money, Mr. Wolfe?"

"I don't give you nothing until I test the shit. Let's see it."

Bernardo produced the quarter-kilo packet of beige powder, the "red shoes," or "red wine."

Ed removed his homemade field testing kit from his briefcase. He dug his pocketknife into the plastic wrapping around the narcotics and selected a bit from the middle of the packet. An inexperienced buyer will often test a sample from a corner of the package, so sellers wishing to cheat will put the highest-grade narcotics in the corners. Ed dropped hydrochloric acid into the first test tube. The acid turned positive purple. Next, the ammonia test showed acceptable levels of heroin and cut.

"Get out of the car," Ed told Bernardo, Luigi, and Peppe.

With everyone standing beside the Pontiac, Ed locked the dope inside the car. He looked at Luigi, schooling him as he proceeded. Never leave the drugs and the money in the same place. He moved to the rear of the car, keeping his eyes fixed on Bernardo. He slipped the key into the trunk lock; his eyes said: Don't make a fucking move, Bernardo. Lupo trusts nobody.

Bernardo had his hands buried in his coat pockets. Ed suspected that one of them fingered a gun. Beside the briefcase in the open trunk lay another 9-mm Walther. He paused as he reached for the money to look over the lid of the trunk at Bernardo. The moment of stillness told Ed, and told the drug dealer, that no one was going to draw. Ed smiled and lifted the briefcase from the well of the trunk. He handed over the $40,000.

"Be sure you settle up with them two," Ed told Bernardo, jutting his chin at Luigi and Peppe. He got into the Pontiac and drove out of Yonkers.

But not directly out of Yonkers. This time, with Bernardo watching, he couldn't follow the FBI van away from El Torrito and he got lost. Trying to work his way back to La Guardia for his flight home, Ed completely separated himself from the surveillance team. Within minutes, he grew mired in the back streets of a bad New York neighborhood. He'd never been to the tough parts of New York, but this was what he thought it looked like from movies—long shadows like black knives dicing across high tenements, spray-painted walls, litter-choked gutters, cascades of iron fire escapes, and meandering men with trouble on their faces. His gleaming Pontiac was easily the best car on the streets and he drove it like a bewildered tourist. His internal alarm signaled an oncoming attack of paranoia; the heroin and handgun tucked under his seat sizzled like a string of firecrackers. He got out of the car only once, to make a pay phone call to the New York Office for directions to La Guardia. The person answering the phone couldn't recognize where he was calling from based on the streets he named. He wanted to speak with the Narcotics Supervisor and was asked, "Which one?" Ed was a Washington agent; he didn't know anyone in the New York Office and he certainly wasn't going to confide in the person on the phone that he was an undercover agent lost on his way back from a buy. Flustered, he got back into the Pontiac.

Tired, fuming that the surveillance team had lost track of him, and disheartened by a maze of wrong turns, Ed finally stumbled to La Guardia. New York agents were waiting for him at the gate to the Washington shuttle. He turned the heroin and car keys over to them and got on the plane.

* * *

Immediately after the sale of the quarter-kilo of heroin to Kurt Wolfe, Michele Bernardo drove to the Bronxville home of his supplier, the man who'd handed him the package at El Torrito, Raffaele Fiumara. That same afternoon, Fiumara had been hustling to find enough heroin for another deal, the one with the California undercover agent in the Sheraton lobby, which had spooked Bernardo earlier that day. Though that buy didn't go down, the FBI soon determined that Fiumara stood in the shadows behind both deals. His was the name inscribed on the next level of the Sicilian drug pyramid.

The deal in Yonkers cemented the first round of cases in Infamita. Luigi, Peppe, Silvio, Bernardo, and Fiumara were now all in the FBI's bag. The El Torrito buy, plus dozens of recorded conversations—from Ed's car and phone, and Gino's and Luigi's bugged telephones—gave the Bureau the necessary probable cause to seek additional Title III wiretaps on suspects' phones and beepers in New York and Washington.

Once the wires went up in the first week of February 1987, Pizza II expanded swiftly. Along with the increasing criminal activity and the growing body of evidence came an old, familiar bugaboo: a turf war between FBI Field Offices.

FBI Offices are judged internally by the quantity and quality of cases they prosecute and the convictions they secure. The same is true of U.S. Attorneys' Offices. Though Pizza II was of nationwide scope involving several cases, Infamita had been the investigation's most productive covert component.

Infamita had been initiated by Glenn Tuttle of the Washington Field Office. Ed Robb was their lead undercover agent and the operation was financed from the Washington Office's coffers. Nonetheless, a large portion of Infamita's illicit enterprises was originating in the Southern District of New York, home of the most influential FBI and U.S. Attorney Offices. The New York, Los Angeles, and Washington Field Offices are the only ones in the Bureau with Assistant Directors of the FBI in charge. In addition, FBI Headquarters has always had a large contingent of New York alumni with a lot of administrative clout. The New York Office coveted Infamita.

Because of his loyalty to Eddie McLaughlin and Glenn Tuttle, Ed had been trying to convince Bernardo to mule the narcotics personally to D.C. to strengthen the prosecutorial venue against him there. Through the wiretaps, the New York Office picked up on Ed's efforts and cried foul to their comrades at HQ. He's trying to steal our case, they complained. As in Coldwater, Ed was again the agent in the street caught in the squeeze. And since it was still his life on the line, he wasn't going to be quiet about it this time. Ed had some clout of his own.

He was now well connected and appreciated in the Bureau's top echelons. He was acknowledged as the FBI's premier undercover agent. The chief prosecutor in the New York U.S. Attorney's Office of Rudolph Giuliani was Louis Freeh, Ed's personal prosecutor during the Manhattan portion of the Coldwater trials. Also, in the New York U.S. Attorney's Office, responsibility for Ed and Infamita had been assigned to Al Pavlese, a University of Virginia law grad and a friend from Charlottesville. Eddie McLaughlin at the Washington Field Office and Tony Daniels at Headquarters were both pleased that their old friend was on the case. Even the supervisors in New York were pleased that Ed was making big narcotics cases in their backyard with Washington's money.

This time, Ed took the lack of Field Office cooperation head on. In a message intended for all to hear, Ed asked how New York had the nerve to complain to Headquarters about how he was doing his job. After that, the New York agents tiptoed around the topic but still did not cooperate.

In addition to the FBI's inter-office squabbling, Ed soon discovered that the DEA had become another threat to his safety. Unknown to the Bureau, a DEA Narcotics Task Force in D.C. had targeted Luigi Visciano and Kurt Wolfe. They had put an informant in place, a man who lived in Ed's building. This new snitch learned of an impending heroin buy between Luigi, Kurt, and Bernardo. He informed his DEA handlers.

Peppe was scheduled to bring the heroin from New York to Ed's apartment. An armed bust was planned; the DEA was prepared to kick in Kurt Wolfe's door, guns drawn. Ed had weapons cached in his apartment, in his car, and often on his person. The potential for a dangerous mishap was great. This was a classic left-hand-right-hand situation but with both hands toting guns. Luckily, Bernardo called on the afternoon of the delivery to say that he couldn't get the heroin. He wasn't coming to D.C.; the buy was canceled.

Ed erupted when McLaughlin told him what the DEA had planned for him. With the DEA supervisors present, he stomped through the list of DEA's deficiencies: They were incompetent, they'd fucked up first class, and they were dangerous. The DEA even had a representative on the Infamita oversight team. The

DEA supervisors, stung by the criticism, complained about Ed to FBI Headquarters. The complaint found its way through channels to the head of the FBI's Criminal Division, Assistant Director Tony Daniels. Daniels calmly told the DEA: Yeah, he's right. You fucked up. Now, be quiet and stay away.

* * *

Next, it was the snitch Gino's turn. On the street, Ed picked up mumblings of threats to Gino. The little greaseball, Ed thought; he's probably playing several ends against the middle and it's catching up with him. One evening, Ed rang Gino's phone endlessly at a pre-arranged time. When the informant didn't answer, Ed feared something had happened to him. He grabbed a gun and his key to Gino's apartment.

He burst in and found Gino spread out on the sofa, watching TV, ignoring the phone. Ed slammed the door behind him and tore into him. Ed was furious. He'd been worried and afraid for Gino, enough so to bound into his apartment with gun in hand to protect him, only to find the snitch safe in his shiftlessness.

Gino decided he'd taken enough abuse. He threatened to reveal Kurt on the street as an agent. That was all Ed needed to hear.

"You are fucking with the wrong guy, you little cocksucker! Believe me, you jeopardize my life or this operation, I'll kill you myself or I'll see that it gets done!"

Back in his apartment, Ed called case agent Glenn Tuttle.

"Get rid of him, Glenn." His voice still shook with rage. "Now."

Within forty-eight hours, the FBI had relocated Gino a long way from Washington, D.C. He was watched and warned: You haven't got a friend in the world except the FBI. So don't shit where you eat.

Gino's sudden disappearance had no effect on the case. The snitch had been an excellent connection to Luigi Visciano but that had been the sum of his usefulness. Luigi, not Gino, had

269

brought in the other brokers, and now Ed had moved beyond Luigi's little sphere of influence. Kurt Wolfe was inching ever closer to the Sicilian sources of the narcotics: Michele Bernardo, Raffaele Fiumara, and the other big money men with their clean, manicured hands.

* * *

Luigi and Peppe set up another "quarter-bottle" buy between Kurt and Bernardo during the last week of February 1987. On the phone with Luigi, Bernardo said he wanted to do the deal that night. Luigi repeated the instructions Ed had given him, that the score couldn't happen for a few more days. Bernardo said that he was beginning to think that Kurt Wolfe was a cop.

"No way. He's no cop." Luigi stuck up for his boss. "He's too fucking crazy." Ed's investment in weirdness had paid off.

Ed made the buy from Bernardo in Yonkers on February 25. As before, when he pulled into the parking lot, Luigi and Peppe were doggedly stalking the grounds, watching for trouble. Ed parked in the far corner of the lot. Luigi, Peppe, and Bernardo huddled with another white male, later identified as Aldo Pastore, beside a Ford station wagon. Peppe split off from the group and came to Ed's car. He handed over a sample of heroin in a plastic bag, wrapped in newspaper. Ed produced his testing kit. The sample tested poorly.

"The fuck is this?" he barked at Peppe. "Go back over there and tell Bernardo this is shit. Tell him I want the good stuff. He's trying to rip me off."

Ed watched from across the lot as Peppe and Luigi held an animated discussion with Bernardo. When they were done waving arms and pointing fingers, the two mopes hurried over to Ed.

"Kurt," Luigi spoke, "Michele says he guarantees the shit. He says it's better than the last time. He'll double your money back if you're not happy with it."

Ed agreed to accept the heroin. He'd only put up the fuss for good form. Luigi handed him the quarter-kilo packet and Ed turned over $40,000 in FBI cash. Luigi and Peppe walked back to Bernardo, and Ed pulled out of Yonkers. The next day, the packet was analyzed at the DEA laboratory. It came up only 37 percent heroin.

Ed returned to Yonkers on March 5 for his third deal with Bernardo. The first two buys had gone smoothly, with only the one complaint he'd lodged last time about the quality of the heroin. Lupo had been a pretty easy customer so far. This trip, Ed decided, Kurt Wolfe would bare his fangs.

He drove into the El Torrito lot and sat still. A battered old Fiat, driven by Aldo Pastore, parked behind him. Ed watched him through the rearview mirror. Luigi and Peppe came out to join Ed in his car, where Peppe produced a taste in a plastic bag wrapped in masking tape. Ed tested the powder; it showed positive for heroin. The quality of the narcotics seemed fine.

Ed turned to Luigi in the back seat.

"It's bullshit again. Tell fucking Bernardo I want to talk to him."

"Kurt, Michele says this is good stuff. The best."

"Tell him."

Luigi knew better than to say more. He and Peppe left the car and jogged to the restaurant. When they returned, Luigi gave Ed a thumbs-up. "In the men's room."

"Tell him to come to my car." The Nagra was in the trunk.

"Kurt, what do you want me to do? Michele says inside." Luigi was apologetic but helpless. "In the bathroom."

Ed cursed and got out. He left the briefcase carrying the money locked in the trunk and walked to the restaurant.

Bernardo waited inside the men's room.

"Michele."

"Marco." For some reason never explained to Ed, Bernardo had taken to calling him "Mark" or "Marco." Perhaps it was for the same reason—a lame try at security—that they called narcotics by code name.

Ed complained. "The last quarter bottle I bought from you wasn't as good as the first. Now this one is even worse. What's the matter, Michele, you don't like my money?"

"I love everybody's money, Marco. I don't know why you say this shipment is bad but I promise you, next time you're not happy with the shit, I'll cut the price in half. There." Bernardo spread his hands like a magician as if to show what wonders he could produce with just a wave of them. "Satisfied?"

Ed spread his hands to mock him. "No. I'll go get your money. And the next time I'm unhappy with the shit, you'll eat it and I'm dealing with someone else."

Ed went to his car where Luigi and Peppe stood vigil. He opened the trunk and handed Luigi the "meatballs," $40,000 in a brown paper sack. Peppe took the quarter-kilo packet of heroin from under his coat and handed it to Ed. This time, instead of ferrying the money across the parking lot to Bernardo, Luigi walked behind Ed's car and turned the sack over to the man waiting in the Fiat, Aldo Pastore. Another fish hits the net, Ed thought.

Luigi came back smiling. Before climbing into the rental car to drive to La Guardia, Ed peeled a thousand dollars off the wad in his pocket and handed the fan of bills to Luigi. The DEA lab revealed the sample to be only 35 percent heroin. Bernardo was still testing Kurt Wolfe.

Over the next month, Ed stayed in regular telephone contact with Bernardo. He remained irate over the quality of the last two heroin buys. Bernardo had been caught trying to pull a fast one and though Kurt had purchased the shit anyway he demanded that Bernardo improve the product. Ed played his hand as the unsatisfied customer: The next deal would go down in D.C. with Bernardo present or it wouldn't go down at all. Bernardo agreed. When this hit the Title III wire, the New York Office threw a fit. They tried to have Ed reprimanded for trying to steal their case by coercing Bernardo to make a sale in Washington. Ed chewed back harder. Beefs were put in left and right: Eddie McLaughlin and his New York counterpart John Walzer, and case agent Glenn Tuttle and his match in New York Ted Wasky, exchanged complaints.

To Ed, the danger of the infighting wasn't just a bureaucratic issue. If the New York and Washington Offices couldn't work together, if vital decisions were left to hang fire, then Kurt Wolfe would appear indecisive to his targets, as someone who wasn't in control. If he were always having to "check with his people" before he came up with money or made a move, the natural tendency of the Sicilians, among the most suspicious of criminals, would be to wonder who his "people" were. Was Kurt an international narcotics trafficker as he claimed, with a million bucks in the bank, or was he merely representing someone else? The stink reached Tony Daniels again and, as before, he showed little patience with such bickering, as well as a great deal of support for the guy on the block. Did Ed say that? Well, he was right. Now shut up, all of you.

Once Daniels had enforced a truce between the two Field Offices, Ed set about the business of cozying up to Michele Bernardo. Bernardo made his first visit to Ed's Georgetown apartment on March 10, 1987. Ed, Bernardo, and Luigi discussed their previous narcotics deals together. Ed again vented his displeasure with the quality of the previous two deliveries. Bernardo waved them off as problems of the distant past. He told Ed he had an unlimited supply of cocaine available in the Dominican Republic; he wanted Kurt to be his partner in smuggling the coke to Italy where it could be exchanged in an even swap for heroin. The heroin would then be transported to the States where it could be sold for a far higher profit than the cocaine.

Luigi sat quietly through most of the meeting. He was not a player at the level of Kurt or Michele; he was merely an intermediary, an illegal alien scooping up a few thousand "meatballs" here and there left over after the big boys had helped themselves. Luigi had dreams of becoming Kurt's lieutenant in his international narcotics operation. Luigi had brought in ring members Peppe, Silvestri, Silvio, and recently another smooth New York waiter pal, Raffaele Iennaco. These men were forming their own *famiglia* and Luigi considered himself just below Kurt in the hierarchy. He listened to Bernardo and Kurt plan smuggling operations between South America, Europe, and the United States, and he felt a pang of jealousy.

Luigi chafed at any indication that he might fall from grace as Wolfe's Number One. Now that the narcotics operation had grown in size and activity, Luigi told Kurt that he wanted to make some of the decisions, especially with Gino gone some-where without saying goodbye. His new guy in New York, Iennaco, claimed to have big coke connections in Ft. Lauderdale with an Italian tile importer named Raffa, and an uncle in Miami who was a made member of an American mob family. Luigi nagged Kurt to explore these new connections. Ed, who couldn't go anywhere near Florida or an American Mafioso, laughed the scheme off and told Luigi to just keep doing his job and forget thinking. He passed the names Raffa and Iennaco on to Tuttle for the Miami Office to look into.

Luigi felt stung. He became more possessive of Kurt Wolfe and their operation, wanting to be involved in every detail. He brought to Lupo's door every drug deal he caught even the merest whiff of, the way a house cat brings mice to its owner. The sur-veillance agents monitoring the taps on Luigi's phones had their hands full day and night with his anxious efforts to stay at Kurt's right hand.

Ed and Tuttle discussed the problem of Luigi's meddling and anxieties. The waiter had to be kept busy and believing he was involved. Though he was no longer pivotal to Infamita and the case against him was well in hand, Luigi remained fully capable of upsetting the FBI's apple cart before it rolled all the way up to Fiumara. Ed and Tuttle set up another scam buy for Luigi, this time with a "Miami Vice" brand of elegance.

After driving to a small airport in the Virginia horse country outside Washington, Ed and Luigi boarded a flashy twin engine private plane Ed told Luigi he'd just bought. An FBI pilot flew them to Norfolk where a luxury car awaited them. The two drove to a secluded dock where, at precisely 2:00 p.m., a high-powered Cigarette speedboat roared around the point. The captain tossed his lines urgently to Ed and Luigi waiting on the quay. Ed accepted a duffle bag containing ten one-kilo footballs of cocaine (talcum powder). He instructed Luigi to keep an eye on the boat and skipper while he carted the duffle to the trunk of the car. For five minutes, he pretended to test the packages, finally declaring them acceptable as he tossed a briefcase out to the Cigarette, which lit up and skimmed away in a blink.

Back at the Norfolk airport, Ed gave Luigi $200 for tagging along and being another set of eyes. Luigi reveled in the private plane and the racy narcotics intrigue. He would do whatever he could to stay in Lupo's good graces and prevent Kurt and Bernardo from forging a relationship that would bypass him.

Luigi rummaged hard for another source to replace Bernardo before Bernardo could replace him. During the last week of March, every conversation between Luigi and Ed featured a section, like a regular editorial in a newspaper, about Luigi's search for new narcotics sources. His inquiries turned up several contacts, including a Sicilian named Pietro, a Chinese girl in the Bahamas, a Peruvian in Florida, and a Colombian connection of Iennaco's. Finally, Luigi told Ed frankly that he didn't think they should deal with Bernardo any more. Behind Ed's back—not behind those of the listening surveillance agents—Luigi had confided in Peppe his fears that Kurt and Bernardo were cutting them all out of deals. Kurt wants to send us back to Sicily, he lamented, so he and Michele can get rich alone. Maybe, he said to Peppe, the two of them should consider contacting the big boss Raffaele Fiumara and cut Kurt and Bernardo out instead.

Luigi was right: Ed and Bernardo were about to start dealing with each other directly. Bernardo called Ed on April 2 to tell him he would be in Washington that evening to sell him a shipment of red heroin personally. The dope waited at a location near La Guardia; Bernardo wanted Luigi to come to New York to meet with Peppe; the two of them would pick up the drugs and mule it to D.C. on the bus to avoid airport security. Bernardo would take a shuttle flight. Bernardo also said he needed to speak with Ed about something very important.

Ed dispatched Luigi to New York. New York surveillance agents watched Peppe and Luigi meet at the bus station, then proceed to a car lot, Sabino Motors in Queens. There, Bernardo gave them the heroin.

At 11:06 that night, Bernardo walked into Ed's apartment. For the next two hours, while they waited for the drugs to arrive with Luigi and Peppe, Bernardo and Ed talked shop in multi-million-dollar terms, on a worldwide level.

Bernardo said that he and Raffaele Fiumara operated a smuggling ring whereby kilogram quantities of cocaine were purchased from South American locales; he specified Santo Domingo. The coke was transported to Italy, where it was swapped for heroin two-for-one. The heroin was then imported into the United States by persons with U.S. passports hired to body-pack it in. Bernardo preferred children and especially obese women with big breasts as his mules. These women would tape the narcotics in the fold under their bosoms; the checkpoint guards never had the nerve to body search there. Previously, he'd imported the heroin in tomato paste cans but the customs dogs had found too many of their packages. His boss Fiumara had made twenty-four trips to Europe setting up such transactions. Bernardo told Ed that, with just three days' notice, he could have "twenty pieces" (kilograms) delivered from Italy. In fact, if Ed wanted to buy cocaine in the States or South America and smuggle it to them in Italy, Bernardo and Fiumara would exchange it there straight up for heroin; Ed could make his own arrangements to bring the H into the States and make a fortune.

At the end of his presentation, Michele offered Ed a one-third partnership in his international operation with Fiumara. Ed said he'd consider it very seriously.

Luigi and Peppe arrived at the D.C. bus terminal at 12:57 a.m. under surveillance. Peppe carried off the bus a rolled-up plastic bag. Luigi phoned Ed to report that they'd arrived, then he and Peppe took a taxi to Georgetown. At the apartment, Luigi took the package from beneath his hat. Ed tested the beige powder, then handed $27,000 to Bernardo. After the dealer was gone, Ed gave Luigi $4,000 and Peppe $3,000. He knew the heroin was shit quality again, with excessive cut—it later tested at 32 percent. He also knew that he may as well have lit a cigar with the thousands he'd just handed Luigi and Peppe for all the good it did the taxpayers. But Ed had just made a major drug buy in front of the cameras and mikes inside Washington's jurisdiction, and Luigi and Peppe were happy and out of the way for a while. If Tony Daniels could keep New York from making any more waves, Ed sensed that Infamita was back on track.

CHAPTER TWENTY-TWO
Rome

In late May, Ed dispatched Luigi, telling him not to come around any more.

"I told you to get a driver's license, you never did it. I tell you to be on time, you're always late. You're bad mouthing Bernardo every time I talk to you. I'm sick of it, Luigi. You're fired. Get lost."

Luigi didn't believe it at first, thinking Lupo was just blowing off steam. But when Ed didn't return his calls, Luigi understood. He left a final, rambling message on Ed's answering machine. In response to Ed's recorded request for callers to "please leave a message at the beep," Luigi began his diatribe with: "At the beep, Kurt, you are a motherfucker."

Now that Luigi was expendable to the investigation, he was no longer secretly protected from arrest. The FBI continued to keep tabs on Luigi, monitoring his calls and movements. Had he become a threat to Infamita, interfering with Ed's relationship with Bernardo, the Washington Field Office would have arrested him. But Luigi was such a mope that he never rose above being an irritant, simply wreaking his vengeance by slandering Kurt Wolfe on the street. By October, Luigi took himself out of the picture and dragged Peppe Vitiello along with him. In New York, he and Peppe were jailed for conspiring to sell five kilograms of cocaine to a DEA undercover agent.

Without the covetous attentions of Luigi, Ed could pursue a closer association with Michele Bernardo and his wife, Katherine. Michele became a regular visitor to Washington, where Ed entertained him with the bustling nightlife of Georgetown's neon streets, trendy eateries, and chic shops.

On May 28th, Ed was again in Yonkers to purchase one-eighth of a kilo of heroin from Bernardo. During the deal, Bernardo called his wife four times to enlist her help in having the dope picked up from their home and transported to El Torrito. The FBI intercepted a call from Katherine to Alfredo Albino of Alfredo's Pizza in Brooklyn. She asked if he were coming. Alfredo said no, he would send an employee. Katherine called her husband back, who instructed her to put the dope in a black briefcase. Soon thereafter, a cab appeared at the Bernardo house-hold. A young man, Gino Dambrasio, entered, then left within minutes carrying a black briefcase to the taxi. New York agents followed the cab to El Torrito where the briefcase was delivered to Bernardo. Inside the restaurant, Michele gave the case to Ed. Ed took the case to his car, tested the drugs, and returned with another briefcase carrying $10,000.

Bernardo asked if Ed wanted to buy some white heroin. He mentioned a big connection of his, "a guy in Brooklyn." Ed was interested; he told Bernardo to get back to him with an offer.

Two days later, the FBI intercepted a call from Bernardo to Alfredo "Tony" Spavento in Brooklyn. Bernardo told Spavento it would be "Monday for the shirts."

Spavento replied that he'd received "the suit that morning."

"I'll pick it up Monday," Bernardo said. "That guy has left already."

Bernardo had bought the shirts, the white heroin, from Spavento for sale to Kurt Wolfe. Spavento was Bernardo's "guy in Brooklyn." Alfredo Spavento was a haberdasher working out of his Brooklyn clothing store, Italian Fashions, Inc. Bernardo used Spavento as a backup source whenever he and Fiumara came up short or needed some narcotics fast.

Once Alfredo Spavento came to the attention of the FBI, it became obvious that Italian Fashions, Inc., was a hub for narcotics trafficking. Many of the deals the Bureau had been watching for the better part of a year in both Washington and New York had passed, at some point, through Spavento's hands. A Title III wiretap was put in place immediately on Spavento's business and home phones and beeper.

Several separate FBI and DEA investigations began to converge on Alfredo Spavento and Italian Fashions Inc. In early June, an illegal alien named Emanuel Adamita shopped some heroin deals with a DEA informant in Florida. Just three months earlier, Adamita had been in an Italian prison serving a sentence for a 1980 conviction on charges of narcotics and Mafia association, in connection with a forty-kilo heroin shipment bound from Milan to the United States. That shipment had been one of the original seizures of Pizza I. Adamita strolled out of jail on a weekend furlough and kept going. Once he surfaced in Florida, the DEA put two of its best undercover agents on him. By July, Adamita walked into Italian Fashions, Inc., to supply the two agents with narcotics.

In addition to Infamita, another of the Pizza II undercover operations, Crimson Sky based in Charlotte, found its way to Spavento. A Crimson Sky undercover agent was brought by his Charlotte connections to New York to purchase heroin in kilogram quantities directly from Spavento. Spavento then introduced him to two other high-level drug dealers, Michael Modica and Vincenzo Miceli. The Crimson Sky agent bought a kilo of heroin from Modica and Miceli for $195,000 in cash. A third FBI covert operative, running a drug sting in South Carolina completely separate and unrelated to Pizza II, was also brought by his sources to Spavento's Brooklyn boutique for a narcotics deal.

Italian Fashions, Inc., was a crossroads of drug dealers. Like dust in a spinning fan, every criminal name and face that hit the store sprayed out into more particles and bits of trails, evidence, phone numbers, meetings, new names, and faces. Bernardo begat Fiumara and Spavento; Spavento begat Adamita, Modica, and Miceli, who begat Calderone, Caruso, Cannavo, Rizzuto, Romano, Catalano, and a host of others. Most of these Sicilian criminals had little networks of their own, each spreading out from Italian Fashions, Inc., in oil slicks of drug dealing.

Ed Robb knew he couldn't work Alfredo Spavento. Italian Fashions, Inc. resided in the heart of Brooklyn, and Tony Rossi was still too notorious and despised there for Ed to risk making regular visits. Besides, the agent from Crimson Sky, plus the South Carolina agent and the two DEA agents, seemed to be mining the Spavento vein very successfully. Pizza II was gathering an immense amount of intelligence from the lead Ed had developed from Bernardo to Spavento.

He concentrated instead on getting next to the kingpin, Raffaele Fiumara.

* * *

Fiumara owned a house in Yonkers. Ed had already made five buys at the El Torrito Restaurant in Yonkers through Bernardo while Fiumara lurked in the shadows. Neither Tony Daniels nor Eddie McLaughlin was going to approve many more trips to New York for Ed; he had already exceeded their wishes. Ed knew their concerns for his safety would eventually override any courtship of Fiumara; the risk of exposing Ed to his former mob enemies in Brooklyn and Manhattan grew with each visit to New York. Taking the next step up the ladder to Fiumara would be tricky.

Fiumara took regular trips to Italy, sometimes staying for months at a time to set up drug transactions. Ed decided to press for a meeting with Fiumara in Italy. There, away from the eyes of the New York City underworld, Ed could slow down and do some in-depth intelligence. In Yonkers, Kurt could do nothing more than drive in, test the drugs, hand over the money, and drive out. He had neither the time nor pretext to meet Fiumara. But in Italy, Ed could get a close look at the drug boss's operation, his European sources, and his methods. Give me a couple of days with Raffaele Fiumara, he was convinced, and we'll be partners. Old pals. Famiglia.

In June 1987, Ed put his foot down on Bernardo. No more buys until I meet your boss. I want to deal directly with Italy. I want to meet the man.

Bernardo was reluctant. This wasn't the way the business was supposed to work; his and Fiumara's operation had been structured specifically to prevent just such an occurrence as a buyer meeting Fiumara. Small-time brokers like Luigi and Peppe found the buyers and brought them around. Bernardo's job was to qualify the buyers, sell to some, and reject the rest. He kept another layer of human insulation in front of him, men like Aldo Pastore, who handled the money and drugs up front. Meanwhile, his boss Fiumara arranged the overall picture, the supply of narcotics through Italy and middlemen like Spavento. Fiumara never touched the drugs, and rarely the money.

But Kurt Wolfe had proved to be a reliable and consistent customer, paying fair prices with few questions. Wolfe was very careful. He'd undergone several of Bernardo's cop tests and passed. In D.C., Kurt ran a crew of street-level brokers. He had been a gracious host to Michele several times in Georgetown, and Kurt's willingness to travel to Italy to meet Fiumara on foreign turf—where, even if he were a cop, he'd be powerless outside of his American jurisdiction—showed a flexibility and commitment too rare to be insincere, too unique to be a cop.

Bernardo continued to stall. Marco, he wheedled, buy some dope, buy some nice leather jackets, how about some stones? Bernardo had to be reminded that Kurt Wolfe was an SOB; when Kurt said no, he made it stick. I want a sitdown with the man, in Italy, Ed insisted. I want to know who I'm dealing with.

One sunny morning in early June, with Michele visiting Washington, Ed took him to the Georgetown bank where he kept the million dollars. Ed slid out the safety deposit drawer. Bernardo's eyes almost fell into the cash pile.

"Go ahead," Ed said, motioning to the brimming basin, "reach in. Feel it."

Bernardo grabbed up a bundle of the bills and let it drop back into the box.

"Jesus Christ, Marco."

Ed joined him and scooped up several hundred thousand

dollars, the packets slipping slowly through his fingers. "You see what we got to play with here?" he said, laughing alongside Bernardo's growing glee. "Get me in with Fiumara. We'll fill up ten of these boxes."

Ed kept up the pressure on Bernardo. He knew the Sicilians had long been hoping to set up a lucrative drug-swap market, cocaine for heroin between the United States and Europe. He saw an opening and surged into it with an appealing offer to Bernardo:

"Look, I'm a businessman like you. I won't touch the shit, I'll just arrange for it to move from place to place. I'll handle the money. What I want to do is take you up on your offer to be partners, like we said. I'll supply the coke from my Colombian connections. We'll get it muled to Italy. I can score coke for twenty-twenty-five a key. In Italy, we trade it two-to-one for heroin, then we import that back into the U.S. We can get, what, as much as $250 a key for heroin here? That's a five to one profit, uncut. We step on it a few times before we put it on the street, we can go twenty to one. I got all the cash we need, Michele, and I got the coke connections. You got the heroin in Italy. We'll do a swap. I'll export the coke, you guys take care of the heroin. Tell Fiumara to let's do a deal, alright?"

Ed hoped he'd touched the right nerve. In mid-June, he learned he'd been right: Bernardo told him that Raffaele Fiumara would sit down with Kurt Wolfe. In Italy.

* * *

During World War II, the Fascists employed secret police and informants throughout Italy. Informing on one's neighbors was a heinous act, rewarded at war's end by beatings and summary hangings across the country wherever the snitches were revealed. The Italians never forgot or forgave their fear of informants and, as a result, the Italian Government did not conduct undercover operations.

Throughout the original Pizza investigation, and for the first year and a half of Pizza II, the FBI, DEA, and INS had coordinated their intelligence with the three principal Italian law enforcement agencies: the Italian National Police, similar in scope and mission to the FBI; La Guardia de la Finanza, the counterpart of the American Customs Service; and the paramilitary police of the Italian state, the Carabiniere.

Once the sitdown was arranged in Rome between Fiumara and Ed, a summit meeting was held in Washington with representatives of the Italian National Police, La Guardia, and Carabiniere. The Italian National Police identified Fiumara as a senior boss of the N'Drangheta, a major Sicilian organized crime family. Intelligence supplied by Ed named Fiumara as a leading narcotics dealer inside Italy and the United States. He was at the center of the effort to create an international exchange for cocaine and heroin. All three Italian law enforcement agencies wanted to nab Fiumara any way they could. The Italian and American agents agreed at the summit in Washington that Ed Robb should be allowed into Italy with both governments' permission for a limited and well-defined undercover objective.

Ed's only demand for the trip was that Infamita Case Agent Glenn Tuttle and Washington Field Office Supervisor Eddie McLaughlin accompany him. These trusted men would be his backup and help coordinate the surveillance efforts. Tuttle and McLaughlin would travel under fictitious identities, also violating Italian law, but it couldn't be helped. The Italians grimaced and concurred.

Even before the meeting at FBI Headquarters had ended, a tug-of-war broke out among the Italian agencies to determine who would take the lead in coordinating the American covert operation inside their borders. The Italian National Police and Guardia de la Finanza both made passionate claims to the jurisdiction in the case, blatantly competing for the credit that might come later.

This skirmish over turf weighed on Ed's mind the evening of June 18 while he settled into his business-class seat next to Michele Bernardo for the flight from Kennedy International to

Rome. Ed had been through enough bureaucratic dust-ups in his career to know how dangerous they could be, and he'd heard more than enough horror stories about the corruption that ran like a genetic flaw through every level of Italian government and law enforcement. He worried about how big an international deal this mission had become, with the details worked out at the State Department level. In the event that he, Tuttle, or McLaughlin got arrested or injured in Italy, or exposed as undercover agents, there was no contingency plan in place. They could easily create a diplomatic incident: American agents conducting covert operations against Italian citizens in direct violation of national law. The FBI would have to let the U.S. Embassy deal with it.

The jet climbed into the night sky. Bernardo nattered away next to Ed. In broken Italian, he flirted with the stewardesses and other passengers and talked a mile a minute into Ed's ear about the millions they were going to make. Ed ordered the first of several cognacs.

Over the Atlantic, his thoughts slowly turned from his worries and calmed. He'd be safe in Italy. Tuttle and Eddie, ten rows behind him on the plane, were at his back. They were good men, tough, professional, proven. He'd been briefed in Italian police powers; they could do things American law enforcement agencies couldn't. The Italians weren't so burdened by the civil rights of their suspects. There were no Miranda requirements. Italian police operated not on the American standard of probable cause but on simple suspicion of criminal conduct. Warrants, wiretaps, searches, arrests—Ed believed that these would surely be easier to obtain in Italy, and the local authorities would use every device at their disposal to guarantee that he, his backup agents, and their operation were safe and successful. Ed Robb was in a critical position; he would definitely be under surveillance 24 hours a day, every day in Italy. They'll bend over backwards to avoid an incident. We'll all be heroes.

Ed had arranged with Tuttle a dead-drop scheme as a means of staying in contact with the surveillance teams. He'd brought along a portable cassette recorder and twenty country music tapes. He planned to record over the music and hide the tapes in phone booths and other unobtrusive locations, leaving them for Tuttle and Eddie to scoop up behind him. These tapes would be his way to tell surveillance his plans for the day or night ahead. During the flight, Ed's mood drifted sleeplessly between apprehension and confidence. The cognacs only intensified his exhaustion. It was early afternoon when they touched down in Rome. After putting his passport on the immigration desk and collecting his bags, Ed just wanted to lie down. Bernardo hailed a taxi and took them to the Excelsior Hotel.

The Excelsior is one of the oldest hotels in Rome. Located next to the U.S. Embassy, it is renowned in international circles as the preferred accommodations in Rome for terrorists and spies. Arriving at his room, Ed watched the bellhop open his heavy oaken door with an ancient skeleton key. None of the rooms in the hotel were secure; they could all be opened with a single key.

Collapsed across the bed, his situation sank onto his chest with his tiredness. He was alone. The FBI and Italian police didn't know his exact whereabouts, though they must know he was in the Excelsior. But which room? He had to get in touch with Tuttle and Eddie. He had the number for the Legal Attaché, in fact an FBI representative, at the American Embassy, but how to call him? He didn't trust the room telephone. There was a pay phone across the street.

Ed lurched out of the hotel to the pay phone. He was too bushed to worry that Michele might see him using a public phone and become curious. He discovered that the pay phone worked only on tokens; he couldn't even raise an operator without one. He walked into a few shops and found no one who sold the tokens. Ed's lack of Italian stretched his patience and his weariness had caught up with him. He didn't want to ask the hotel desk clerk or a bellboy for a token; the Excelsior, he suspected, must be a teeming marketplace for information peddling. Instead, he taped a note under the counter of the payphone for Tuttle, who was probably watching Ed's every move. The note explained which room he was in and where he would leave his first recorded message.

Ed left the public phone, wobbling from fatigue. He noticed a man nearby reading a Roman newspaper. This must be the surveillance, he thought. Good. Once Tuttle picks up the note, the Italian National Police and La Guardia will get to work wiring my room and telephone, and Bernardo's too. I'll go take a nap, give them a couple of hours to get the jobs done, and let Tuttle and Eddie settle in wherever it is they are right now.

Ed's room, No. 521, was spacious, with high ceilings and heavy, worn furniture. The bed, overstuffed chair, and armoire creaked with age, reeked of intrigue. Ed tumbled into a deep sleep. He awoke after two hours to the ringing phone. It was Bernardo; a meeting was set for 8:00 that night in the Excelsior lobby with Raffaele Fiumara. Ed figured that all the electronics were in place by now. He lay on the bed and made his report to the hidden microphones.

"Well, what can I tell you? Michele just called. The meeting with Fiumara is tonight, downstairs in the lobby at eight. I don't know if we'll go somewhere else but you ought to be ready to follow us. At this point, everything is cool."

To be certain that his watchers got the message, Ed picked up the telephone receiver, heavy and antique. He dialed zero to get rid of the tone, then retold his intelligence. He went into the bathroom to take a shower, wondering all the while if a pinhole camera lens were observing him through the light fixture.

At eight o'clock, Ed got a phone call as he was leaving his room: Bernardo and Fiumara were coming to his room instead of meeting in the lobby. This was a lucky break since Ed knew the room would be bugged.

Within moments of shaking Raffaele Fiumara's hand, Ed knew this was a boss. Fiumara's blend of suavity, confidence, and toughness came through instantly in his handshake; his cunning came through in the little nods of his head and his darting eyes. His build was similar to Ed's, with a thick chest and broad shoulders; he was a keg of danger and guile. Like Bernardo, the man seemed without rough edges; everything was polished, slicked, and held firmly in place. Dark sunglasses perched in his thick, jet hair waiting to be lowered like the portcullis of a castle to guard his eyes.

Ed took the initiative. Kurt Wolfe was not a man to dwell on niceties; he was a businessman and this was a business meeting. He laid down the deal for Fiumara as he'd stated it many times already to Bernardo. He worked in the wine business and wanted to establish an ongoing trade of wines. White wine would be supplied by him, exported from the States to Italy, then swapped there two-for-one for Fiumara's Italian red and imported back into the United States by Ed.

"Raffaele, you don't know me and I don't know you. But I guarantee you everything is on the up and up from my end. Your man Mike here believes we can work a deal or I wouldn't be sitting here." Ed recalled Bernardo's delight at the million in cash in the Georgetown safe deposit box. "Mike knows what I can do," he added.

After only a fifteen-minute talk, most of it spent on Kurt's self-promotion, Ed rose from his seat.

"You two go ahead and do what you gotta do," he said politely but with a touch of distance. "I'll see you later." Fiumara shook his hand and bade him good evening.

Leaving after he'd said his piece was the right move. Don't force your way along or hang around trying to listen to every word. Don't fall all over yourself being buddy-buddy. That's what a cop would do. Walk away. Not too curious, not too pushy. Let Fiumara come to you.

Back in his room, Ed spread-eagled across the bed and gave his report to the air. Hope you got all that downstairs. I gave him the pitch, he didn't say much. We're gonna get together later. I'll drop a tape off under the pay phone across the street tonight. Again, because he wasn't sure exactly where the microphones had been installed in his room, he picked up the phone receiver and repeated the details.

Ed slipped out of his suit. The hour was still early but the demands of the traveling day carried him quickly into sleep. When the phone rang just after 10:00 p.m., he answered it half asleep.

"Marco?" It wasn't Bernardo. Fiumara's voice. "Come down to the lobby, will you?"

"Yeah. Sure. Gimme a minute." Ed cleared his head to dress. He spoke to the walls. I'm heading down to the lobby. Fiumara wants to see me.

He descended the steps into the grotto-like lobby. In the center of the room, seated at a coffee table, was Fiumara and, next to him, a priest. Save for these two, the lobby was empty.

A priest? Ed approached the table where the two men sat smiling at him. What is going on here, he wondered. The presence of the padre bewildered him. A man as good as a priest should not be sitting next to a man as bad as Raffaele Fiumara. The symbols of good and evil were out of kilter.

Ed put out his hand, the priest extended his. Fiumara introduced the man as Father Lorenzo Zorza.

"Please," the priest smiled, "call me Father Lorenzo."

By his accent, Ed judged him to be American. Zorza had the fleshy face and flaccid, pale skin of a pampered man of the cloth, plainly a stranger to physical exertion. He stood just under six feet, mid-fifties, and balding.

"Marco," Fiumara said, "let's go across the street to a little outside café. The Excelsior has too many ears."

Ed looked around the lobby. Not enough ears, he thought. He wasn't wearing a Nagra or a transmitter, wouldn't wear one in Italy. He was far too unsure of the quality of his backup in this country to take the chance of being caught with a wire. Also, because of the insecure skeleton lock on his hotel room door, it would be risky to even have a recorder or transmitter anywhere near him. The lifeless lobby resounded with his isolation: If trouble struck tonight, there would be no rescue.

The three ran through an evening shower to a crowded bistro. Inside, Fiumara's brother greeted them; seated at a table with him were two young, beautiful women. Michele Bernardo was still absent. Ed read that as a bad sign. This early in a criminal relationship, it was unusual for mob guys to sit down with a new middleman without including the original connection—in this case, Bernardo. Ed glanced about the café as he sat; no Tuttle or McLaughlin but two guys hanging out at the bar with furtive eyes looked as if they might be surveillance.

Fiumara and Zorza noticed the watchers too. Fiumara laughed. "We must move you out of the Excelsior tomorrow. Too many terrorists. Too many counterterrorists. The last thing I want to do is be arrested accidentally by the Israelis."

"OK. I'll do that in the morning."

"We'll move you to the Sheraton by the airport."

"Great." Yeah, great for Tuttle and McLaughlin, Ed thought. All that installation work in the Excelsior was down the drain.

After five minutes of small talk, inquiring how Ed's flight had been and how he liked Rome so far, Raffaele directed the conversation to the red wine business. Ed glanced mistrustfully at Father Lorenzo.

"Marco, Father Lorenzo is with us. He's also with a very respected famiglia in Brooklyn."

Ed nodded, impressed. Fiumara had an authentic, mobbed-up priest working for him. The brother and the girls stayed huddled at their end of the table, giggling and smoking. They weren't listening as Fiumara continued.

"First, I want to tell you that, even though you've been dealing with Michele all this time, I've actually been behind all your purchases. Michele brings your money to me."

Ed only nodded. The priest nodded too.

Fiumara continued. "Michele and I have been buying our cocaine in the States for cash and importing it back to Italy. We've had to develop several sources in America." Ed recalled the Brooklyn clothier Tony Spavento and his Italian Fashions, Inc.

"I very much like the idea of dealing with one source for cocaine. You, Marco. You bring cocaine to me here. We'll swap it for heroin and smuggle the heroin back into the States. The cocaine we'll sell in Europe, the heroin you sell in America, and we both get rich."

Raffaele explained that his heroin came from the Middle East, through the seaports in Sicily, then into his home in Calabria on the southeastern coast of Italy. From Calabria, where he owned a house, the narcotics were driven in cars bearing NATO tags—so they wouldn't be stopped—north to Milan where his sister's husband maintained a stash house. In Milan, the drugs were packaged into kilo bags that Raffaele called "soles," plastic wrappings smashed flat to resemble the soles of shoes. The heroin was then strapped under the breasts of female mules, specially selected for their girth, and driven across the Alps into Switzerland. From there, the drugs were body-packed and flown to America. Switzerland was chosen as the European point of departure because the Swiss did not stamp passports at departure; Fiumara seemed certain that would obscure the origin of the drugs if they were seized on arrival in the States.

The discussion soon turned from drugs to Father Lorenzo's criminal specialty, stolen artwork. The priest said that he had access to a great many priceless works of art long thought to be missing or destroyed. When the Nazis first gained control of Italy, Hitler brought back to Berlin thousands of treasures of the Italian master painters and sculptors. Most of this art was never returned to Italy; the pieces were eventually lost or stolen during the war's final years. Father Lorenzo claimed to be hooked into an Italian crime ring that had possession of several of the masterpieces, including paintings, statuary, and artifacts. Zorza dropped a few artists' names; the only one Ed recognized was Caravaggio. A subsequent check by the FBI revealed a 1982 conviction against Lorenzo Zorza in the Southern District of New York on a customs charge of smuggling stolen artwork from Italy into the United States. The priest had served no time in prison.

Fiumara patted Father Lorenzo on the back and spoke up, to add more items to the priest's crooked resume. Zorza sat quietly, humble, as the boss bragged about him.

Father Lorenzo had been born in Naples but had become a naturalized American citizen. He'd served as a priest for a number of years in New York City where he'd made his mob connections. He rose through the ranks of the Church to become a diplomatic liaison and envoy between the Vatican and the U.S. government. Zorza transported Fiumara's money from illegal sources back and forth between Italy and the States. The priest placed the cash in his diplomatic pouch, which by international law was free from customs scrutiny. Zorza also moved money for his Mafia connections in Brooklyn. Raffaele claimed that Father Lorenzo had never been searched.

Fiumara and Zorza waxed at length about what a good thing they had going. They professed to have an information source in the DEA's Rome office. Ed winced; this was not good news, since the DEA was an inside party to Pizza II and Infamita. They regaled him for half an hour with tales documenting how corrupt and cooperative the Italian government was. Fiumara had a line on some national contracts to build apartments on the Isle of Capri. Fiumara knew of Ed's construction background: Between the two of them, Fiumara figured they could land the contracts, throw up a couple of apartment buildings, and rake in profits from kickbacks and creative accounting.

At last, Fiumara and Zorza rose and said goodnight. The brother and the girls paid no attention. Ed left them and hurried through the drizzle to the Excelsior. The moment he walked into his room, he realized it had been tossed. Nothing was missing but little items and traps he'd set by habit before he left for the meeting betrayed a stranger's search. A burned match had been left leaning against the medicine cabinet door; he found it on the floor. His shaving kit had been positioned carefully on a stand in the bathroom; the kit had been rotated. He'd noted where a suit was hung on the rod inside the closet; it had been slid aside. And two dresser drawers he'd left slightly ajar were now closed all the way. That's why Michele Bernardo wasn't at the meeting with Fiumara and Zorza. He'd been occupied elsewhere, in Ed's room.

Ed lay on his bed and gave his evening report to the hidden microphones. He described the details of Fiumara's operation he'd learned in the bistro and asked for background information on Father Lorenzo Zorza. He repeated this intelligence into the phone. Lastly, he selected one of the country tapes and recorded his report over the music. He carried the tape out into the wet night, checked to make sure the coast was clear, crossed the boulevard, and taped the cassette to the bottom of the pay phone counter.

CHAPTER TWENTY-THREE
It Comes Down to "Louie"

The phone rang early. "Marco?" It was Bernardo.

At the sound of his voice, Ed wanted to say: Fuck you, you greaseball, you tossed my room! He shook off the cobwebs and stayed in control.

"Yeah."

"We gotta move. This morning." His tone was animated, insistent. Obviously, Fiumara had given Bernardo his orders, and he intended to follow them with urgency.

"Too many fuckin' cops here. It's dangerous. Pack up."

Ed gathered his clothes and effects, explaining to the walls as he packed and then the phone receiver that he was on his way to the Sheraton. Sorry, but you guys will have to start over there.

Ed rang for a bellboy to fetch his bags. Downstairs, the Excelsior lobby looked like a training session for surveillance agents. A dozen people walked about the massive room with purpose, checking in or out, coming or going, while an equal number stood around or skulked with sunglasses on, newspapers up, heads bobbing, swiveling left and right. The scene struck Ed as a burlesque of connivance on a grand scale. But it didn't make him feel any better to see so many secret cops when none of the watchers was Tuttle or McLaughlin.

Bernardo arrived in a cab and ferried him to the Sheraton where reservations awaited Kurt Wolfe. He and Bernardo had rooms on the same floor, several rooms apart. Ed tossed his luggage on the bed. Figuring it would again take the Italian National Police or La Guardia de la Finanza several hours to install the wires, he took Bernardo down to the hotel bar to hang out until lunch.

After an hour, Fiumara swept into the lounge dressed in a flowing white linen outfit, perfect for the bright Italian day. He could only stay a minute. He wanted to set up another meeting for that evening to confer further about the wine business. Father Lorenzo had more he wished to discuss with Kurt regarding art and other enterprises. A casual listener might have judged these three men to be cultured, international dealers in fine wines and priceless paintings, not global criminals discussing narcotics and stolen artwork.

* * *

Just as Ed had dumped Luigi Visciano once his relationship with Michele Bernardo had flourished, he was now rising beyond Bernardo as he closed in on Raffaele Fiumara. And just as Luigi had responded with envy and bile to Ed's abandonment, so too did Bernardo. Bernardo began to make passing but disparaging comments about Fiumara, imploring Ed not to trust the man too far. He advised Ed to remember that Fiumara was first and foremost a made Sicilian mobster. His loyalties would always be to the N'Drangheta famiglia and his fellow Calabrese, not to the American Jew Kurt Wolfe. Ed could only surmise what doubts and scandals Bernardo whispered about him into Fiumara's ears, like a poisonous serpent.

Bernardo's carping made things even dicier for Ed. It was only his second day in Rome, and he felt the anxiety of not knowing where his surveillance team was. So far, Tuttle and Eddie Mac had been invisible; he couldn't tell which, if any, of the seemingly ample supply of Italian watchers were assigned to watch him. He was alone, a stranger in a strange land dealing with dangerous animals in their own jungle. His mere presence in Italy under a fictitious name constituted a crime. He thought of his family: Gretchen had no idea he was even on this side of the Atlantic. He went again to a pay phone, this time with several tokens in his pocket. He dialed collect to a "hello phone" in the Washington Field Office.

He asked for Carol, Glenn Tuttle's partner. She came on the line. Ed emptied his bag of woes. He'd been abandoned. He hadn't seen his guys since they'd landed in Rome. He could use a glimpse of them just for comfort, for Christ's sake! Carol, do something!

Carol tried to soothe her agent, but she had nothing concrete to tell him. She hadn't heard from Tuttle or McLaughlin either. Carol became Ed's lifeline. Because of the eight-hour time difference between Rome and Washington, they set times to speak. Ed wouldn't talk with anyone else; he wanted only Carol, someone who knew the case and the Italian shit he stood neck-deep in.

That night, Fiumara, Bernardo, and Zorza stood him up for dinner. He waited in his room at the Sheraton until Raffaele called and apologized for the delay. We can't make it tonight, Marco. Tomorrow, alright? Bene. Ciao.

Ed was aggravated at the slight but not surprised. He'd always believed it to be a blessing that criminals were not more diligent in the conduct of their businesses. If they were disciplined and precise, they might run the world. But now he grew impatient. He wanted to get the deal done and go home. He reported his dismay to the walls and the telephone and took out another country tape to record his report, then decided against it. Now that he'd established contact with Carol, there was no need to risk leaving tapes in phone booths for Tuttle. The case agent would surely call his partner, Carol.

The next day, Ed relaxed with Michele at the Sheraton pool to wait for dinner that night with Raffaele. At dusk, a man in a dented, rusted out, pea-green Fiat not much larger than a roller skate picked Ed and Michele up to drive them to dinner. Ed folded into the front; Bernardo gathered into a ball in the rear seat. The driver took off like a maniac, bombing around the bowels of Rome, making crazed, squealing U-turns, diving in and out of wheeling traffic, grinning the whole time like a child playing hide-and-seek. Ed looked out the tiny rear window every few minutes to check if any surveillance car might be surviving the ordeal. None were.

They arrived in a dark part of the ancient city where the buildings loomed over Ed's shoulder as if to listen in. The restaurant was small and hidden, a classic Mafiosi den, a favored eatery where local gangsters were treated like gentry and guarded by the staff. Dinner was an elegant affair of Chianti, breads, cheeses, pasta, raviolis, meats, fruits, and spumoni. Raffaele and Michele were in expansive moods, toasting their fortunes, Ed, each other, life, money.

After dinner, the three climbed into Raffaele's red Mercedes and he, too, drove like a madman in Rome's insane traffic. He ignored every precaution; Ed's only consolation was that it seemed all the other Roman drivers were doing the same with grace and ease.

Back at the Sheraton, his hands at last able to unclench, Ed led Raffaele and Bernardo into the hotel lounge for several rounds of drinks. Ed nagged Fiumara about getting the deal done. Raffaele responded with monumental braggadocio, exhorting Marco to look beyond their planned cocaine-for-heroin exchange to the future. Fiumara claimed he and his connections could buy and sell anything Ed wanted, including hi-tech firearms, tanks, even an F-16 jet fighter. Ed let his mouth hang open in mute admiration of Fiumara. He raised his glass in silent tribute, thinking Yeah, yeah, bullshit. If this guy's an international arms merchant, why's he dealing horse? The only thing he's going to be buying and selling is cigarettes in prison. The fuck.

Ed steered Fiumara back to reality, to the wine business.

"Yes, alright, Marco. There are some very important people I want you to meet. Tonight was for our enjoyment. Tomorrow, I will start to put together the deal."

That night, Ed gave the walls and phone of his new room an intense rendition of the evening's events. He drifted off to sleep believing that, in the morning, he would meet some heavy Italian hitters and move closer to finalizing the deal.

He was wrong. Raffaele left him to soak his heels by the

pool for two more days with no contact other than short messages apologizing for the delay. Ed didn't know what was going on. Perhaps Fiumara was checking him out further or was busily pulling things together on his end. For all Ed knew Fiumara was setting up a whack on Kurt Wolfe. In any event, Ed didn't wander away from the Sheraton to sightsee or shop. Kurt Wolfe had come to Rome only to make a score, not play tourist. He stayed close to the phone. He placed periodic calls from a nearby pay phone to Carol. She had still no news of Tuttle or McLaughlin.

Finally, Fiumara arrived in the early afternoon to collect Ed and Bernardo. He drove them in his Mercedes, again, driving like a man on fire—no way could surveillance keep up—past the secluded mob restaurant and on into the surrounding neighborhood. He parked in the middle of the street, then escorted Bernardo and Ed around the bustling sidewalks and shops, stopping in several stores and stalls. At each, he was greeted cordially by name, by proprietors and shoppers alike. Raffaele played the role of Godfather; he picked up fruits, trinkets, and souvenirs and handed them to Ed or Michele, whispering, "Go ahead. Take it." Raffaele either paid nothing or an exorbitant amount for each item; either way, the shopkeepers nodded and smiled.

They returned to the Mercedes to pick up two more people. One of them was introduced as a Count. This man smiled as he climbed into the back seat next to Ed and greeted him as "Lupo."

The men rode around the clotted, twisting Roman streets, dueling with traffic like go-carts. They talked about everything but business. Most of the chatter was in Italian until Ed insisted they speak his language. The Count looked hurt; he knew no English.

Fiumara drove them to the restaurant. Inside, a table was set for seven. Father Lorenzo waited along with two others Ed didn't recognize. Fiumara sat at the head with Ed at his right hand. The priest held court at the opposite end while Bernardo, the Count, and the two newcomers filled in along the sides.

Ed had given Carol the name of the restaurant, but he'd been so turned around by Raffaele's driving that he couldn't begin to guess where it was in the city. Perhaps surveillance had somehow made their way here and could photograph this assemblage for later identification. But in his heart, he held little hope that there was any backup within striking distance.

Like the first night in this restaurant, the meal was some of the finest food Ed had ever tasted. The vigorous conversation was a tapestry of Italian and English. When Fiumara switched to English, it seemed not for Ed's benefit but so that some others at the table wouldn't understand what he said. At last, an extended period of English ensued. Zorza brought up the topic of a woman who had disappeared with $100,000 he'd given her to mule back to the States. She'd last been seen in Miami. Zorza recommended beating her with a stick, not enough to kill her but to bruise every inch of her body and make her wish for death. She would serve, he said, looking righteous in his habit, as an example to the other couriers of the price of betrayal.

Fiumara agreed. "This is the only way we can deal with this type of situation."

The remainder of the meal was given over to joking, and Chianti. Ed wasn't able to learn a lot about the strangers at the table, or the Count, but Fiumara confided that he needn't worry who they were; they'd already approved of him.

After dinner, Fiumara catapulted his Mercedes, with Ed, Bernardo, and Father Lorenzo, back to the Sheraton. In the lounge over drinks, Raffaele resumed his boasting of what he'd done and what he could do. He said he had available millions in counterfeit hundred dollar bills. He mentioned a diamond mine he owned a piece of that gave him access to uncut stones. Fiumara claimed membership in both Sicilian and American mob families; he also mentioned that he was a licensed private detective. He and Father Lorenzo revisited the topic of priceless paintings and artwork obtainable through the underground market. Ed wanted to have these conversations recorded. Trusting that his room was wired by now, he insisted that they leave the lounge and go upstairs for an in-depth talk about the wine business.

In the room, Fiumara, Zorza, Bernardo, and Ed went over the proposed heroin-cocaine exchange point by point. Ed told his partners that he owned a colonel in the U.S. Air Force. The colonel was a high-ranking official in Military Intelligence who could transport narcotics in and out of Italy and the States on Air Force transport planes in his duffle bags. His bags would be free from customs or security searches because of his lofty status with the Pentagon. Ed's strategy was to use the colonel to ferry the cocaine to a U.S. air base near Venice. The drug swaps would take place at a location off the highway between Milan and Venice. Ed planned to travel there in the next few days with Bernardo to locate the perfect site where their couriers could meet and make the exchanges in privacy.

Ed arranged for Father Lorenzo to send him photographs and descriptions of the stolen Caravaggios. He told Zorza he'd confer with his art authorities and get back to him with prices and shipping plans.

After his criminal colleagues left the room, Ed asked the walls if they'd gotten everything. To make certain, he gave the room a review of the salient points of the meeting, then repeated his report into the telephone. After he was certain that Bernardo had gone to sleep in his room, Ed snuck down to the Sheraton's lobby and called Carol on the pay phone. He told her that he and Michele Bernardo were flying to Milan the following morning to scout locations on the Milan-Venice autobahn for the coke-for-heroin swap.

*   *   *

Ed and Bernardo rented an Alfa Romeo at the Milan airport. Ed insisted on driving. In case there actually was surveillance following this time, he didn't want any more deranged Italian driving to lose it.

The Alfa was fast. The road out of Milan ran straight and without speed limits. Ed roared east toward Venice, checking his rearview mirror. Several kilometers out of town, he noticed

300

behind him a boxy Fiat straining to keep up under the weight of four large men crammed into a space any two of them might have filled. Gradually, so Bernardo wouldn't notice, Ed slowed the Alfa to keep the diminutive tail car from falling too far back. Bernardo became impatient with the pace. He bugged Ed to speed up; it embarrassed him to have so many cars passing them on the freeway. Ed hit the gas to shut him up. When the surveillance car—the "sardine tin," Ed branded it in his mind— disappeared for too long in his rearview mirror, he pretended to Bernardo that he had to take a leak and stopped along the shoulder of the road.

West of Venice, they located the U.S. air base. Just before it on the highway was a rest stop with plenty of parking. Ed and Michele agreed it was an ideal spot for their mules to make the narcotics transfers without fanfare. There was plenty of open ground to spot surveillance and it was convenient to the base for Ed's Air Force colonel.

Once they'd concluded the business part of their trip, Ed and Bernardo decided to drive a little further and spend the rest of their afternoon and evening visiting beautiful Venice. At the out- skirts, Ed drove around looking for a place to park the Alfa; they wanted to take a gondola ride in the city. One of the streets he turned down became a dead end after a few blocks. He backed the Alfa out. The surveillance car chugged into the street behind him, blocking his path.

Bernardo leaned out his window, shouting in vituperative Italian at the men behind them to back up, get out of the way! Ed couldn't believe what he was seeing. It was a scene right out of a Pink Panther movie.

The tiny Fiat crept backwards. The four husky surveillance cops looked stupidly and sorrowfully at Ed. Careful not to let Michele see him, Ed smiled and flashed them a thumbs-up sign. He was glad to see even buffoons on his tail. It meant that some- body had gotten his messages. He learned the next day from Carol that Tuttle had finally contacted her.

Walking around Venice, Ed discovered he'd broken the partial upper plate in his mouth. He couldn't remember when it had happened. Most likely, he thought, it was from all the teeth grinding he'd been doing from having either no visible backup or Italian idiots following him, or from all the waiting, or the several madcap car rides he'd endured. He'd been as tense as a tuning fork from the moment his plane had lifted off from JFK. He and Bernardo located a drug store along a canal where he bought a tube of superglue to effect a temporary fix. Ed shook his head in amusement as he repaired the split plate; it seemed just another prop in what had become a week-long act from an Italian Comedia del Arte.

* * *

Back in Rome, Ed met with Raffaele and Father Zorza. He'd now been in Italy for eight days. Bernardo and Ed weren't scheduled to fly home for another two days, but Ed claimed that a situation had cropped up in Washington that required his immediate return. Besides, he told Fiumara, he was eager to go home and get started on his end of the heroin-coke swap. In truth, Ed had arranged through Carol to spend one more day in Italy. He was to be debriefed by the Italian National Police and La Guardia de la Finanza. A taxi driven by an Italian National Police agent would pick him up at the Sheraton.

At ten in the morning, in the muggy, rising Roman heat, a cab stopped in front of the hotel where Ed waited with his luggage.

"Hey!" the driver shouted to him. "You froma Pittsa'burgh?" This was, roughly, the code phrase. "Yeah." Ed gave the required answer. "Take me to the airport."

Ed put his bags in the trunk and climbed into the taxi. The driver slid Ed's photograph back into his pocket.

After another rollicking ride, the cabby let him off downtown at a newsstand in front of a monument. Ed waited there, sweating, breathing the carbon monoxide of the swirling Saturday morning traffic. After half an hour, a dilapidated green

Fiat drove up. The driver leaned over and asked, "You wanna go to Pittsburgh?"

Ed laughed. "Sure." He stowed his luggage and they took off.

The driver, who introduced himself as Renato, an agent with La Guardia de la Finanza, flung the little sports car about like the teacup ride at a carnival. Renato chatted cheerfully in fluent English—he'd been educated in Canada—while he sped between jostling cars and trucks, skirting walls, jumping sidewalks. Renato was clearly a cut above the others who'd chauffeured Ed around Rome. He'd actually been trained to drive like this. Ed tried to appreciate Renato's frenzied skill but he couldn't stop thinking that, after all he'd been through, he might still be killed in Rome, smashed flat in a crappy little Fiat driven by a cop.

Renato barreled down narrow one-way streets, dead ends, made U-turns, and ducked into side streets to clean himself of anyone who might be following. After thirty minutes of bone-rattling swerves—Ed feared he would bite through his plate again—the Fiat pulled into a tight, dark alley, a desperate look-ing, empty place with dirty water running in a deep ditch. At the far end of the alley, a gigantic grey gate swung open. Renato drove into the courtyard of what appeared to be a fortress con-cealed in the heart of Rome. Several guards armed with auto-matic rifles strode along catwalks.

Renato helped unload the bags. Ed's spirits began to warm. He was finally near the end of his trip. He was going home, but not before receiving the congratulations and thanks of the Italian law enforcement community. He had made airtight cases for them against Fiumara, the man they wanted, and the dirty priest and art thief Zorza. He'd also brought several other criminal faces before the hidden cameras and microphones (though he never knew where they were) and he'd done it all on his own, with no help or any Italian backup agents. He'd had no trans-mitters and code words to bring the troops running; he'd hung his ass out on the line for eight days straight, alone and exposed in a country foreign to him. This was heroic stuff. Surely the Italians knew that.

Renato escorted Ed into a white room deep in the forbidding building. He was left in the room, actually a holding cell, with four blank walls and one chair. He sat ignored for an hour: no greeting, no coffee. Renato returned with three uniformed officers who seemed by their medals, stripes, and piping to be of high rank. There were no smiles or handshakes.

One spoke. "Come with us." Ed followed them down a hall into another, equally grim enclosure. He was left alone with Glenn Tuttle and Eddie McLaughlin. Ed jumped on them.

"Where the fuck have you two been? I haven't seen either one of you for a week!"

McLaughlin returned Ed's fire. He and Tuttle had been having their own tough time. "Who the hell do you think you are, you selfish son of a bitch? You think you're the only person in the world?" Tuttle pitched in. "We've been over here, too, Ed. It's been a bad scene. We don't know what the fuck's been going on!"

This was not the reception Ed had anticipated. The Italians, rather than kiss his cheek, had almost slapped it. Instead of a rousing reunion with Tuttle and McLaughlin, they were fighting. Renato entered and beckoned. They followed him in surly silence to a large, sparse room where three dozen men in various uniforms were seated and waiting. An interpreter stood by their sides as Ed, Tuttle, and McLaughlin sank onto metal folding chairs.

The gaudiest uniform, a general, identified himself as the head of La Guardia de la Finanza. His words were interpreted into English in a curt, clipped manner.

"Tell us what you know."

Ed related the sum of his eight days with Fiumara, Bernardo, and Zorza. He told the stern assemblage about Raffaele's narcotics operation, the planned coke-for-heroin swap, and the location at the rest stop near the air base outside Venice. When he ventured onto topics other than drugs, such as Zorza's illegal art dealings or Fiumara's proposed construction scam on the Isle of Capri, they steered him back to drugs. They wanted to know more about Fiumara's brother and that fellow called the Count. When Ed said that Fiumara claimed to have a government official in his pocket, the general grunted that they didn't care about corruption, what about drugs? Fiumara professed to have a connection in the DEA's Rome office. That's not our concern, they told Ed in a firm tone. Tell us about the heroin.

His Italian inquisitors made little effort to disguise their dislike of Ed, Tuttle, and McLaughlin. Several of the uniformed men, when speaking to or about Ed, did not address him by his undercover name Kurt Wolfe but called him "Louie." They browbeat him for answers and treated him as if he were not a fellow officer but a low-life bad guy. Ed worried that the sneering police interpreter was editing his report as he repeated it in Italian.

After a four-hour grilling, the three Americans were dismissed. None of the Italian officers stood; no one thanked the FBI agents when they filed out.

In the hall, Ed grabbed Renato.

"Alright, what the hell does 'Louie' mean?"

"Sorry." Renato shrugged. "It means informer. It is an insult."

The Italian law enforcement community, which Ed had hoped would applaud, had instead labeled him the most despised creature in the undercover world: a rat.

That evening, Renato booked Ed into the same hotel where Tuttle and McLaughlin had spent their agonizing week. He took Ed out to dinner and did his best to calm him down, apologizing for the attitude of the Italian National Police and La Guardia.

The next day, Ed hung out with Tuttle and McLaughlin to make peace. They'd had a rough time of it, as well, they said. The Italians had cut them out of everything. They weren't allowed to come along on surveillance and were told little about Ed's movements. The only way the two agents received any significant information about Ed was through Carol. By the time they could catch up with her because of the time change, her information was often stale, at least a day old.

Tuttle told Ed how pissed off he'd gotten when he heard that

Ed and Bernardo had taken off to Milan and Venice to sightsee. The Italian cops were furious as well. Ed explained that he and Michele had gone to Venice not to play tourist but to locate a drop point for the deal. He'd been setting up the heroin-coke swap; it was a business trip. And when he and Bernardo were done, they decided to spend the night and see the town. Big fucking deal.

"Didn't you get my reports?" Ed asked.

"What reports?"

Ed was stunned. "The reports I made in my room. To the mikes."

"Ed, there were no mikes in your room."

"What about the tap on my phone?"

"There was never any wiretap."

Ed flashed back to the many detailed, and now ridiculous, narrations he'd given to the deaf hotel walls and telephones. He had only been talking to himself.

Deep in his gut, his pride cringed. An inner voice mocked him. It laughed and called him "Louie." He shook his head, clapped his two friends on the back, and chuckled again at the undercover Italian comedy.

"Let's get the fuck out of here."

Tony Rossi (Ed Robb) emerges from lounge of the Tahitian Motor Lodge in Holiday, Florida, bringing plans for the expansion of King's Court.

Benjamin "Lefty" Ruggiero in front of his room at the Tahitian Motor Lodge.

Sonny Black and Santo Trafficante at the Tahitian Motor Lodge.

John "Boobie" Cerasani at the Tahitian Motor Lodge pool, displaying the bird tattoos on his chest, in photograph later used as evidence in his conviction in the burglary of Princess Ashraf Pahlevi's apartment in New York.

Sonny Black discusses expansion of Bonanno operations in Florida with Tony Rossi.

From left, Sonny Black, and Tony Rossi, followed by Judy Brown.

Sonny Black followed by Tony Rossi heading for the Tahitian Motor Lodge pool.

Santo and brother Fanno Trafficante.

Tony Rossi takes notes for Sonny Black at the Tahitian pool patio.
Judy Brown, Sonny's girlfriend, sits between them.

Benny Husick with Sonny Black. Husick handled all gambling for Trafficante in Florida including, but not limited to, sports booking and bingo.

Tony Rossi (Ed Robb) and Donnie Brasco (Joe Pistone) consult strolling by the pool.

From left, Donnie Brasco, Sonny Black, and Tony Rossi head for the lounge at the Tahitian Motor Lodge.

Lefty in pensive mood before heading to dinner at the Tahitian Motor Lodge.

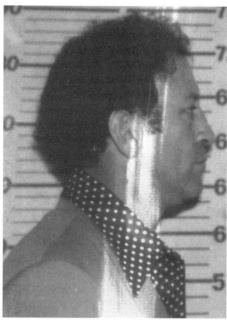

Tony Rossi, photographed by Pasco County Sheriff's Deputies, after being charged with operating an illegal gambling operation.

The photo shown to Sonny Black of Tony Rossi and Donnie Brasco with FBI agents. From left, Jerry Loar, Joe Pistone, Jim Kinne, Ed Robb, and Doug Fencl, whom Sonny knew to be an FBI agent.

Luigi Visciano, narcotics broker and courier for Kurt Wolfe, admiring the Ferrari belonging to Gino, the full time FBI informant who provided entree for Ed Robb to the drug cartel targeted by Pizza II.

Giuseppe "Peppe" Vitiello and Michele Bernardo, with his ever-present briefcase, arrive for meeting at Kurt Wolfe's Washington apartment.

1.

2.

3.

4.

photo sequence above: 1. Kurt Wolfe (Ed Robb) approaches El Torrito Restaurant in Yonkers to arrange heroin buy from Michele Bernardo. 2. After extended meeting with Bernardo, Kurt Wolfe brings out heroin in briefcase for testing in car. 3. Bernardo comes out of El Torrito to check on progress of test. 4. Wolfe returned to El Torrito with Bernardo and a briefcase of money and, the heroin buy consummated, both then exit the restaurant. Bernardo does not notice Wolfe's satisfied smile for the camera.

Father Lorenzo Zorza emerges from a 1987 ⟶ hearing in New York's Southern District Court.

CHAPTER TWENTY-FOUR
Wrapping Up Pizza

While Ed worked in Italy, Infamita kept the FBI busy in Washington and New York.

Ed's activities in Rome had sparked a brushfire of trans-Atlantic phone calls, monitored by the several Title III wiretaps in place. Ed was "tickling the wires" from Rome. The Crimson Sky undercover agent spent the afternoon of June 24 with Tony Spavento in Brooklyn trying to buy a "suit," a kilo of heroin. Pizza II was cooking and soon would be done.

Ed reached Charlottesville on June 28 and slept for two days. His ten-day absence had been his longest stretch away from Gretchen since The King's Court. The look on his face at the front door when he arrived was one Gretchen had seen frequently throughout her husband's seventeen-year undercover FBI career. It said, "Don't ask."

Four days later, Ed returned refreshed to Kurt Wolfe's Georgetown apartment. Despite his chilly send-off from Rome, he was pleased with the results of the trip. Though still jealous, Michele Bernardo soon stopped his whining and adjusted to Kurt's new position above him on the narcotics supply ladder. Ed was careful to remain solicitous of Bernardo; he stayed in daily phone contact with him and included him in every deal he discussed with Fiumara.

Fiumara made several junkets from New York to Washington where, along with Bernardo, the three continued to map out their international heroin-cocaine exchange. On Raffaele's first visit, only a week after Ed had returned, Ed showed him the million dollar stack of cash. Raffaele wanted to dip into the fund and borrow a hundred g's out of it. Ed said no. Raffaele made a commotion but Ed held his ground. Raffaele was just like all the other mobsters, just like Lefty and Sonny, trying to bleed every connection, suck money up from every possible source without regard to responsibility or reason. As Coldwater's Tony Rossi, Ed had played the role of a mark, an open wallet for the mobsters he courted. But Infamita's Kurt Wolfe was nobody's mark.

By July 1987, Infamita was far ahead of schedule compared with the other Pizza II investigations spread across the country. McLaughlin, Tuttle, and Daniels were prepared to close Infamita down. The surveillance teams of the Washington Field Office, New York Office, and the Roman Italian National Police had collected more than enough hard evidence against Fiumara, Zorza, Bernardo, Spavento, Luigi, Peppe, Silvestri, and several other players such as Modica and Miceli to put them away in either American or Italian prisons. But because the Charlotte, Los Angeles, and Boston operations were still in mid-stream, Ed had to string his subjects along until the rest of the investigations could catch up.

*   *   *

On July 21, Fiumara again appeared in front of the cameras in Kurt Wolfe's Georgetown apartment. He showed Ed photos of three stolen paintings he said were stored at his house in Calabria. Raffaele also displayed a folder containing secret Italian government documents. During the discussion, he explained how he'd hidden his money in pizza restaurants up and down the East Coast. He also claimed to own a 55-foot sailboat with compartments to smuggle narcotics up from the Caribbean.

Raffaele had put pressure on Ed for several weeks to make another deal. Several times, he'd questioned why Marco hadn't brought a few kilos of heroin back from Italy with him. It had been readily available there at good prices. Ed needed to keep the ball rolling with Raffaele. He struck another deal to purchase a kilo of white heroin the next day in Yonkers. Raffaele said the dope would come from "the guy in Brooklyn," Spavento.

Ed and his New York Office backup van arrived in Yonkers. At 11 a.m., he pulled into the El Torrito parking lot and met Fiumara and Bernardo. The two gave him a sample of white heroin to test but apologized that they didn't have the full kilo on hand. It would take a few more hours. Would Marco mind waiting?

"Get it in two hours," Ed replied, "or forget the deal."

Fiumara and Bernardo took off, leaving Ed to kill time at the restaurant. Soon afterward, the FBI intercepted a phone call from Fiumara to Tony Spavento. Spavento had no white heroin for sale; he was fresh out but instructed Raffaele and Michele to go to the Marriott Hotel near La Guardia Airport. There, they could find a man Spavento called Salvatore D'Angelo. Spavento said he'd just sold D'Angelo some heroin for a deal D'Angelo was doing with a guy coming in from North Carolina. Spavento told Fiumara that if he could get to the Marriott first, he could buy D'Angelo's dope for his own deal.

Ed stayed put. By 2:30 in the afternoon, he had waited at El Torrito long enough. When Bernardo called to give a progress report, Ed scotched the deal. He'd buy the shit at a later date. He was going home. He drove directly to the airport while one of the New York Office surveillance team went to the La Guardia Marriott to pay for Ed's one-night stay. While in the lobby paying the tab, the New York Office agent spotted another FBI agent, a friend of his who also worked undercover on Pizza II but had been assigned to Crimson Sky, based in Charlotte. What was his friend doing in New York, the surveillance agent wondered, in the lobby of Ed's hotel?

The New York Office agent watched the Crimson Sky operative meet with a man later identified as D'Angelo. The agent negotiated with D'Angelo and arranged to buy a half-kilo of heroin later that evening. Within minutes of concluding his business with the agent, D'Angelo met with Fiumara and Bernardo, the two men the New York Office surveillance agent had spent his morning watching out in Yonkers.

Fiumara hadn't gotten to D'Angelo in time; the dealer had no china white left to sell. Fiumara and Bernardo left the Marriott empty-handed. The New York Office surveillance agent returned to his Manhattan office to report his amazing discovery: By happenstance, he'd watched D'Angelo meet first with an undercover agent from North Carolina and then with the two large New York dealers, Bernardo and Fiumara.

The New York agents pieced together what had happened. First, they knew that a major share of the dope flowing around New York City emanated from Tony Spavento and his Italian Fashions, Inc. They had traced Emmanuel Adamita, the Italian fugitive, from Spavento's Brooklyn clothing store to Florida. Next, Fiumara and Bernardo were known to be major suppliers in both Washington and New York, with big Mafia hooks in Italy and the Middle East. And now that Spavento had been linked to a narcotics deal originating in North Carolina, it became clear that Tony Spavento's operation was huge, extending far beyond New York, all the way down the eastern seaboard and across the Atlantic. The FBI began to see how the many slices of Pizza II fit together.

* * *

For the remainder of 1987, Ed worked to stay close to the narcotics ring a while longer, spending as little of the FBI's money as he could. He purchased one more quarter-kilo of heroin in Yonkers and bought a few tastes. Father Lorenzo continued to hound Ed to buy some stolen artwork while Fiumara pouted that Ed wouldn't lend him a hundred g's from his mountain of cash. In September, Ed went with Fiumara and Bernardo to Miami and Key West to locate additional cocaine supplies for the proposed narcotics exchange in Italy. In each instance, Ed used all of his undercover skills to stall their constant urging for bigger, faster deals. He maintained that he was interested only in really big scores now, the kind that, unavoidably, took several months to set up.

On the streets in Washington, Kurt Wolfe had become a powerful name. "Lupo" was known in the local underworld as an international financier, with the cunning and unpredictable nature of his namesake, the wolf. Scam after scheme came his way, many of them from unexpected, and even respectable, quarters. A banker gave Kurt a pitch on buying a controlling interest in a troubled bank in Texas. The man explained that falling oil prices in 1987 had ruined a lot of Lone Star State fortunes and the bank would be a distress sale bargain if Kurt could act quickly and in cash. A businessman from Cleveland sought out Kurt to convince him to use his financial services, which consisted of making available large amounts of international currencies, laundered through the Middle East. His clients were anxious, he said, for "aggressive investments." He meant drugs.

While waiting for the end of Pizza II, Ed and the Washington Field Office agents discussed a final direction in which to take Infamita. Should Kurt lend Raffaele the one hundred g's or buy some hot art from Zorza to keep them in line? Or could Kurt make one more effort to leap above Fiumara, to begin dealing directly with the suppliers in Rome, Sicily, New York, and Florida?

Pizza II was scheduled to end in January of 1988. There was not enough time and not enough Group 1 money left to adopt any more grandiose goals for Infamita. The Washington Field Office decided that Kurt should spend his final months forging ahead with his end of the cocaine-heroin swap. He would search out other domestic suppliers of coke, operators on the same level as Fiumara. A flurry of activity by Kurt would rivet Raffaele's and Bernardo's attentions, forcing them to proceed with their own efforts to come up with supplies of heroin for the exchange, with the FBI, Italian National Police, and La Guardia de Finanzia watching and listening closely. Ed also needed to maintain his involvement and status in Washington criminal circles. Even though he had less than a few months left, Kurt Wolfe might still develop a few more names or connections that could lead to subsequent investigations after Infamita's curtain dropped.

The word needed to be circulated that Lupo was looking for multi-kilo amounts of cocaine. Ed knew he didn't have time to be mired at the bottom of the coke pyramid buying the narcotics in dribs and drabs as he'd done a year earlier when he'd bought his first heroin. He would refuse now to deal with any more brokers, mopes like Luigi Visciano, or dealers and middlemen like Bernardo. Kurt would buy only large quantities and work exclusively with big suppliers.

Ed, Tuttle, and McLaughlin created some tension between Bernardo, Fiumara, and Kurt Wolfe. They made plans for a massive fake coke buy to go down in the Florida Keys. The purpose was to turn the tables on Fiumara and Bernardo: In one impressive deal, Ed would have his end of the coke-heroin swap in hand— to the tune of forty kilos. This would put the pressure on his two partners to come up with their portion of the bargain, perhaps making them careless enough to lead the Bureau or Italian agencies to their heroin sources. It would at least keep them busy. Ed figured it ought to take Raffaele a good three or four months of intercontinental finagling to come up with twenty kilos of heroin. That should be all the time the Washington Field Office needed to see Infamita and Pizza II to their conclusions.

Also, Ed wanted to send Raffaele and Michele a signal that he was maneuvering to outgrow them. Marco intended to start dealing directly with their sources and would inevitably cut them out. If he could shake things up, he might send a serious tremor through the Sicilian network and flush out some fresh faces from Spavento's operation or another narcotics ring eager to get a profitable piece of the powerful and ambitious Kurt Wolfe.

Ed told Bernardo of his impending big cocaine score. Though he'd hated to do it, the coke-heroin swap scheme had made it necessary for Ed to go back to his old Colombian connections. He disliked dealing with the Colombians, he said they were wild men, with violent ways and unstable temperaments.

But they had the coke and they had plenty of it cheap. Ed asked Bernardo to accompany him on a quick trip to the Florida Keys to make a buy, forty kilos of high-quality South American cocaine at twenty-two per kilo, $880,000, paid in cash. Ed needed Bernardo to cover his back. And, he added in confidence to Michele, don't tell any one what's going down. This is just between us.

Raffaele Fiumara grew furious when he got Bernardo's call. Marco had cut him out of a gigantic deal and was working with the fucking dirty Colombians again. Marco had a million dollars for coke but wouldn't loan him, his partner, a measly hundred grand. Raffaele saw Marco slipping away from his influence.

Bernardo felt caught between his old partner Raffaele and the hard-charging Marco who was suddenly making things happen in a big way. Michele told himself he could play both sides of the equation. He informed Fiumara that he would go along on the Florida trip with Marco but he'd keep his eyes open for opportunities for their own operation.

Fiumara felt spurned, by both the interloper Marco and his longtime henchman Bernardo. His mortification turned to treachery. He called the FBI.

Though Raffaele didn't identify himself, the wiretap on his phone flagged him. He informed the New York Office of Kurt Wolfe's drug trafficking and described Wolfe's impending trip to the Florida Keys to purchase a million dollars worth of Colombian coke.

The New York Office alerted Ed of Fiumara's betrayal. He wants me out of the way, Ed thought. Raffaele's hoping the Feds will bust the coke buy with guns drawn, and the crazy Colombians will start a gunfight. Fiumara wouldn't mind seeing me dead, Bernardo, too. The Sicilian bastard.

* * *

Before dawn on a morning in early February, Ed and Michele stood on a secluded point of the lush island of Key

West. They watched over the moonlit Gulf waters for a blinking signal: two red lights, two greens, two reds, then two greens. Just before daybreak, Ed caught the sign. The boat carrying the dope approached the island. Ed and Michele headed for the stash house on one of the canals that carved Key West, where residents moored their sport fishers and sailboats beside their front lawns.

When they arrived, the speedboat was already docked in front. A half dozen Colombians came to attention—an equal number of AK47 assault rifles rattled in their hands—when Ed and Bernardo entered. The atmosphere in the stash house was charged with malice and threat. The Hispanic FBI agents posing as Colombians played their roles to perfection. No names were used, few words were uttered. Ed nodded to one of the Colombians and strode to the table. Forty footballs were laid out for inspection. Ed took out his testing kit and cut into the middle of each package, mumbling to himself as his tubes and liquids did their alchemy. The Colombians milled about, ordering each other in tough tones to go here or there, watch for this or that.

After thirty minutes of feigned scrutiny, Ed put away his kit and turned from the drugs. He walked out the door without a word or ceremony, with Bernardo at his heels.

They drove to their hotel, the Key West Marriott. In front of Michele, Ed dialed the number of a hello phone at the Miami FBI Office.

"OK," he said, "let's do it."

They waited an hour in Ed's hotel room. A knock came and a dark man entered with two briefcases. He laid them on the bed; Ed clicked the cases open, looked inside, and nodded. The man left.

Ed showed the contents to Bernardo; the cases appeared lined with money. In fact, only the top few bills were real. The rest was paper. No way was Ed going to allow Bernardo to touch the stacks. He snapped the cases shut.

After thirty minutes, another mysterious, silent man entered the room. He hefted the cases and walked out. Ed explained to Bernardo that twenty of the kilos were already gone and the other twenty had been stashed, for use later in their coke-heroin exchange. These kilos of cocaine were ready to be transported overseas by the Air Force Intelligence colonel under Ed's control.

Bernardo was flabbergasted at the size of the deal he'd just witnessed and the convoluted machinations swirling around Marco. Colombians with AK47s, mute, hard men coming and going in their hotel room, hundreds of thousands of dollars switching hands without a word, and Marco sat in the middle, conducting it all like a maestro.

"You'll never see the whole puzzle, Michele," Ed said afterwards. "There'll always be a piece missing." Ed instructed Bernardo to call Fiumara and tell him to come to Florida. Marco wanted to start setting up the deal right away. After Bernardo put down the receiver, Ed wondered what Raffaele must be thinking. Was he surprised that Marco and Michele were still alive, or at least not in handcuffs, after ratting them out to the Feds? Whatever his concerns, regardless of his reluctance to take orders from Marco, Raffaele flew out the next morning. Ed and Bernardo met him in Ft. Lauderdale where Fiumara owned a house.

Soon after he arrived, Ed told Raffaele to score two kilos of heroin immediately. He wanted Raffaele to take some action while they were in Florida, to identify some new names and numbers for the Miami Field Office. Raffaele busied himself with phone calls from Ed's hotel room. The FBI would acquire a subpoena register to identify the numbers he had dialed.

By the end of the day, Fiumara had come up empty. Ed was magnanimous. Don't worry about it, Raffaele, old pal. Let's go party. Which they did, on a private yacht anchored in Ft. Lauderdale, owned and operated by the FBI.

* * *

The conclusion of Pizza II was postponed three times, first from January to mid-February, and again to mid-March. Finally, the decision was made that, no matter where things stood, the investigation would be shut down in a blizzard of raids on April Fool's Day, 1988.

The raids were coordinated between FBI Offices in five American cities, and with the Italian National Police and La Guardia de la Finanzia in Rome and Sicily, to strike simultaneously. The raids began on April 1 at 4:00 a.m. New York time. In New York City alone, two hundred and sixty FBI and DEA agents moved in on forty homes and businesses.

By breakfast in Los Angeles, lunchtime in New York, and dinner in Rome, the Sicilian Mafia had been hit hard on both sides of the Atlantic. One hundred and sixty-four arrests were made in Italy, including Raffaele Fiumara and Father Lorenzo, and sixty-nine more in the United States.

At an afternoon press conference, Attorney General Edwin Meese said the investigation was "the largest international drug case ever developed by the Justice Department." U.S. News & World Report described Pizza II as "the biggest drug bust in American history." Frank Storey, a New York Office Supervisor who had coordinated most of Pizza II, went one better, calling the April 1 sweep "the largest arrest ever to take place in the history of mankind."

*   *   *

The night before the arrests, March 31, Michele Bernardo visited Ed in Georgetown. Ed had told him to come down to discuss some business. He wanted Bernardo to be arrested the next morning by Washington Field Office agents. During dinner and afterwards in his apartment, Ed was wrathful. He picked arguments with Michele. He knew this was his last opportunity to ventilate, to tell Bernardo what an asshole he was and how he genuinely despised him.

After Ed's insulting behavior, Michele had no intention of spending the night in Washington. Around midnight, he insisted that Ed take him to the airport to catch a late flight back to New York. Ed had calmed; he didn't argue. Bernardo would be collared the next morning in Yonkers, along with his wife Katherine.

In the car on their way to National Airport, Bernardo rekindled the quarrel. Ed didn't respond; he'd had his say. The game and the ruse were over. As they drove into the airport, Bernardo grew quiet. He looked at Ed, gazing for a long moment.

"Marco," he said, "I think you might be an agent."

Ed looked back. "It just goes to show you, Michele. Things aren't always what they seem. Like I said, you'll never see the whole puzzle."

* * *

Weeks after his arrest, Michele Bernardo appeared before a judge in a federal courthouse in New York, handcuffed and hobbled in leg irons, flanked by U.S. Marshals. Ed approached him in the courthouse hallway.

"Michele."

Bernardo glared at the man who'd brought him down.

"The FBI wants to make you an offer," Ed said. "You could help us out and save your own ass at the same time. What do you think?"

Bernardo shook his head slowly, not to disrupt the aim of his stare at Ed Robb.

"What I think," he said, "is that I will kill you when I get out of prison."

Ed did one last time what he had done for most of the past two decades: He showed this criminal only what he wanted him to see. He showed him nothing.

"You ruined my life and my family," Bernardo said, holding up the shackles so Ed could see his handiwork. "One day, I'm going to do the same to you. I'm going to ruin your life and your family."

The Marshals led Bernardo away. Ed shrugged.

CHAPTER TWENTY-FIVE
Incarnations

The Pizza II trials took two years. Ed stayed busy preparing for the trials and testifying in Washington and New York. In between, he traveled to FBI Offices and law enforcement seminars to lecture on undercover techniques.

At the outset of his testimony in New York, the team of defense lawyers requested Ed's confidential personnel file from the Bureau. They claimed that Infamita's Special Agent Edgar S. Robb had done far too much undercover work in his career. He'd become a paranoiac and a split personality, also a drug user and an alcoholic. He was crazy and therefore an unreliable witness. The file would show it.

The FBI had never before given up a complete personnel file on one of its agents. It was an unheard-of request. Nevertheless, the judge in the federal district court for the Southern District of New York took note of the seriousness of the allegations against Ed and the severe weight of evidence against the defendants, most of it hinging on Ed's credibility. The judge ruled that the file be brought into evidence, over the strenuous objection of the prosecution team, led again by Assistant U.S. Attorneys Al Pavlis and Louis Freeh. The judge would review Ed's record not in the open courtroom but in his offices, in camera, alone with Mr. Pavlis. The court adjourned for a day.

The following morning, the court announced to the assembled defense attorneys out of the presence of the jury that, in his estimation, the defense did not want to go into the FBI file of Agent Ed Robb. He advised the lawyers that he'd never seen "a more spotless record." The matter ended there.

* * *

Raffaele Fiumara was indicted in the Southern District of New York and charged with narcotics trafficking. He was arrested in Reggio di Calabria, a seaport in southern Italy. He remained in custody in Italy for two years and was released by the Italian authorities. In 1995, he returned to the United States and, for reasons unknown, turned himself in. He was arrested, tried, and convicted; he received a sentence of forty-five years.

Michele Bernardo was sentenced on narcotics trafficking charges to two hundred and sixty-two months in a federal penitentiary plus six years of probation upon his release. Katherine Bernardo, as the mother of their two children, was not sentenced as the result of a plea agreement between the government and her husband.

Father Lorenzo Zorza was arrested in Italy on narcotics charges. He was tried, convicted, and incarcerated there but did not serve his entire sentence.

Luigi Visciano was convicted of conspiracy to distribute narcotics and sentenced to four years. He served his time but disappeared immediately after his release from prison and was later confirmed to have been hit. Guiseppe Vitiello was sentenced to serve eleven years on narcotics charges, with deportation upon release. Luigi Silvestri was sentenced to serve five years for heroin trafficking.

Aldo Pastore was sentenced to six years with three months' probation on narcotics charges. Mario Digrazia was charged with murder for hire and heroin distribution. He plead guilty and was ordered to serve six years with a four-year probation. On July 27, 1988, Ed Robb received the Attorney General's Distinguished Service Award.

* * *

On February 23, 1990, Ed left the FBI. At his retirement party in Charlottesville, Ed was surrounded by more than one hundred and fifty agents, men and women who'd been either close behind him or at his side during his twenty years of service. His life, at one time or another, had been cradled in every one of their hands.

He gazed over the crowd. The familiar faces sent his mind back over his two decades in the Bureau, to search among the exhilaration, frustrations, perils, and pitfalls for a defining moment.

He had been one of the Bureau's first criminal undercover agents. In three Group 1 investigations, he had pioneered the tactics, techniques, and procedures that continue to guide FBI covert operations. His first major undercover operation, Coldwater, resulted in a major blow to the American mob, wreaking havoc in its inner sanctums at its highest levels. He'd climbed to within one sitdown of the untouchable Old Man, Santo Trafficante. Because of his work at The King's Court, Ed became the first undercover agent to be elevated to the position of boss with his own territory and crew. Ed and Joe Pistone became the first and only FBI undercover agents ever to be offered membership in a Mafia crime family.

Later, as the central undercover agent for Infamita, the spear point case of Pizza II, Ed had been at the heart of the biggest drug bust the FBI had ever engineered, and was the only agent to have successfully penetrated both the American and Sicilian mobs.

Tony Daniels, now an FBI Assistant Director, stepped to the podium and said that Ed Robb was "the greatest undercover agent the FBI had ever seen." The band struck up an emotional rendering and the crowd sang to Ed, "Did you know that you're my heeee-ro?"

Comrades young and old drank to his health. They reminisced about Ed's many incarnations as Robb, Rizzi, Ritz, Rossi, Nesbit, and Wolfe. During the toasts, Ed's ranging thoughts dredged up one quiet, undramatic episode from Infamita, a chance encounter with a stranger on a plane. Calling the scene to mind, he realized that the incident was the perfect summation, the epitome of his lengthy and satisfying undercover career.

In the spring of 1987, on a flight returning to D.C. from Miami, Kurt Wolfe sat in first class reading a book. Well into the flight, he hadn't spoken a word to the man seated next to him. Nonetheless, the fellow struck up a conversation.

The man introduced himself as an 11th vice president of the Teamsters Union. The federal government, he explained uninvited, had recently kicked out most of the Teamsters' leadership and placed the union in receivership to clean up suspected widespread corruption in the organization's higher ranks.

Ed put his book down and bought the guy a drink. The man continued with gathering steam. He expressed his belief that the new caucus of Teamsters leaders, himself included, could rebound and take the union in new and profitable directions. If, for instance, they could make some inroads into police and fire department unions, they could "run the country."

In Washington, Ed stayed in touch with the guy. One evening, they met for dinner in Georgetown. At the restaurant, the man introduced Kurt Wolfe to four persons claiming to be Teamsters officials from Chicago. They acted and talked, to Ed's practiced eye, like gangsters.

Ed reported the encounter to the FBI. Those Teamsters guys were dirty, he said. I know it. Let me see where they can lead us. The supervisors talked it over and told him, no.

Ed, they said, sorry, but you can't do it all.

It was the first time in his FBI career that the thought had struck him. He knew then it would soon be time to move on to a new line of work. He'd find something worthwhile where perhaps he could start over, where he could again try to do it all.

* * *

In 1991, less than two years after retiring from the Bureau, Ed was elected to the Virginia Legislature as a state senator from

Charlottesville. After serving in the Legislature for four years, and four more years as Governor George Allen's appointee as Inspector General of Virginia's Department of Correctional Education, Ed was elected Sheriff of Albemarle County, Virginia, a position he currently holds. Ed Robb remains a law man.

SOURCES

Information for this book was developed through several sources, including extensive interviews with Ed Robb and many FBI agents who participated in the events described in this book, plus Bureau surveillance records, internal reports, court transcripts, and newspaper and magazine reportage.

Several law enforcement professionals with personal knowledge of the operations described in this book have contributed their comments for additional detail and accuracy. They are Tony Daniels, Ty Cobb, Bill Baker, Jim Kinne, Glenn Tuttle, Bill Garner, Jack Case, Mike Lunsford, Bill James, Jim Kossler, Charlie Rooney, Sean McWeeny, Steve Salmieri, Phil McNiff, Greg Devlin, Jules Bonavolonta, Ed McLaughlin, and Joe Pistone. The author, publisher, and Ed Robb wish to express their gratitude to each of these men for their attention and support of this project. Apologies are extended to anyone we've left out.

In a few instances, the words of Agent Joseph Pistone have been drawn on, as expressed in his book, Donnie Brasco: My Undercover Life in the Mafia; New American Library, 1987.

APPENDIX: CAST OF CHARACTERS

OPERATION COLDWATER
TAMPA
The FBI Agents
Ed Robb - Tony Rossi
Jim Kinne - Contact Agent
Ty Cobb - Vinnie Russo and Tony Conte
Jack Case - Case Agent
Joseph "Joe" Pistone - Donnie Brasco
Mike Lunsford - Surveillance
Eddie McLaughlin - Eddie Shannon
Bill Garner - Records and Documents
Steve Salmieri - Steve "Chico" Navarro
Tony Daniels - Supervisor
Richard Holland - Dick Stauder

The Luccheses
Vincenzo "Jimmy East" Ciraulo, *capo*
JoJo Fitapelli, associate
Rick Mazzenga, associate
Bernie Agostino, associate

The Bonannos
Phillip "Rusty" Rastelli, incarcerated family boss
Stefano "Stevie Beef" Cannone, *consigliere*
Dominick "Sonny Black" Napolitano, street boss
Joe "Joey" Massino, captain
Benjamin "Lefty Two Guns" Ruggiero, *capo*
John "Boobie" Cerasani, associate
James "Jimmy Legs" Episcopia, associate
Dennis Mulligan, ex-NY cop, associate
Frankie Foggia, associate
Nicky Santora, associate

The Bonannos *(continued)*
Carmine Rufrano, Sonny's cousin
Johnny "Spaghetti" Tagliarini, Lefty's associate
Mimmie Matchicote, Lefty's associate
Rafael "Ralph" Puig, Sonny's and Boobie's associate
Joe Puma, family member in Miami

The Trafficante Crew
Santo Trafficante, head of Florida organized crime
Bennie Husick, associate
Billy Jones, professional dealer
Barry "Winter" Bienstock, professional dealer
George Petry, bodyguard
Henry Gonzalez, attorney

The Acquafredda Crew
Vincenzo "Jimmy" Acquafredda, Gambino associate
Lindsey "The Kid" Cherry, associate
Joseph "Joe Pete" Pullicino, associate
Anthony "Fat Sonny" Santangelo, associate
Eddie Trascher, associate
Ricky Trascher, associate, Eddie's son, a Las Vegas dealer
Joseph Donahue, captain, Pasco County Sheriff's Department

The Chicago Outfit
Johnny Cascio, associate
Michael "Mike" Condic, associate
Tony "Nags" Panzica, associate
Michael "Mike" Spilotro, member, Cascio's *compare*

Narcotics Dealers
Theo Nicholis, pilot
Rick Renner, airline baggage handler and Nicholis's partner
Bill Sakelson, shrimp boat captain, associate of Capt. Donahue's
Freddie Cataudella, associate of JoJo's
Pete Solmo, associate of JoJo's
Tom Solmo, Pete's son

OPERATION FAST HIT
CHARLESTON
The FBI Agents
Ed Robb - Tony Rossi
Charles "Charley Chains" Gianturco - Charley Sacco

The Targets
James W. Rogers, Berkeley County Sheriff
Ray Scarboro, Goose Creek businessman
Nick Tsachilis, businessman
Gus Flamos, drug trafficker

PIZZA II INVESTIGATION
WASHINGTON, D.C., NEW YORK, ITALY
The FBI Agents (Infamita)
Ed Robb - Kurt Wolfe
Eddie McLaughlin - Supervisor
Glenn Tuttle - Contact Agent
Gino - FBI informant

The Targets
Raffaele Fiumara, member of N'Drangheta crime family of Sicily
Michele Bernardo, narcotics dealer, Fiumara's partner
Katherine Bernardo, Michele's wife
Father Lorenzo Zorza, Catholic priest, courier for mob, dealer
in stolen art
Aldo Pastore, Bernardo's Brooklyn associate
Mario Digrazia, Bernardo's Brooklyn associate
Alfredo "Tony" Spavento, Brooklyn narcotics supplier
Luigi Visciano, D.C. narcotics broker and courier for Kurt Wolfe
Guiseppe "Peppe" Vitiello, Luigi's New York associate

INDEX